MW00587564

Flight
For
Safety

Global Air Lines merges with Coastal creating the largest airline in the world. In the fallout Captain Darby Bradshaw's 4th stripes are ripped from her shoulders as she is bumped to first officer. Leaving her Boeing behind she is checked out on the Airbus A330. Compliments of sitting reserve she has not flown for nine-months.

But when Pacific Airlines Flight 574 is found in a watery grave, a Boeing 777 crashes short of a runway, and Global Air Lines implements a 'train yourself at home' program, Darby decides it's time to take action before another crash occurs.

Darby tells the world, on her training blog, why the Pacific Airlines A330 crashed and all hell breaks loose.

Forced to pull the post she is called into the chief pilot's office and her career threatened. But when her boyfriend, a Global check airman, disappears and numerous airline incidents are covered up, Darby realizes she has stepped into the heart of a far-reaching conspiracy, where each flight has turned into a game of Russian roulette.

Flight
For
Safety

AVIATION. INSPIRATION. MOTIVATION.

BY KARLENE K. PETITT

AT

WWW.KARLENEPETITT.COM

FLIGHT TO SUCCESS

 **KiloPapa**Productions

KARLENE PETITT

Flight
For
Safety

*Paul!
Enjoy all you
flights ... they're
all good!
xo Karlene Petitt
2/23/2014*

JET STAR PUBLISHING INC.
SEATAC WA

Copyright ©2014 by Karlene Petitt

All rights reserved. No part of this publication may be reproduced or transmitted in any form or by any means, electronic or mechanical, including photocopy, recording, or any information storage and retrieval system, without permission in writing from the publisher.

Requests for permission to make copies of any part of the work should be submitted online at JetStarpublishing@gmail.com

978-0-9849259-4-0

www.JetStarPublshing.com

Printed in the United States of America

Cover Design By Kayla Wopschall

DEDICATION

Flight For Safety is dedicated to anyone who has ever lost a loved one in a plane crash—passengers and pilots.

While this story is a work of fiction, it mirrors life, and as the case may be—death. When a loved one dies in a plane crash it's hard to move forward. Guilt, anger, and the need for accountability fill your heart. We want answers. But when there are none and the accident could have been prevented, it makes moving forward all the more challenging.

We may not have control of all events that occur in our lives, but we do have control of how we deal with them. While we cannot bring anyone back, I promise to do my best to not allow aviation deaths to be in vain. As I journey through the remainder of my career, I will work toward making aviation the safest possible and will be a guardian of our future pilots and their careers.

Flight
For
Safety

PROLOGUE

NARITA TO SINGAPORE
PACIFIC AIRLINES FLIGHT 574

DECEMBER 14, 2009

BRAD LIFTED HIS WRIST and squinted, trying to bring the numbers into focus. Twenty-five minutes of his three-hour break remained and he was still awake. *It's going to be one hell of a long night.* The Airbus A330 jolted and bounced. The seatbelt sign illuminated with a chime. A couple female passengers squealed, but the laughter continued.

The party in the business class section of Pacific Airlines flight 574 started shortly after departure and he was stuck in the middle of it. This was the place to be if you were on your way to Singapore and part of the Princeton wedding—which he was not.

Brad was one of the pilots responsible for the lives of these passengers. A task he was proud to be part of. With over 4500 hours flying the A330 he had twice the Bus hours as the captain. But what did those hours mean? Nothing. Other than being a really good button pusher. Reality was, the Airbus took both good pilots and shitty pilots and made them all average.

They told him it could take up to three years to feel comfortable flying the plane. He'd been on the plane for twelve years, but he never flew it. He was nothing more than a programmer. Tom, the other first officer, was only six months into his three-year training plan. Tonight Brad would be babysitting both plane and pilot.

Listening to the laughter reminded him of the responsibility he held. Pilots needed to be at their best. Which was impossible without sleep.

Pacific Airlines removed their crew bunks for additional business class seats. How the company expected pilots to sleep in a passenger seat was beyond him. He was just thankful he had a job with the downsizing going on worldwide. He glanced at his watch, again. Maybe volunteering for first break was not the smartest idea with the meal service in progress.

This was day ten of his twelve-day trip. The flight to Singapore was under nine hours, but multiple ocean crossings with accumulated fatigue left the entire crew dragging. He started tonight's flight behind the power curve.

Brad shifted to his right and adjusted his pillow. He should be grateful he got a break at all. Normally this flight was flown with a single crew, but due to the weather conditions they were scheduled longer than normal. He rubbed a hand over his face.

Brad turned to his left and pulled a blanket over his head. If he could just catch a few minutes...

"Brad," the lead flight attendant said touching his arm.

"What the…," he said a little too loud, jerking from her touch.

"Sorry to startle you. Captain Wilbur said to give you your ten-minute notice."

"Thanks," he mumbled. Glancing at his watch, he struggled to see the time. Maybe a few minutes were not better than nothing. He felt like shit.

"I was hoping you'd get some sleep," Janice whispered. "Sorry for the noise tonight."

"Yeah...thanks, Jan." Sucking a deep breath he pressed the button to up-right his seat. "Think I could get a large, black, and very strong coffee?" he asked pulling on a shoe.

"Might keep you up all night," she said with a laugh.

"Good. Then I'll take two."

Brad stood and yawned. He tipped sideways when the airplane jerked with the turbulence. Holding the seats for balance, he worked his way up the aisle toward the lavatory.

Once inside, he placed his hands on the edge of the counter and closed his eyes willing himself strength to suck it up so he could make it through the night. When he opened them, blood-shot slits returned his stare. He considered the bacteria swimming in the water tank for a moment, then splashed water over his face.

"Get a grip buddy," he chided himself.

Outside the lavatory he stood at the flight deck door and Janice handed him his coffee. He picked up the handset and pressed the intercom button, ringing the boys up front.

He gave the captain the code to gain access to the flight deck. Sipping his brew, he waited for them to open the door to what would be his home for the next six and a half hours.

The door opened, he stepped inside and closed it. "Everyone doin okay?" he asked.

Captain Wilbur turned. "Looks to me like we're doing better than you. You look like hell."

"Yeah, well, I didn't get much sleep in the party zone."

"Why didn't you go to the aft bunk?" Tom asked.

"The hell if I'm going to sleep in the cargo compartment," Brad said. He had forgotten that this was one of the planes converted for long haul flights—those needing four pilots. But sleeping in the cargo compartment was less appealing than trying to snooze in a business class seat.

"Well, that's where you boys will find me," Wilbur said climbing out of his seat. "Away from the noise."

Captain Wilbur stepped out of the way, and Brad climbed into his seat and buckled in. The turbulence was now a continuous, moderate chop.

"What the hell is that?" Tom asked, staring outside his window.

"St. Elmo's fire," Captain Wilbur said, putting on his tie. "A phenomenon often found with thunderstorms at these latitudes."

Everyone starts somewhere. Life was a learning curve, especially in an Airbus at 37,000 feet. Despite Brad's hours flying the Princess, he still did not understand half of what the plane did. Thank God for automation—especially on nights like this.

Once Captain Wilbur was out of the flight deck Brad said, "How about you fly and I'll work the radios."

It was easier being the pilot flying and Brad did not mind being the pilot monitoring. Besides, the most challenging part of this flight was usually trying to stay awake. Doing nothing in the middle of the night had a sleep inducing effect all its own. But tonight there would be no sleeping with mother nature's wrath.

"Yeah. Thanks," Tom said. "This is one hell of a storm…look, we're right in it—"

"Why the hell are we flying through the storm?" Brad watched his navigation display as the radar painted the cells in front and to the right. "I'll call 'em in the back and let 'em know."

He pushed the call button. "Jan, it's Brad. In a couple minutes we'll be in an area where things will get exciting. Make sure the passengers are seated."

"Should we sit down too?"

"Definitely. And give everyone a heads-up," Brad said. "I'll call you as soon as we're out of it."

Brad pressed the progress button on the navigation computer. "We should've been at our final cruise altitude by now."

"Captain Wilbur said we've got abnormally warm temperatures keeping us down," Tom said.

The plane jolted and Brad tightened his seatbelt. He glanced at the temperature indication—minus 57 degrees. He shivered, turned on the landing lights, and squinted into the moonless night. Within seconds snow attacked the plane and they both jumped.

"Let's go for the anti-icing system," Tom said.

"We seem to be at the end of the cloud layer, it might be okay." Brad reached overhead and turned the anti-ice on. It couldn't hurt. He turned off the landing lights and glanced at the radar system.

One of the most automated planes in the world, but Pacific Airlines would not put in a radar system with the automatic feature. They had the older radar system—WXR-700—that depended upon pilot selection of an appropriate setting to paint an accurate picture.

Captain Wilbur set it at a standard calibrated setting. Brad's eyebrows furrowed and then he took another look.

Is this right? He twisted the knob to max gain and his mouth dropped open. The true nature of the storm blossomed before him on the radar display.

"Holy Shit! Looks like we're headed directly toward an area of intense activity! Can you possibly turn a little left?"

Brad startled as the plane was attacked by what sounded like rocks hitting the windshield. They were flying through an ice storm.

Tom yelled, "Sorry, what?"

"Pull it to the left. You're headed directly into the heart of the storm."

Tom reached up and pulled the heading knob and turned it left and the plane followed.

Out of nowhere an electrical aroma flooded the cockpit and the temperature inside the flight deck increased.

"Something's wrong with the air-conditioning system," Tom shouted.

"It's not the AC. The odor is from the weather. Just fly the plane." They should not be flying this close to a storm. What the hell were they doing while he was taking his break?

Brad turned on the landing lights again and what appeared to be mini hailstones pelted the aircraft. He thought they were going over the top of the clouds. The indications said they should have been above the storm, not in it.

The plane jerked and bounced.

Ice crystals slapped the fuselage and competed with the rushing of blood through his ears and the pounding in his head. His heart rate increased to match the speed of the plane. He wiped his hands on his pants and then placed them on the glareshield.

"I'm going to reduce the speed," Tom said. "Should we turn on the ignition so we don't flameout the engines?"

Brad looked at the ECAM. The ignition was already on. *What the hell?* The switch was off. He reached down and turned the ignition switch to on, and the autopilot disconnected. A warning screamed like a cavalry charge that the pilots were in control.

Jesus fucking Christ!

Red warning lights flashed. ECAM messages filled the screen. The plane tossed about like a small boat in the middle of an ocean.

"I have the controls," Tom yelled. Immediately the plane rolled to the left, and then to the right, and then left again…and the nose pitched up.

"Stabilize!" Brad yelled trying to figure out the best way through the storm, while Tom fought to control the plane.

Another tone blared—an altitude warning alert. They were climbing. "Maintain your altitude!" Brad snapped.

Their airspeed indication was gone. *What the fuck?* The plane chirped, chimed, dinged and cried from one alert to another. Brad wanted to scream.

"What's this?" Tom yelled.

"What's what?" Brad snapped and yelled, "There's no good... there's no good speed indication. Jesus Christ what's happening?"

"We've lost the...the...the speed then?" Tom cried.

As quickly as it disappeared the airspeed indication returned displaying 85 knots. The plane screamed, "Stall. Stall. Stall."

Brad tried to digest the list of procedures on the ECAM that were uploading and prioritizing as failures occurred. He began to read... "Alternate La..."

"What's happening?" Tom yelled.

"Stall. Stall. Stall," the plane cried.

"Pay attention to your speed. Pay attention!" Brad yelled. The plane climbed and they were getting slow. They could not fly without airspeed. The A330 was not supposed to be able to stall. Why were they getting that warning?

He hung onto the glareshield to maintain balance while he tried to figure out what was happening.

"Okay, okay, I'm descending," Tom yelled.

The speed increased to 185 knots, but it should have been 275. Brad's eyes darted from the ECAM's many warning messages to Tom, and then outside and back to the instruments.

The damn pitot tubes had to have water in them from flying into the storm. But they were flying through ice, not water.

The plane rolled left again and Tom jerked, and then it rolled in the opposite direction. Brad hit his head on the window.

"Stabilize!" Brad yelled, as he braced his left arm against the seat.

"Yeah—"

"Descend...it says we're going up," Brad yelled. "It says we're going up, so descend!" He wasn't imagining this. The plane was climbing. But why?

The thought of grabbing the stick flashed through his mind. But two pilots flying would either double the stick input or cancel out the other stick making things worse.

"Okay," Tom yelled, "I got it!"

"The hell you do. You're climbing again! Descend!" Brad yelled.

The plane screamed, "Stall. Stall. Stall." A ding sounded every few seconds and he had no idea why. Ice pounded the plane and Brad could not hear himself think.

If he knew how to fly this piece of shit without the automation he would have...

"Here we go, we're descending," Tom yelled.

"Gently."

The plane gained speed and the pitch attitude decreased. They were accelerating. The speed increased. The stall warning fell silent. That damned dinging continued, but Tom had the plane under control. And then...

"What the hell?" Brad said, as the nose pitched up again.

"We're...we're in a climb," Tom yelled.

What's wrong with this plane? "Enough of this," Brad cried, and pushed the call button to get the captain to the flight deck.

CAPTAIN WILBUR HUNG UP his uniform and climbed into his bunk. He closed his eyes. Within minutes he rolled left with the plane, slamming into the wall. Seconds later he rolled the opposite direction and dropped out of the bunk.

Standing he smacked his head on the ceiling. "Shit!" He pulled on his pants and zipped them. Bent forward, he worked his way through the tunnel to get upstairs.

The crash at the top of the ladder, followed by screams, was anything but good. The plane shook violently and the pitch angle... it was wrong. *What the hell are they doing up there?*

He found his footing and climbed the ladder. Turning the knob, the door only opened an inch. It was blocked. He pounded and yelled, but his voice could have been one of the screaming passengers.

The plane jerked left, then right, and pitched up again. He pressed his full weight into the door and it flew open.

Emerging from the cargo bunk he saw the source of the crash and what had been blocking him. Pinned beneath a food cart, Susanne's head was twisted backward and blood trickled from her mouth. Her barren eyes stared his way.

Captain Wilbur climbed over the cart and headed toward the flight deck fighting the uphill battle of pitch. He ran against time. He fought a congestion of bodies and carts in the aisle. People standing were being tossed about with the rolling of the plane. Others held tight to their seats, screaming, as the aircraft jerked them against their seatbelts.

Moving quickly he stepped over a woman in the aisle and fell backward. Grabbing for a seat he wrenched his shoulder and landed on his back.

Tom slammed the thrust levers forward and the plane pitched up. Brad grabbed the glareshield.

"Dammit, where is he?" Brad yelled, wishing the captain were with them. Captain Wilbur might know what to do. The screams coming from the passenger cabin gave reason to why he wasn't there.

Tom yelled, "I'm in TOGA, right?"

He was trying to increase his speed. But he shouldn't have max power at this altitude. *Should he?*

"Dammit, is he coming or not?" Brad yelled again. *Shit! Shit! Shit!* He had no fucking idea what to do. The plane took on a life all its own.

Despite Brad's insistence to descend Tom continued to pitch up. Then their altitude began spinning down. How the hell was the plane descending? The nose was sixteen degrees up. They had forward motion. But the altimeter spun down rapidly.

"We still have the engines. What the hell is happening? I don't understand what's happening," Tom cried.

The wings rocked left and right, up to 40 degrees each direction. Turbulence buffeted the plane violently. Brad was covered in coffee mixed with sweat. The altimeter indicated the plane was in a descent. But how could it go down if they were pitched up with max power? This was a fucking nightmare.

"We have a speed problem," Tom yelled, and pulled the speedbrake lever toward aft.

"No! Leave the speedbrakes alone," Brad shouted and pushed the lever forward.

"Damn it, I don't have control of the plane, I don't have control at all!" Tom yelled above the noise.

CAPTAIN WILBUR JUMPED to his feet, catching his breath. He continued his upstream fight to the flight deck, praying he could get there in time. He fell left into a passenger's lap. Ignoring the profanities he pulled himself upright, stumbled forward, and then fell right. He caught a seatback in his rib, but pressed onward. Steps from the cockpit door, he climbed over the last cart lying in the aisle.

Wilbur punched the emergency code into the door. He waited for what felt like forever, then slammed the door open. "What the hell are you two doing?"

"We've lost control of the plane!" Tom cried.

"We've totally lost control of the plane," Brad yelled. "We don't understand at all! We've tried everything. What do you think? What should we do?"

"I don't know!" Captain Wilbur yelled. They had engines and full power. The plane was pitched up. *What the hell is happening?* He had never seen anything like this.

"Climb...climb...climb...climb...," Brad yelled, as they passed through 9000 feet in a descent.

"But I've had the stick back the whole time!" Tom cried.

Oh shit! "No! No! No! Don't climb!" Captain Wilbur yelled. They stalled the plane. Falling at an excessive rate, they had to get the nose forward, if only...

"Left seat taking control!" Brad yelled and pressed forward on the stick dropping the nose from 15 degrees above the horizon to just below, as they passed through 7000 feet.

DUAL INPUT blared in a synthetic voice. The green CAPT and F/O lights flashed respectively in front of each pilot, indicating they were both on the controls as they fell through 6000 feet.

"Watch out, you're pitching up," Wilbur shouted, descending through 5000 feet. They needed to get the nose down further.

"We need to…we're at…four thousand feet!" yelled Tom.

"You're pitching up," Wilbur yelled. "Get the nose down."

The plane pitched up to 12 degrees and dual input blared again. Wilbur's eyes darted to the altimeter—they were descending through 2500 feet.

"SINK RATE, PULL UP, PULL UP," the plane screamed.

The A330 yelled, "Pull up," for one reason only—they were minutes from impact. Unfortunately there was not enough altitude to recover, and nothing they could do would make a difference.

Wilbur gave the boys something to do in their final moments. "Go on pull," he said. The best they could hope for would be a painless and quick death for all on board.

Tom yelled, "Let's go! Pull up, pull up, pull up!"

"PRIORITY RIGHT," blared over the audio and a red arrow appeared in front of Brad's seat pointing right.

Tom pressed the priority takeover push-button and locked out the left stick, taking control of the plane. A green CAPT light illuminated in front of him indicating Brad had no clue his inputs were useless. Yet Brad fought the plane and Tom.

Brad yelled, "Damn it, we're going to crash…This can't be happening! I don't want to die!"

"But what's happening?" Tom cried. "I don't understand."

Captain Wilbur closed his eyes and placed his face into the palms of his hands. *God forgive us.*

GLOBAL TRAINING CENTER
SEATTLE, WASHINGTON

SEPTEMBER 28, 2012

THE TEMPERATURE DROPPED inside Darby's car as quickly as it fell outside. She pulled her wool cap over her ears and then turned on the ignition to warm up her home away from home. She tapped the buttons on the radio and then turned it off and pulled on her gloves. Her mood sank deeper than the day before.

Each day she moved her car to a different location. During her watch she would start it every two hours for warmth, listen to tunes and eat something non-healthy. Most of the time she would sit in silence. Today the silence was replaced by the growl of her stomach as Starbucks crept into her mind.

She sat on her butt for a living, but doing it in a car left a lot to be desired. She looked at her watch and figured she could escape for twenty minutes. What were the odds of his coming out the minute she left? Zero to none.

She put her car into gear at the same time her passenger door opened.

"Going somewhere?"

Darby startled. Her mouth opened, but nothing escaped. She choked on her reply, staring into the barrel of a gun.

CHAPTER 1
SEATTLE WASHINGTON

DARBY BRADSHAW SPRINKLED cocoa into a pan of warming milk, then picked up a wooden spoon and stirred with one hand while she logged onto her company's website via her iPhone with the other. Popcorn crackled in the microwave and 'Santa Baby' played in the background, but her smile came from the laughter in the living room.

Once logged onto GlobalAir.com she entered her employee number and password to gain access to the top-secret portal. She scanned her messages and her eyes narrowed at an email from the director of training. As she read, the smile fell from her face and she dropped the spoon, splattering milk over the counter.

"No f-ing way."

"Aunt Darby," Jessica said from the doorway. "Fifty cents for the swear jar."

Darby looked up and covered her mouth in one swift move so nothing else would pop out. "I thought it was twenty-five cents," she said, picking up the spoon. "Besides, I didn't technically swear."

"Intent. It's a double fine for an F-swear," Jessica said as she peeked into the pan.

"Looks like I'll be financing your and Jen's college education,"

Darby said wiping milk off the counter.

"Hmm…another six years at the rate you're going, I'm thinking we'll both be able to go to graduate school," Jessica said as she pulled a bowl from the cupboard.

"In your dreams," Darby said with a grin.

The truth was, it would be her greatest pleasure to help with the girls' education. Something she planned on. When the microwave beeped Darby rushed across the room and popped open the door. She pulled the bag out and bounced it between her hands.

Jennifer walked in the room and yelled, "Don't drop it!"

"Under control," Darby said. She emptied the bag into a bowl and gave it a close inspection, picking out the black pieces as she did. Splaying her hands she said, "See…perfect. Did we think anything less?"

"Not from you," Jennifer said.

"Maybe you just got lucky." Jessica smirked.

"Better to be lucky than good," Darby said with a wink. "Why don't you two take this to the living room, and I'll be right out." She handed the bowl to Jessica and napkins to Jennifer.

Darby pulled down three mugs from the cupboard and set them on the counter. She glanced over her shoulder, and as the girls left the room she opened the memo and read.

MEMO: Training Canceled
To: Global Air Lines Pilots
From: Frank Dawson, Director of Training

Date: December 17, 2011

As of January 01, 2012, 'on location' pilot training will cease to exist. Instead of traveling to the schoolhouse and staying in a hotel away from your families you will be able to train in the comfort of your home.

After cutting last year's annual recurrent training, we realized the huge benefit this is to you and your families. We are now capable of training all initial checkouts at home.

Details to come. On behalf of the Global Air Lines's Training Department we wish you a Merry Christmas.

Darby's blood pressure skyrocketed with each word. *No friggin way.* Initial training was the classroom portion of flight training. Somewhat like medical school before doctors practiced on patients. Pilots would learn their planes without instructors.

She stuck her phone into her pocket, lifted the pan, and poured cocoa into a mug. This had to be someone's idea of a joke. They cracked the core of safety when they killed recurrent training, and now they were murdering systems training. What would be next?

With one mug filled, she started on the second. This was a huge hit to safety. Of all the cheapskate ways to save money. What were they thinking? She filled the third mug then set the pan in the sink.

Darby dropped a handful of mini marshmallows into each cup then sprayed a mound of whipped cream on top. She sucked down the angst that rolled her stomach and placed the mugs on a tray. Pushing the crisis to the back of her mind, she plastered a smile on her face and carried the cocoa into the living room, while the knot in her gut tightened.

"Thanks," Jennifer said, reaching for a cup.

"You're welcome, Sweetie," Darby said.

The girls set their cups on the coffee table beside the illegal paraphernalia, and Jessica picked up a lipstick and pressed it to her lips. "How's this?" she asked, puckering.

Darby grinned. "Let's see." She slid to the floor with the girls and stuffed a handful of popcorn into her mouth before she took a closer look. She had given them makeup for an early Christmas present despite their mother's wishes, and they were practicing putting on their faces.

It had been two years since Kathryn told them that ten was 'too early' for makeup. For the life of her, Darby could not remember what Kathryn's definition of 'old enough' was. So technically this was not a violation of the rules, just an innocent mistake. Besides, Darby had a lot on her mind with the new plane she flew. How was she supposed to remember the finer details of childcare?

Kathryn was the expert at parenting, but tonight she was at her company's Christmas party—someplace Darby would have paid any price for admission.

The Federal Aviation Administration's annual Christmas party was a huge event—the biggest of the year. Seeing the Feds let down a few hairs was something she wanted a backstage pass to.

Unfortunately, being so close to the holidays everyone was having a party, Jackie was out of town, and there was nowhere for the girls to go. Instead of attending as Kathryn's guest, Darby stayed with the twins. She told them they were 'hangin out' and there was no place she would rather be. Which was true.

Jennifer and Jessica were as close to her own kids as she would ever have. But being 'Aunt Darby' suited her well. Compliments of their psycho dad, they'd had a tough couple of years and deserved a little fun. Darby was fun and the girls' savior all in one.

She wiped her hands on a napkin and lifted a brush to Jennifer's hair wondering if it were they who were her savior.

"Looking pretty sweet ladies," Darby said, glancing at her watch. She had hoped Kathryn would be home early so she could prepare for her flight. Now all she wanted to do was tell her about Global canceling training.

Darby sipped her cocoa and grinned as Jessica put purple eye shadow on Jennifer, hoping Kathryn would not blow a gasket. But some things were worth the risk.

"Are you sure you have to work over Christmas?" Jennifer asked.

"Yeah. With the buyout I've lost too much seniority and can't hold it off," Darby said.

She chose to stay in Seattle as a junior first officer to help with the girls. She could have maintained a junior captain position—if she relocated to New York and downgraded to the MD-80 to sit reserve. But her ego to wear that fourth stripe did not overpower her need to help her best friends.

"Where will you be?" Jessica asked, giving up on her makeup and stuffing popcorn into her mouth.

"Hawaii." Darby stuck a finger into her whipped cream then sucked it clean. "Maybe I'll get a suntan for Christmas."

"How's Santa gonna find you?" Jessica asked, with a glint.

"Oh God Jess. You're such a putz," Jennifer said, rolling her eyes.

Darby loved these girls. She also had a lot of work to do to extend their childhood. Which in hindsight, giving them makeup might not have been the brightest of ideas. But twelve years old? Seriously? Their friends were light years ahead of them.

"Well…when Mom gets home, you can just ask her," Jessica said with a wink at Darby.

"Ask her what?" Kathryn asked, standing in the doorway.

"You're home early," Darby said, scrambling to her feet.

"I can see that," she said, removing her coat. "So what kind of art project do we have going on here?"

"Aunt Darby's teaching us how to put on makeup," Jennifer answered.

Kathryn knelt beside the girls and took Jessica's chin in her hand and shifted her face taking a good look at both sides and said, "hmm." Then she did the same to Jennifer. "Well ladies, all I can say is you both look beautiful. But why do you have to grow up so fast?" She kissed Jennifer on the head and rubbed Jessica's back.

"How was the party?" Darby asked, hugging Kathryn.

"Not bad. Office rumors were running rampant," Kathryn said sitting on the couch and kicking off her shoes in one movement. "Not for publication yet, but they found the Pacific Airlines black box."

"No kidding," Darby said, with eyes wide. "How long until they pull it up?"

"Probably months." Kathryn sighed. "Other than that, nothing exciting. I left early so they'd have opportunity to talk about me." She laughed a warm earthy tone that Darby loved.

"You won't believe the latest rumor at Global," Darby said, still standing. "The only problem is, it's not a rumor." She fought to keep the emotion out of her voice. "They're canceling training again. This time, initial!"

With hands on her hips she said, "This plane is confusing enough. Pilots need ground school. They're marketing it as a stay at home with your family deal. But it's training—it's supposed to be painful," Darby said exasperated. "And away from distraction."

"So…how do you really feel?" Kathryn asked with a grin.

"Ha. Ha," Darby said. "Seriously, we have to do something." She sat heavily on the couch. "How could the FAA have allowed this? More than that, how could our management pilots let it go through, let alone our union?"

"I have no idea. I'd heard rumbles at work that some of the carriers were petitioning this, but I never thought it would be approved. I'd have fought it all the way." Kathryn chewed on her lip and said, "Barring an accident, I don't know if I can undo the decision once made."

"But I've got to do something." Darby scowled. "For how little I fly, at least I had a solid foundation with my initial training. Set safety aside, think about the new hire pilots. If they don't pass their probationary check it's their career. We owe them better than this. Especially if this is their first airline job." She folded her arms.

"Besides, we learn so much better as a team. During initial we figured shi…" Darby glanced toward the girls and then said, "We figure the systems out together with an instructor who knows the plane. If a student learns something wrong, chances are they'll remember it incorrectly when it matters."

"I wish I could do something," Kathryn said. "They must have slipped this through while I was working on that special project."

"Well, it's wrong." Darby stood, this time to move her butt home. "I hate to ditch this party, but I've got to study for my flight." There was a lot she wanted to review one last time before strapping on the plane for the next eleven days. Especially since she had not flown for far too many months.

Darby reached her hand deep into her purse and found two quarters, then dropped them on the coffee table. Kathryn raised an eyebrow and Darby shrugged. "I try." The girls were busy sorting nail polish when she said, "Bye girls."

They scrambled to their feet and gave her hugs and then Kathryn walked her to the front door.

"I wish you didn't have to fly over Christmas," Kathryn said with such an expression of grief that Darby had to laugh.

"Me too," Darby said, pulling on her coat. "But pilots get the 'holiday flu' and passengers must travel. We reservists must carry them safely to their destinations in times like this. We're kind of like Superman that way." She pulled her wool hat on with a big grin. "Or Santa as the case may be."

"Can you call in sick?" Kathryn asked.

Miss Work Ethic herself did not really expect a response.

The answer to a perfect schedule was a sick call away, but Darby prided herself on a twenty-year career and never missing a day of work. She was not about to start just because of a merger and loss of seniority.

"Think you're going to have a white Christmas?" Darby asked stuffing her hands into her gloves to change the subject.

"It would be fun. Plus I've got the week off after Christmas with the girls."

"Seniority does have its benefits," Darby said and grinned.

"You'll get there again," Kathryn said and hugged her. "Did you ever hear back from Mr. Patrick?"

"Nope," Darby said opening the door. "I'm kind of surprised."

Mr. Patrick, the CEO of Global Air Lines, had been the CEO of Coastal Airlines once upon a time. He had always responded to Darby's emails in the past. His silence was unusual, but this time of year was busy for everyone.

"I'm sure he'll get back to you."

"I think so too," Darby said. "We've got eight days to work it out." She stepped onto the front porch and turned toward Kathryn. "Thanks again for my early Christmas."

The story of the pilots' life—holidays rarely happened on the actual day. Kathryn and their best friend, Jackie, made sure Darby had the full-meal-deal Christmas the weekend before.

"Are you kidding? The girls are ecstatic to have two Christmases. I think it was just about the best pre-Christmas anyone has ever had," Kathryn said. "Thanks for staying with them."

"Anytime." Darby hugged her once more, and she held on long and hard. Then said goodbye.

She stepped onto the porch and closed the door.

The temperature had dropped a few degrees since she arrived.

She shivered, but the chill came from Dawson opening Pandora's box. How could he cancel ground school?

How could the union have bought off on it?

Pilots were responsible for the souls on a plane. They needed to be trained properly and by professionals. Shivering, she wrapped her scarf around her neck and glanced through the window. Kathryn was sitting on the floor with the girls. Darby smiled and turned away.

She stepped off the porch and ran down the path toward her car. Shifting focus to her flight, she stuck the key into the car door. Tomorrow—Tokyo, her first flight in five months.

Opening the door, her scarf blew across her face. She pulled it away and glanced up. The sky darkened before her eyes as the moon slid behind the clouds. She climbed into her Subaru, turned the key, and cranked up the heat.

She had been checked out on the Airbus, A330, short of a year since the merger and she loved the technology, but on reserve she never flew. How could a pilot not fly for five months and stay proficient? They couldn't. Especially on the Airbus. This had been a concern of hers for many months.

Tomorrow would be her test.

Darby accessed her email on her iPhone while the car warmed. Scrolling through the messages, she saw the name that reminded her daily to never get into another relationship with a pilot—Neil Jordan.

She rolled her eyes. Looking over her shoulder she backed down the driveway. She had more important things to think about right now, like preparing for her flight. She also had to figure out what she was going to do about Dawson murdering yet another training program.

CHAPTER 2
OKLAHOMA CITY, OKLAHOMA

DECEMBER 17, 2011

CEO LAWRENCE PATRICK slid a hand over his mahogany desk, a piece in his game of Monopoly. He reached for his bottle of 18 year Macallan and poured himself two fingers.

He place the DVD into his computer and pressed play. Leaning back, he brought the crystal to his lips as he watched the video that would go live New Year's Day on every flight.

"Ladies and Gentleman, welcome aboard the largest airline in the world. We are delighted that you've decided to travel with us.

"As the CEO of Global Air Lines, I am proud to be sitting at this desk." He placed a hand on the surface and smiled into the camera. "Where history and dedication to an industry and its people began over seventy-five years ago. We at Global Air Lines value honesty, integrity, and taking care of our customers, as well as our employees. Our promise is one of safety and exceptional customer service…"

Lawrence pressed stop and ejected the disk. "Perfect," he said.

He raised his drink. "Hank, wherever the wind blows you…to your health." He tipped back his glass and emptied it.

Hank Dyer, the man who taught the rest of the world how to dismantle an airline, loved single malt scotch. He loved it so much, that it sent him to the drunk-tank one too many times. Lawrence Patrick, an attorney in another city at the time, was called to make Dyer's problems go away.

He had done his job well. He also learned of a world that was ripe for the picking—airlines. Dyer used deregulation to destroy Universal Airlines. Lawrence, however, saw far more potential than breaking apart an airline. Instead he ate other airlines, parted out services, and built the largest airline in the world.

With a quick glance at his watch, he pushed back from his desk. He strode across his office toward his eighteenth century armoire. Lawrence pulled on his coat, and removed black leather gloves from the pockets.

As he glanced around the richly furnished office, he smiled. He had come a long way. Thanks to Dyer, he closed up his law practice and joined Coastal Airlines. Starting at the bottom, he left at the top as the CEO. A fall guy took his place during the bankruptcy—an illusion the problems occurred after he was gone. Life was filled with smoke and mirrors. He turned off the light and pulled the door closed behind him.

Lawrence Patrick arrived at the hotel thirty minutes later. His driver pulled in front of the building, apologizing for taking longer than expected. He jumped out of the car and opened the door.

Palming the driver a healthy tip, Lawrence assured him it was fine. He wanted his boys relaxed and a few extra minutes with an open bar would take care of that. He turned and headed for the historic Colcord Hotel.

Built in 1910, the Colcord was the first skyscraper in Oklahoma City, and one that held great memories. Marketing believed history was needed to successfully merge the two airlines. He agreed.

Creating an illusion of history, connecting him to the legacy and the people, they would love and trust him.

Stepping into the lobby, he glanced at the black and white marble columns, admiring the architecture as he removed his gloves and slid out of his coat.

A beautiful blonde approached and took his outerwear. "Your party is waiting, Mr. Patrick," she said extending her arm toward the Flint restaurant.

"Thank you," he said and headed that way.

When he left Coastal, he took a side trip before arriving at Global Air Lines—a twenty-three million dollar year with Green Leaf Health Care Insurance, tied to a promise of combining both airlines and bringing Green Leaf on with the largest healthcare contract known in the world, made him a wealthy man.

The move also removed him from the line of fire during both airline bankruptcies. He returned to the airline industry as the savior of Global Air Lines and the welcoming committee to Coastal.

"Good evening, Gentlemen," he said approaching. "I trust you're enjoying yourselves." Smiles, expressions, and a variety of responses answered his question.

Mingling with the group, he said hello to each manager, laughing and joking as he did so. He asked about their wives and children, remembering every detail.

Once the niceties were done Lawrence said, "Gentlemen, shall we sit?" He extended his hand toward the table and took his place at the head. Vice President Todd McDermott sat on the opposite end and tilted his glass once their eyes connected. Lawrence nodded in response—a team that could not be beat.

To Lawrence's right sat the director of flight operations, Captain George Wyatt. Beside him was Captain Rich Clark, manager of flight operations. To his right sat First Officer Dick Foster, director of flying. Lawrence questioned the intelligence of putting a first officer into such a high position, but the price tag was right as was the commitment.

To Lawrence's left sat Captain Frank Dawson, managing director of training—Global's tourniquet to the airline's bleeding problem. Beside Dawson was a new face, Captain Burt Armstrong. He would take over the last of the Coastal director positions as the A330 fleet training captain.

Between Armstrong and McDermott sat Captain J.R. Roanoke, the head of Global Air Lines' Airline Pilots Organization, ALPO. Lawrence would miss their working arrangement. But Roanoke in Washington, as the head of all ALPO airline unions, made a much more powerful tool.

The only person missing was Miles Carter, the chief operating officer. He was the portal that connected flight operations to the corporation. These were Carter's boys sitting in from of him, and Lawrence was sorry that he was unable to join the party.

"Gentleman," Lawrence said, "This previous year was a challenge for all, compliments of the merger. But we made it. And with great success at that." Glancing at each person as he spoke, his eyes landed on Captain Armstrong's and held.

This was not a dinner that a fleet training captain normally attended. But Armstrong was new, and this event would impress upon him the role he played. Besides, throwing a dog a bone bought loyalty.

"Join me in welcoming Burt to our team," he said raising his glass. "We know you will take the future of our airline to new heights. The A330 is the foundation of Global, and we need a solid fleet training captain. A soldier. Frank tells me that's you."

"Well, I hope so, sir," Armstrong said. "I'll do my best."

"I know you will, son."

Lawrence turned his attention to Captain Roanoke and said, "And we'll miss you, our friend, as you run off to bigger and better things."

"I will always be part of your team, sir. Global's where my roots are firmly planted and always will be. Nothing will change while I'm away." Lawrence and Roanoke exchanged a knowing look.

"Here's to roots," McDermott said, raising his glass, "that run deeper, and stronger than the oak tree sacrificed to bring our scotch to life." Everyone laughed and they all raised their glasses.

"Gentlemen," Lawrence said, lowering his voice and allowing his eyes to moisten. "Tonight is about you. About your sacrifice and commitment to the success of Global Air Lines.

"It's because of you that we are the leaders in the industry. You are the best and everyone wants to be you. Make them earn it."

Three waitresses arrived and placed dinner salads in front of the men. Once the women were gone, Lawrence said, "We have a contract coming up, further integration of company procedures, development of Next Gen, and a few Coastal pilot issues to contend with. Nothing we cannot handle. But tonight is about celebration.

"Tonight is about rewarding yourselves for excellence as the leaders you continually prove to be. You are sitting at this table for two reasons—for me to say thank you, and to raise our glasses to your future and the future of Global Air Lines."

He lifted his glass, as did everyone.

"We are the largest and most successful airline in the world. I will do whatever it takes to keep us there." His eyes scanned the table and then he asked, "Will you?"

CHAPTER 3
SEATTLE, WASHINGTON

DECEMBER 18, 2011

D ARBY ROLLED to her side and hugged a pillow. Within minutes she was on her back with the pillow on her face. She tried not to think about anything, especially that memo and the ramifications of what Dawson was doing. But that was all she could think about.

She peeked out from under the pillow and squinted at her clock—0700. Her alarm was set to go off in two hours. Closing her eyes she tried to think of nothing and drift back to sleep. But the day's pending activities raced behind her eyelids and deep within her brain. Then Dawson slammed into center position.

The previous night she stayed up late in a solid attempt to study, but her mind was distracted with thoughts of their cutting training.

Then inspiration smacked her in the head. Pulling the pillow off her face, she jumped out of bed and rushed to her desk. Why hadn't she thought of this sooner?

She would write a blog—something to supplement the lack of training. It was not the perfect solution, but it was something.

Opening her laptop, she Googled Blogspot.com and then flashed over to GoDaddy.com and purchased a domain name. Her blog would be a forum where pilots could share stories and exchange information. This would be a virtual classroom—a place to discuss flying issues.

Once her blog was set up, she began to write.

Flight For Safety:
December 18, 2011

Welcome to the world of an A330 virtual classroom. Many airlines are no longer conducting ground school. Pilots are expected to learn their airplanes and remain current via the computer. But a thumb drive does not share stories or exchange ideas. Disks do not provide feedback. Plastic does not think critically. I am opening up this venue for pilots to come together and discuss aviation related issues and share information.

Together we will learn, grow, and keep the skies safe.

For now, I have a question for all Airbus Pilots about the following performance chart. What power setting and pitch attitude should you hold at flight level 340 if you lose your airspeed indication? What about you Boeing pilots, do you know what power settings and pitch attitude you'll need? Something to think about before the situation occurs.

Welcome aboard your Flight to Safety!

Fly Safe. DB

Darby uploaded a photo of her plane and a copy of an Airbus performance chart. Sitting back in her chair, she folded her arms and smiled at her handy work. It was not a perfect answer, but it was definitely better than nothing.

Four hours after her blogging moment Darby was dragging her bags through the parking lot on her way to check-in.

Merging airlines changed many lives, hers being one of them.

But change was a good thing. Well...maybe not always good, but inevitable and everyone needed to adjust.

The jury was still out, however, on which was more painful—dropping off her Boeing, or having her fourth stripe ripped from her shoulder in her step back to first officer.

Once inside the terminal, she dodged passengers and ran toward the elevator as the doors were closing. A foot stuck through the opening and stopped them from their mission. That foot belonged to one of her favorite captains—Jack Barton.

"Thanks, Jack," Darby said, squeezing herself and her bags into the small compartment filled with more of her kind—airline employees leaving home for the holidays.

"Didn't you get the memo we don't have to carry flight bags anymore?" Jack asked.

"I did. But I've got holiday contraband inside."

"Huh?"

"Christmas phallic symbols." Darby grinned.

Two flight attendants giggled. It was obvious that Jack's mind was not traveling down the same path as the women. "What's sticky and sweet and red and white all over?" Darby asked.

"Ah, candy canes," he said. "Give an old guy some time, we'll eventually get there."

"I have faith in you," Darby said. "And for need to know info, they are not the little ones. They're the good six inchers." The door opened and Darby backed her bags out to the mezzanine. "When it comes to holiday phallic symbols, size *is* an issue." This time everyone laughed, and Jack turned three shades of red.

"Happy Holidays," Darby said to the flight attendants, as she and Jack turned down the hallway in the opposite direction.

"Where'ya headed today?" Jack asked.

"Tokyo. You?"

"Looks like I'll be your captain. They nailed me on reserve two hours ago."

"Sorry about that," Darby said. "The good news is I can teach you more about the art of celebrating holidays on the road."

Jack chuckled. "What happens on the road stays on the road."

"Absolutely," Darby said as they reached flight operations. She punched in the security code and held the door open for him. He rolled his bag in and she followed.

The room was far too quiet for how many people lingered. This was the week everyone would be leaving home for the holidays. Only the very lucky, or very senior, would be returning before Santa came.

Darby placed her hands on her hips and drummed her red nails. A bad attitude would not be tolerated during the holidays. Not on her watch.

"Hey guys, anyone know why Santa doesn't have any kids?"

"I'm sure you're going to tell us," Jack said with a grin.

"He only comes once a year, and it's down a chimney." A couple of pilots laughed and the room became more animated. *Mission complete. Tension broken.* "My job here, is done."

"The hell it is," Jack said, with a laugh. "We've got a plane to carry across the ocean."

Darby relocated her bags and parallel parked them against the wall and stepped into the glassed-in flight planning room. Eight other pilots stood around a large oak table as they performed their task of flight planning.

She located their paperwork, which led her to the other first officer. He was busy highlighting the chart for their flight. Darby stood beside him.

"Hi, I'm Darby."

"Nate. Nice to meet you," he said, with a glance.

"Thanks for doing the paperwork."

"No problem."

"You want first break?" she asked, working on the power of positive suggestion, as she picked up the release. Nobody wanted the first break at 1400. It was too early to sleep and far too noisy with a meal service in progress.

"Nope. Arrived eight hours ago. Been dozing on the couch all morning."

Okay, second break it is. Her night's marathon study session combined with her over-active mind had put her over the edge of fatigue. Despite the hour and the noise, she was sure if she stuffed earplugs far enough in she might get some sleep.

"I need a takeoff, anyway," he said, "or I'll go non-current."

The story of a pilot's life on an international plane. Darby settled into a chair and reviewed the flight plan when a knock on the window startled her. Everyone in the room looked up. The assistant chief pilot pointed at Darby, then turned his finger and pulled it toward him like he was tickling a dog's neck.

Darby pointed at herself, eyes wide, and he nodded. Then he turned and walked away.

"Oooh…Darby's in trouble," someone said.

"What'd ya do now?" another pilot asked with a grin.

"Ha. Ha," Darby said. "He probably wants to give me my Christmas bonus."

"Good luck," Jack said giving her a blessing with an invisible cross and a wink. "We'll wait for you."

Darby stepped inside the assistant chief pilot's office. "You wanted to see me?"

Roy Sutton, a first officer just like herself, wore the hat of assistant chief pilot and dealt with issues when the chief pilot was away.

"Yes. Please sit down." Roy folded his hands on the top of his desk. "You wrote an email to Mr. Patrick."

"I asked him if I could have a room to host a Christmas party, and—"

"You've really upset a lot of people."

"For writing to the CEO? Why? That was never an issue before." She narrowed her eyes, trying to understand the problem.

"You violated the chain of command."

"What chain of command?" Darby asked, a little too loudly. "We have an open door policy."

"No, we don't." Roy cleared his throat.

"That's not what Mr. Patrick said. Besides, where's this chain of command policy written?"

"It's not. But that's the way they do things here."

"They have policies that aren't written?" Darby's eyebrow lifted.

Roy shifted in his chair. "Management pilots at Global are military. The chain of command is the way they run things."

Like she would know, never having been in the military. "So who's upset with me?"

"Captains Wyatt and Clark, and First Officer Foster."

"Who the heck is Foster?"

"Your director of flying. He's the chief pilot's boss."

"A first officer's the chief pilot's boss?" Darby asked raising an eyebrow, trying to understand how that worked. "So whose Foster's boss?"

He hesitated then said, "Clark."

"So you're the fifth link in the chain?" Darby asked. "And I pissed you all off?"

"More or less."

"Which is it?" Darby asked, "More…or less?"

"More."

"What about your boss. Did I piss the chief pilot off too?"

"Only because shit falls down hill. They called him on the carpet to find out why you went over his head."

The chief pilot was one of the few remaining management pilots from Coastal Airlines. Causing him problems with the new regime was the last thing she wanted, but this discussion was stupid on so many levels.

"Maybe I should write apology letters to the victims of my crime," she said sarcastically, fighting hard not to laugh.

"That's exactly what you should do," he said, leaning forward. "They do things differently here, and the sooner you figure that out, the better off you'll be."

"Seriously? I was kidding."

"This is not a joking matter. An apology would put this behind you."

"Okay. Is that it?" She glanced at her watch, wanting out of the room before her mouth opened and something slipped out that would cause her more problems.

"No," he said. "Your email brought attention to your blog."

"I just started it this morning. How did—"

"I don't care if you started it five minutes ago. You put a Global chart on it. You need to remove it."

"It wasn't a Global chart. It was an Airbus chart that I pulled from the Internet."

"Doesn't matter. They want it gone."

"Who's they?"

He gave her the stink-eye and she held up both hands in

surrender and said, "Consider it done. Will you send me the email addresses to the guys you want me to write those apology letters to?"

"Of course," he said. "Have a nice Christmas."

Darby left the room. She pulled out her laptop and logged onto her blog and removed the chart. The point was to enhance training. One would think that running an airline, management would have better things to do with their time than read blogs.

Had she really just been called into the chief pilot's office for emailing the CEO? Darby shook her head.

We don't have an open door policy?

She repacked her computer, then poked her head into the flight planning room and said, "Guys, I'll meet you at the plane." She did not wait for a response, but headed out the door.

CHAPTER 4
INBOUND—JFK AIRPORT

DECEMBER 18, 2011

WALT SIPPED THE LAST FEW DRIBBLES of cold coffee and tossed the empty cup into the garbage bag. Glancing at the captain, he stifled a yawn.

He did not mind the captain sleeping. But Walt could have used a couple minutes of shuteye himself. Seniority had its privileges—something that he would never again see in his career.

Walt lived through a couple mergers, but finally upgraded to captain at Coastal. Then Global took over. He ground his teeth. After he was stapled to the bottom of the seniority list, he was bumped out of his captain's seat. Unable to make ends meet, he checked out on the highest paying first officer seat he could hold—the Airbus, A330, in New York.

Sucking a deep breath, he hoped the oxygen would slap him awake. He was a sixty-four-year-old that needed to be in bed sleeping. Staying up all night on ocean crossings was killing him. This was a younger man's sport.

Walt closed his eyes, and then shook his head as he opened them. He squinted out the window into the afternoon sun. His brain hurt. But falling asleep while the captain snored was the last thing any of them needed.

Losing both his pension and his seniority with the merger was the final slap in the face to his career. His time was running out for the career he once loved. One more year and he would be forced to retire. Hell...he would have been gone now if he could have afforded it.

He would have to take a training position after retirement to make ends meet. That would be the only job he would be qualified to do, having given his life to aviation. Qualified was open to interpretation on this plane.

Walt yawned and closed his eyes. Their flight was scheduled for under eight hours without a relief pilot. He had been awake for the previous twelve, and monitoring the plane for the last seven and a half. The captain had been sleeping for two. Walt could not blame him. Besides he would rather have the captain rested than falling asleep on approach.

"Global 54, contact New York Center on 135.8."

Walt startled. His eyes popped open. "Shit," he said, fumbling with the hand-mic, as air traffic control repeated the clearance.

"Uhh, sorry. Wrong button for Global. Global 54 is going to center on 135.8." He changed the radio and contacted ATC. "Center, Global 54 is with you."

"Good afternoon Global 54, turn left heading one nine zero for traffic. Descend to flight level two one zero."

After repeating the clearance Walt reached up to the flight control unit and pulled the heading select knob and turned it to a heading of 190. Then he spun the altitude down to 21,000 feet. He hesitated a moment, wondering which would be the best course of action—pull or push the knob.

When he pressed the altitude selector knob, telling the plane to go down, nothing happened so he pulled it. The power came to idle and the plane started down toward the selected altitude.

He was way too tired to contemplate the finer points of flying this plane. He felt like a passenger on the A330. There was truth to the saying that you can't teach an old dog new tricks. Especially if the tricks were on a foreign, computerized airplane.

The captain's brief, that occurred eight days prior, had gone something like—"I don't like this plane. I miss the Boeing. I'm on reserve and there's a reason, so I don't have to fly. Once in awhile scheduling gets me, but that's when it's your job to fly. Keep me out of trouble."

"Global 54, contact Kennedy Approach on 127.4."

Walt jumped. "Going to approach," he said, flustered. "Approach, Global 54 is with you out of, uh…flight level two nine zero for two one zero."

"Global 54 direct PARCH, ROBER ONE arrival. Descend to niner thousand, cross CALVERTON at one two thousand, two hundred and fifty knots. Expect ILS 22 left."

Walt replied to the clearance and then selected direct to PARCH. He turned on his interphone speaker for the cabin PA and cranked up the volume. He lifted the PA and said, "Ladies and gentlemen, this is your first officer speaking. We've started down. The winds are about sixteen knots out of the west, and the temperature is forty-three degrees. I hope you had a good flight. Flight attendants prepare for landing."

The captain didn't move. *Jesus, what's with this guy?* Then he looked at the instruments. *Why is the plane leveling at 21,000 feet? Shit.* He scratched behind his ear, then realized he had forgotten to put in the lower altitude. He quickly dialed in 9000 feet and pressed the altitude knob. The plane started down.

They were supposed to cross CALVERTON at 12000 feet and 250 knots. He typed 250/120 and hesitated, unsure if that was the correct format. At least with the Boeing aircraft they could insert and analyze. The Airbus was an all or nothing.

He quickly added two more zeros, took a deep breath, and entered 250/12000 on the flight plan page. *Shit.* They were above profile and not going to make their crossing altitude. He pulled the speedbrake handle full aft to help get down quicker.

They would be on the ground within 30 minutes and he needed to brief the approach.

"Captain, you alive over there?" When he didn't respond Walt reached out and smacked his arm.

"Whaaa...what the hell? " The captain said glaring Walt's way with two bloodshot eyes. "What'd ya need?" he asked, before closing his eyes again.

"We've started down and we'll be on the ground in less than thirty minutes."

"God dammit!" The captain yelled sitting up and opening his eyes wide. "Why in the hell didn't you wake me?"

"I tried."

"Try harder next time."

"Some things are easier said than done," Walt mumbled.

"Global 54, turn right heading two six zero radar vectors ILS 22 left," ATC announced.

Walt keyed the microphone the same time the captain did—if looks could kill. Walt spread his hands and mouthed, "You got it." Technically it was the pilot monitoring's job to talk on the radio. Which was impossible when that person was sleeping.

"I've got the radios. You're flying the approach!"

"Got it boss. It's just been a long night flying solo. I forgot." He pushed the speedbrake handle forward.

"Sorry," the captain said.

Captain Snooze was definitely not a morning person, despite it being the afternoon. But on their time clock it was late at night somewhere. Or perhaps early morning. Hell if he knew.

"Ready for a brief?" Walt asked.

"Yeah, go ahead."

Giving the fastest brief in history, Walt set the minimums and compared the approach in the computer with the approach plate. Their runway was only 8400 feet long. He pressed medium on the autobrakes, then pulled the airspeed selector and dialed it back to 240 knots.

"Global 54 turn right heading three one zero, radar vectors for ILS 22 left, descend and maintain three thousand."

Walt spun the heading to 310 and the altitude to 3000 feet and pulled the speedbrake lever full aft again.

"Global 54, four miles from ROSLY, turn left heading two four five, maintain two thousand until established on localizer, cleared ILS runway 22 left approach. Contact the tower on 119.1 over ZALPO."

The captain confirmed the clearance while Walt turned the heading selector, pressed the approach button, and activated the second autopilot.

"Shit, we're fast," Walt said. "Flaps 1." He dialed the speed back to 200 knots. "Gear down." When the speed passed through 205 knots he called, "Flaps two." Then he dialed the speed to 180 knots.

The captain lowered the gear and said, "Gear down," as he selected the flaps.

"Flaps three," Walt called passing through 185 knots and dialed the speed back to 160.

"Let me give you full flaps," the captain said, lowering them. He contacted the tower and received a landing clearance.

They were on a three mile final when Walt finally felt under control. He pushed the speedbrake lever forward and set it to arm, then pressed managed speed. *What the fuck?*

The power increased and the speed bug moved up to 250 knots. The speed bug was supposed to go to landing speed.

"Go around!" the captain yelled.

"Go around thrust, flaps three, positive rate gear up," Walt yelled, as he pushed the thrust levers forward to TOGA. The captain raised the flaps and gear, and called the tower to alert them they were on the go.

The speed bug dropped from 250 to 203 knots and Walt had no fucking idea why. He pulled back on the stick and the autopilot disconnected. Warnings flashed and associated dinging warned him he was flying the plane.

"You're going through your missed approach altitude!" yelled the captain. "You need to turn."

Walt pushed the nose forward trying to recapture 3000 feet. They had forgot to set the missed approach altitude. Then he banked, trying to follow the green line on his map. "Get me radar vectors."

The captain dialed 3000 into the flight control unit. "Tower, ahhh Global 54 is on the missed. Request radar vectors."

The control tower passed them back to approach control who said, "Global 54, state your intentions."

"We'd like to come back for another approach," the captain responded. Then he snapped at Walt. "Think you can get her under control this time?"

"I have no idea what happened."

With their power in TOGA, they were seconds away from

over-speeding. Walt pulled back the thrust to the climb position. As the speed came back Walt called, "Flaps 1." He reselected the autopilot and took his first breath since the craziness began. What the hell was that all about?

Approach control gave them radar vectors, with plans for another approach to ILS 22 left.

Walt pulled the speed knob and dialed it back to 190, then to 185 knots.

"Give me flaps two. We'll get her stabilized well in advance." The excessive blood flow pounding inside Walt's head made it hard to think. He had never flown an actual missed approach before, and had no clue why the speed bug went to 250 knots, and then to just above 200.

With his heart in his throat, ringing in his ears, and adrenaline firing in all cylinders, he thought he was going to have a heart attack. Confusion slammed through his brain. *Why the hell did it do that? Why wouldn't it slow down? Why did the speed bug come up?*

They were cleared for an intercept heading for the ILS approach. Walt turned the heading selector to the intercept course, selected the second autopilot, and pressed the approach button. He was on course, on speed, and on the glide path. He had it wired. ATC passed them back to the tower.

"Tower, Global 54 is on final for landing 22 left," the captain said.

"Global 54, cleared to land 22 left," Kennedy tower replied. "Wind two seven zero at fifteen knots."

Walt called, "Flaps three." With hands sweaty and heart racing, he called, "Gear down," and then, "Flaps full." But his nightmare continued when he selected managed speed and the power increased. This time the speed bug jumped to green dot.

"What the hell are you doing?" the captain shouted.

"I'm not fucking doing anything!" Walt yelled. "Check the speeds in the computer." *What is happening with this fucking plane?*

"We've got 132 knots in the box," the captain said. "But the thing is running over 200. Why?"

"Hell if I know," Walt snapped and pushed the nose over to follow the glideslope. The speed was at 185 knots and increasing. This was a nightmare. The plane would not slow down. "I'm going around." Walt pushed the power forward. He called for gear and flaps to come up as he pulled back on the stick.

They executed the missed approach.

Hands sweaty and body visibly shaking, he glanced at the fuel— 8980 pounds and decreasing. He was on a downwind again—this time they stayed in the pattern with the tower.

"Do you know what in the hell it's doing?" Walt asked. "I've never flown this plane without autothrust before, but maybe we should…" He looked at the captain, and asked, "Do you want to do it?"

"Hell no. I'm better monitoring."

Walt had never flown the plane in manual thrust and was not starting now with Captain No-Fly beside him.

He flew around the pattern with the automation connected. He configured the plane and confirmed their speeds. They received landing clearance and he pushed the buttons for their approach. But when he pressed managed speed on short final the same thing happened—the speed bug jumped to green dot, just above 200 knots, as the power increased.

Walt pushed the nose forward to maintain a path to the runway. It was a hell of a pitch attitude down. The A330 sat 'nose low' as it was, but this was crazy. He felt nothing less than a commander of a missile headed toward the ground. The power came back a bit, but the speed continued upward toward 200 knots.

"She's not slowing down," the captain yelled.

They were cleared to land, and he was damn well going to put this piece of shit plane on the ground. "Flaps full," Walt said.

"You're going to over-speed the flaps."

"Then pull them up. I don't fucking care. We're landing."

The captain lowered the flaps to full. But the flaps did not move beyond the three position.

"Go around!" yelled the captain.

Walt glanced at the fuel. They did not have enough to make another go around. Or did they? Either way, he was landing.

They were close to 200 knots. If he flared too much, the plane would fly again. If he did not flare enough, the impact would be ugly. They should have landed on the longer runway, closed or not.

Walt pulled the power to idle as he crossed the threshold. He kicked off the autopilot and pushed the nose forward. The runway was coming at them at high speed. His death grip on the stick stopped the blood flow in his hand.

The plane called out, "Fifty. Thirty. Twenty."

With the power at idle the plane slowed, but not nearly fast enough. They had 8400 feet to stop and were eating up runway. He pushed the stick forward.

The main gear hit first with a jolt, stabbing pain into his spine. He held the nose off and went for reversers and stepped on the brakes as hard as he could all at the same time.

Walt pushed the nose forward. It hit hard and vibrated violently. He held the brakes on full, but the end of the runway approached rapidly. There was no way in hell they would be able to stop before they ran out of pavement.

CHAPTER 5
SeaTac Airport

December 18, 2011

Darby pulled her suitcase and flight bag behind her as she stormed into the bathroom. She shifted from upset to max pissed as she rehashed the stupidity of the situation. Of course she was overreacting, but her emotions took control.

Maybe it was that time of the month—time to realize everything the pilots said about Global management might actually be true.

She turned her back to the mirror, leaned against the counter, and folded her arms. If she were going to get spanked, she damn well better get kissed too.

Darby pulled her phone out and pressed speed dial. When Kathryn answered she said, "You won't believe what happened." She gave Kathryn the *Reader's Digest* version of the meeting.

"Nobody treats my friends like that," Kathryn said. "Don't worry, I'll take them down."

Darby laughed. "I'm overreacting, huh?"

"Maybe a little. But I could still give them a surprise inspection."

"That'd be nice, but not necessary," Darby said with a chuckle. "It'll be okay. It's just an almost twenty-year career and I've never been called into the chief pilot's office before."

"Don't let it get to you," Kathryn said. "Just keep up your Darby joy, and the world will be perfect."

"Ho. Ho. Ho," Darby said. "I just feel like an idiot."

"Don't. They're the ones who should feel stupid."

Shifting gears, Darby told Kathryn about her online training idea, then gave her the address to check it out. After saying goodbye she sucked a deep breath, and wheeled her suitcase filled with holiday joy toward security.

She worked her way through the security line receiving special treatment, compliments of her knee replacement. Raising both hands she was patted down and began to laugh at the irony of her criminal status.

"I'm sorry," Darby said between giggles.

"Quite all right," the TSA agent said. "But I have to say it's a first."

When they were done, Darby gave the woman a candy cane and wished her a Merry Christmas.

Darby was the first to arrive at the plane and she stowed her bags up front. She removed the bag of candy canes from her flight bag. 299 to be exact—enough to give one to every passenger, and then some. She pulled on her Santa hat, adjusted her tie and stepped into the forward galley.

"Nice tie," a flight attendant said.

It was pretty cool. Made out of green sequins, it sparkled. "When the guys say they like it," Darby whispered, "I tell them that it matches my underwear."

Laughing, the flight attendant said, "You're my kind of girl. It's nice to meet you. I'm Bethany."

"Darby. Great to meet you too. Do you mind if I stand at the door and hand out candy canes when we board?"

"Are you kidding? That'd be awesome."

Darby wandered down the aisle and arrived at the entry door

just as her crew approached. "Welcome to Global Air Lines," she said. "I hope you enjoy your flight today. We're the airline that spanks its employees with compassion and respect."

"Funny," Jack said. "So what was that all about?"

"I violated the chain of command."

"How?" Jack asked.

"I emailed the CEO to get a room for a Christmas party on my Honolulu layover."

"Since when do we have a chain of command?" Nate asked.

"Since now," Darby said. "And I'm fairly certain it trumps the open door policy."

"Where the hell's that written?" Jack stepped onto the plane.

"In some military manual." Darby handed Jack a candy cane.

"Well this place is run by a bunch of Airline Nazis," Nate said, dragging his bag over the threshold. "Not sure what you expected."

"Expected? Maybe a little holiday spirit, or a 'Thank you for working the holiday while I'm home with my family.' How about... 'Sure, it's the least we can do!' How about—"

"Whoa, Tiger." Nate raised a hand. "How about I take my candy cane and go to my cave?"

"I know where you could stuff this candy cane," Darby said handing him one, with a grin. Both Jack and Nate laughed.

"I'm glad I'm not on your bad side," Nate said.

"Hell, Darby doesn't have a bad side."

"Maybe not," Darby laughed. "But I might be suffering from work related stress."

"I wouldn't joke around here," Nate said, with a scoff. "I'm just sayin, these boys don't play nice with anyone who one ups them. Watch your back."

"They don't know what can of whoop ass they opened," Jack

said over his shoulder, pulling his bag down the aisle.

"A Ho, Ho, Ho, bunch of whoop in this ass," Darby said, placing a hand on her hip. "Wait, that didn't come out right. Retract that statement."

While the flight attendants laughed, Darby stuffed earplugs into her ears, pulled the flashlight out of her pocket and headed out the door and down the external stairs for her walkaround.

Focusing on her plane she looked for anything that might be wrong. The only thing wrong was she had a bag full of gifts and no room at the Inn for her party. Plan B would soon be in effect. As soon as she figured out what that was.

When finished with her outside duties she ran up the stairs, then walked quickly down the aisle and into the cockpit. "You guys need anything?"

"Nope. I'm good," Jack said, and Nate shook his head.

With her bag of candy canes she headed back to the entry door before the first passenger boarded. By the time all passengers were seated Darby had given out 239 candy canes, helped three families with their luggage, and held a baby.

She returned to the flight deck, hung her jacket in the closet, and sat on the jumpseat. She slid her seat forward and punched buttons on the ACARS, Aircraft Communication and Reporting System, to input their flight number, fuel, date, and employee numbers. She requested the local weather.

When the data arrived, she ripped the paper off the printer and tossed it up front.

"Thanks," Jack said picking it up. He slid his highlighter over the altimeter setting and then set his instruments. "I still find it hard to believe they called you into the office. That's bullshit."

"Called in?" Bethany asked from the doorway. "For what?"

"Darby wrote the CEO," Nate said. "Some really bad shit. She actually wanted a crew room for Christmas party."

"Seriously?" Bethany said. "What'd they say?"

"I'm writing apology letters to my victims."

"They can't make you do that," Jack said.

"I know what I'd tell them, if I were you," Nate said, "I'd tell them to get their asses out here on the holidays."

"But I thought the CEO was doing dinner parties for everyone who was working on Christmas this year," Bethany said. "I'm going to the party in Tokyo."

"He is," Darby said. "Honolulu was an oversight because it's not international, but still impossible to get home."

"Can you say pool party?" Nate said. "As in naked?"

Darby grinned. "I thought it might be a better idea to keep the fun away from the public eye, in case the naked part happened."

"Don't worry Sweetie, those guys are nothing but bullies." Bethany squeezed her shoulder. "If you guys don't need anything, we're good to go."

"Standby," Jack said. "Looks like we're sixteen-hundred pounds over max taxi weight."

"No kidding, why do we have so much fuel?" Darby asked.

"Global doesn't know what to do with the Airbus," Jack said. "They've loaded us with at least fifteen thousand pounds more than we've needed on every leg I've flown in the previous three months."

"They love to waste money," Nate said.

Darby glanced at Nate. Everyone was on edge from losing their seniority. The only reason Jack still held his captain position was that he and a handful of captains would remain on their planes until they checked out all their replacements. Then the snowball would roll down hill and displacements would be many.

She could have held onto the 757 for a few months, but in New York. Instead, she jumped ship, bailing early, and ripped that bandaid off in one swift pull.

Jack called dispatch. "Hey, Pete, 47, any chance of removing some of this fuel? We're overweight and...Yeah...But...Okay. We've got about...But we don't need it." He closed his eyes and shook his head. "You want me to remove passengers?"

"Are you serious?" Darby said.

They could make four approaches into Tokyo and still go to an alternate and land. The expense was crazy. The more fuel a plane carried, the higher the burn. Fuel was like payload, the only difference was it cost money instead of making it.

"Why can't they just take it off?" Darby asked.

"Idiots," Nate said.

By the time they pulled six passengers and their baggage, an hour had passed. They started engines and pushed back. Ground control cleared them to taxi to 16 left, and the tower cleared them into position for takeoff.

"Global 47 taxi clear of the runway at high speed mike," the tower controller said. "Your company wants you to return to the gate. Contact ground on 121.7."

What in the world is going on?

Once clear of the runway, Nate contacted ground control, then performed his after landing procedure.

"Darby, get on the ACARS and send the company a message and find out what the heck is going on," Jack said.

She typed as quickly as she could—*heading back to the gate. What's up?*

The reply came immediately.

"Guys, you're not going to believe this."

CHAPTER 6
TOKYO, JAPAN

DECEMBER 19, 2011

DARBY'S HEART SPED WILDLY as she lifted her suitcase off the luggage cart in the lobby of the Narita Radisson hotel, three hours late. Maybe an energy drink at 1730 local time was not the smartest of ideas—0130 her time zone. But the landing had been hers and that was the best option to bring her alertness to hyper-aware. Two hours after consumption, she still buzzed.

Energy drinks sparked her mind, but she never drank them in the evening. Unfortunately she had been on the other side of the fatigue wall and close to falling off. Her Starbucks refresher pulled her back. Albeit teetering.

She headed toward the front desk. The crew would meet in the Sports Bar and then head down the street for dinner. Chances were they would never leave the hotel. Popcorn and beer, the dinner of champions, would be hers.

Fatigue and energy drink combo with a night of drinking might not be the best idea. But staying awake would be her only option to shift her body into the new time zone.

She accepted her key and autographed the crew sign-in sheet. Pulling her bags through the lobby she passed the twenty-foot Christmas tree without stopping. Twinkling lights and red balls would have to be appreciated another time.

She made her way through the hallway to the elevator and pressed the up button. Moments later the doors opened and she pulled her bags off and dragged them around the corner.

Stopping at the vending machine she dug through the organized chaos of her purse, looking for 450 yen to buy a Sapporo. But the lack of foreign funds meant no beer, so she pressed on down the hall.

With first break she expected to sleep, especially with their extensive delay. Unfortunately, great customer service in the business class section prevented the sandman from visiting. Her mind joined the sleep depravation party as she attempted to justify leaving all those people at the gate in Seattle.

They had been called back to remove two more passengers, as the first extraction included too many children. Then the chain of command issue slipped in, as did her concern that she forgot how to fly. After three hours of a brain battle, she went back to work and seven hours later landed the plane.

Darby unlocked the door and entered her room. She set her computer bag and purse on a twin bed and then tipped her suitcase onto the floor and unzipped it. She found a bottle of Tylenol.

After popping two pills she loosened her tie and pulled it off. Five months was more than enough time to forget how to fly a plane, and yet she did okay. Darby knew better—she got lucky. They all lived and she did not embarrass herself. Life was good.

Yawning, she glanced at her clock—2000 local. She had been awake for over twenty-two hours, yet the only way she would survive the Singapore flight the next night was if she forced herself to stay awake, so she could sleep until noon tomorrow. There was nothing worse than a good night sleep and waking up early, when you had to fly all night.

She pulled her computer from its case, plugged it into the adapter, then stuck the plug into the wall. She opened iTunes and clicked Dierks Bently, *What was I Thinking?* She kicked off one shoe, sat on her bed, and kicked off the other.

She unbuckled her belt and took a deep breath. Standing, she unzipped her pants, wiggled a little allowing them to fall, and kicked them across the room. She closed her eyes and swung her butt to the music as she unbuttoned her shirt. She was about to pull it off when a knock at the door stopped her. She danced toward the knocking and stuck an eye to the peephole and saw a fingerprint.

"Who is it?" she said, rolling her eyes.

"Room service."

Grinning, she pulled her shirt closed, stood behind the door and opened it just enough for a hand with a 16-ounce can of Sapporo to push inside. She smiled at the offering of Tokyo's version of Budweiser and pulled the door open a little further and peered out.

"Thanks," she said, taking the beer. "Just what I needed."

"You're welcome," Jack said. "You've got 10 minutes to get your butt down to the Sports Bar."

"Yes, sir!" Darby saluted with the can. "But I've got something important to do first."

"Don't start without me," Jack said with a grin, and clearly no intention of moving.

"See you soon," Darby said closing the door in his face, as she began to moan. "Ohhhh...Ahhhh..." Then she pounded on the closed door and cried, "Yes! Yes! Yes!"

"I can hear you," Jack said. "I like it."

Darby rolled her eyes as she laughed. "I'll see you in fifteen," she shouted. She had to write the letters of apology and put that chapter to bed. Then she could go play.

CHAPTER 7

GLOBAL AIR LINES,
SEATTLE TRAINING CENTER

DECEMBER 19, 2011

NEIL SAT AT A TABLE in the back of the room as Captain George Wyatt, director of flight operations, stood in the front with his chest puffed out. His lips were moving, but Neil doubted any of these senior captains were listening due to a severe shortage of respect.

Respect was not for Neil to judge. He was one of a handful of first officer instructors on the A330. First officers would soon be the majority of instructors. Global Air Lines business plan—cut the training department's budget by hiring first officers and non-seniority list pilot instructors and cancel classroom training.

Neil was not sure if joining the department was such a good idea, but it would be one way he could see Darby. Since the merger he slid toward the bottom of the seniority list and ended up in New York. Darby opted to bump back to hold Seattle.

He could not get her to move back east with him, despite higher seniority. Not after his lies. With time she would forgive him. But for Darby to sit a junior position and not fly would eventually eat her soul. She would make a move sooner than later. Darby was worth the wait.

"Gentlemen," Wyatt boomed, "before we put this year to rest

I want to personally thank you for the extra effort you've put into this department toward the success of the merger. We've got a long way to go, but with your support we can keep Global as the industry leader."

"Excuse me," someone in the front row said. Neil leaned forward to see who it was, but he could not tell from the back of his head. "Support? We've been trying to convince you guys of the degradation to safety with the current procedures…or lack of, but nobody will listen. You want my continued support? I want to know when you're going to reinstate SOP?"

SOP was the acronym for Standard Operating Procedures— the way the pilots should fly the plane so that everyone was on the same page. A choreographed play. Something that Global apparently did not believe in.

Another captain said, "And this bullshit about our not being allowed to call for takeoff flaps, what's that all about?"

Captain Wyatt raised a hand as the volume of the crowd increased. "Gentlemen," he said flatly, "if we make that flap call scripted, then we've taken away our captains' flexibility."

"Flexibility over safety?" the guy next to Neil snapped. Wyatt flashed his attention their direction. Neil turned and scowled at the guy to his left. He was not getting in this fight.

"We are not going to tell our captains how to fly their planes," Wyatt countered. "Global Air Lines has professional pilots. We are the best in the industry and leave those decisions to the captain."

"This has nothing to do with telling your pilots how to fly their planes, but everything to do with standardization," Captain Brock Townsend, a senior check airman, said. A low murmur filled the room. "Have you read any of the studies on standardization?"

Captain Townsend was more than a check airman—he wrote

the manuals and put the A330 into service at Coastal Airlines. He knew more about the systems of the Airbus than Neil could ever hope to know.

Wyatt shifted his weight from one foot to the other and said, "This is how we do things at Global. If you don't like it, you know where the door is."

Captain Townsend stood, his face red. "Airlines have standard operating procedures for a reason. So everyone knows what everyone else is doing." He folded his arms and shook his head. "We've got too many *new* crewmembers flying together. We can't have everyone doing their own thing."

Neil cringed as he witnessed political suicide. He respected Townsend, but highly doubted he would survive the treason of speaking out against the fuehrer, George Wyatt.

"We've been flying airplanes for a long time," Wyatt said to Townsend. "Our captains have experience enough to manage their own aircraft."

"This is not about managing their own planes, sir," Townsend said calmer. "This is about standardization and safety. Global has never operated an Airbus before. You need to listen to our experts," he said, opening his hand to the room. "We had a great program at Coastal. Don't throw that experience, or lessons learned, away."

"Well…," Wyatt said, placing his hands on his hips. "You're in my world now. If you don't like it, you don't have to live here."

Neil's mouth dropped open.

Frank Dawson, the managing director of training, moved to the front of the room and stood beside Wyatt. He raised a hand quieting the crowd, and whispered something into Wyatt's ear.

Wyatt nodded and laughed.

"It's been a pleasure, Gentlemen," Wyatt said. He headed toward the door and said, "Happy holidays," as he left the room.

Dawson turned to the group and said, "God dammit. Wyatt is not the man to air your dirty laundry with. If you have problems with anything, you bring them to Simpson and he'll discuss them with me." His eyes flashed at Simpson, the A330 fleet training captain, who nodded.

"We've got problems right now," Captain Williams, a senior instructor, said.

"Which are?" Dawson asked.

"The manuals to start with. They suck," Williams spat. "We need the color back. The symbols have different meanings depending upon the color. How the hell do you learn this plane in black and white?"

"You don't," someone from the back of the room said.

Dawson placed his hands on his hips, took in the room and said, "They're good enough."

"Are you serious?" Captain Townsend said. "They're—"

"I'll deal with this," Simpson said to Dawson.

Once Dawson was gone, Simpson walked to the back of the room and closed the door. He returned to the front of the group and said, "Gentlemen, we're not in Kansas anymore."

"This is bullshit," Townsend said. "They said they'd implement our procedures after we were on a single operating certificate."

"They lied," someone snapped.

"I think the sooner we learn that this is not Coastal Airlines, the better off we'll be." Simpson looked directly at the guy sitting to Neil's right. "Why don't we call it a meeting."

The largest airline in the world was in the dark ages where captains were gods and first officers would follow them into a burning hole. Do what I say because I am a captain and said so.

Even Neil knew eliminating standard operating procedures was a deathtrap. Crew resource management be dammed.

Neil turned to the guy to his right and asked, "What was that all about?"

"What do you mean?"

"That look from Simpson when he said we weren't in Kansas anymore. Shit man, you couldn't even look him in the eye."

"I'm a G.O." The term for a Global original.

"I didn't know we had any of you guys instructing on the 330 yet," Neil said.

"I think Dawson hired me for political correctness."

"How long have you been on the plane?" Neil asked.

"Five months," he said, extending his hand. "Stone."

Neil shook Stone's hand. "How long have you been with Global?"

"Twelve years."

This guy was flying captain at twelve years. Neil had been with the same fucking union for over fifteen, and this piece of shit was now senior to him. He bit his tongue. The only good news was Captain Stone would be shut out of training before long.

Pricks like Stone would hold him back the rest of his career. They were not only scrapping all elements of safety by losing their standard operating procedures and cutting training, but hiring the most inexperienced to teach. Unfortunately, Neil was included in that equation.

"Good to know you," Neil lied, not having the balls to tell him how he really felt. "You do know you don't need to wear your uniform to instructor meetings don't you?"

"Yep. Just getting ready to get on a plane."

"Have a good one," Neil said, to the loser. He wandered to the front of the room and stood a few feet away from the pilot pod and waited to talk to Simpson. When their eyes connected, Simpson excused himself from the group and joined Neil.

"Merry Christmas," Simpson said extending his hand.

"You too," Neil said, shaking firmly.

"Quite a show, huh?"

"Wouldn't believe it if I hadn't see it." Neil stuck his hands into his pockets. "By the way, thanks for hiring me."

"You may end up hating me when it's all said and done."

Neil shrugged. "How the hell did you slip me through anyway?"

"Wasn't hard. I was told to hire their boy." Simpson looked over his shoulder and lowered his voice. "They also told me to hire the least experienced first officer applicant. No offense."

"None taken." Neil grinned.

"I'm sure they wanted to offset the image of their guy coming in without experience on the captain side. Won't matter for long anyway. When they're done with us, they'll have all non-seniority list simulator instructors anyway."

"Money wagging this dog's tail, eh?"

"That it is," Simpson said, glancing over Neil's shoulder. "The truth of the matter is that Global's culture is entrenched in a 'we won' attitude and they certainly don't want to be reminded of who made it possible for them to be where they are. I've seen a steady exodus of former Coastal people from this place, whether they're management pilots or administrative types."

"How long are you going to stay?"

"I'm done," Simpson said, with a sigh. "This place feeds on a soup of politics and self-promotion. Quality be dammed. Talk about corporate bigotry and narrow-mindedness. They've had their fill of me already. Burt Armstrong, some putz who's never flown the A330, is taking my place the first of the year."

Chapter 8
FAA Office, Seattle, Washington

December 19, 2011

Kathryn sat at one end of the oak table while her boss, Tom Santos, stood with arms folded at the opposite end. Twelve coworkers fidgeted in their chairs between them. Coffee cups, pens, and legal pads were in position for action.

Santos had just received the safety audit concerning the FAA's oversight of air carrier training programs and pilot performance. His red face and stance indicated that he was anything but happy. Kathryn suspected this might be the case, but she hoped he would take it better than this.

Once everyone was quiet Santos said, "The assistant inspector general thinks that our department is to blame for the Regional crash." He looked directly at Kathryn.

Her husband, Bill Jacobs, was sitting in prison for the accident that brought on this safety audit during his psychopathic attempt to fix the airline industry. His attack opened a can of worms on insufficiencies in training and tracking pilots. Worms that buried themselves in the walls of bureaucracy that Kathryn was determined to fix.

"What I've got in my hand," he said, as he stepped behind each federal employee, dropping a packet over their shoulder, "are the findings. Apparently we need to establish approaches to strengthen the oversight of our airlines."

He walked to the side of the room and all eyes followed. He stood in front of the window and stared their way.

The problems were far more than oversight. They had everything to do with airline training programs. Something that Kathryn was proud to have the opportunity to be involved in fixing. For the bruising of egos these accusations caused, finding the solution would make the pain worth it.

Santos began to pace, holding the report in one hand as he read. "They say, and I quote, that our programs lack the rigor needed to identify and track poor performing pilots and address potential program risks.

"The administrator says these oversight gaps are largely due to *our* inadequate guidance and policies for tracking and gathering data on pilots who fail proficiency tests."

Kathryn glanced at the document and flipped a page as if she were reading. Truth be told, she knew exactly what the report said because she had been instrumental in gathering the data and wrote the recommendations. What she learned was fascinating.

Airlines did not have easy access to pilot training records. The FAA structure forced them to contact two different offices within the FAA to obtain all pilots' records. There was also no centralized process for receiving and responding to pilot record requests.

This had not been an issue with the stagnation in pilot hiring due to the retirement age increasing to sixty five. With the pending pilot shortage everything would change, and the FAA would need solid procedures in place.

Santos returned to the table. All eyes followed him. He stood, assessing the faces before him. "Apparently I have not prepared any of you to oversee the use of the data-driven proficiency-based systems for training and evaluating."

He held full responsibility for the current system.

"Please take a few minutes to look over what I've set before you. Then we'll talk." Santos sat and folded his arms. He turned his attention toward the window that overlooked SeaTac International Airport. Kathryn doubted he saw anything but red.

And I thought Darby overreacted.

She glanced at the document, turning the page to AQP— Advanced Qualification Program. An excellent program if the airlines would use it correctly.

Traditional pilot training programs were expensive. Despite the ability or experience level, pilots were required to fulfill the same number of training hours within a set curriculum. AQP, on the other hand, enabled airlines to train pilots to proficiency. Airlines had the option which program they would use.

AQP was a no-brainer for financial reasons. It also provided quality training for the pilots, enabling them to see abnormal conditions in the simulator that were taken from real life.

Airlines pulled those situations from related airline safety databases and systems such as Flight Operations Quality Assurance (FOQA) and Aviation Safety Action Programs (ASAP).

Kathryn looked up. All eyes were focused on their documents, except Tom's. He stared her direction. When their eyes met, he did not look away. She forced her lips into a slight smile and returned her attention to her packet. Her foot began to tap with a mind all its own.

AQP was also designed to provide airlines access to resources within the larger community with a free flow of information among airlines and FAA resources. Kathryn knew how often they shared this information in today's world—never. They were all too busy negotiating mergers, and the FAA was being cut to the bone.

None of this addressed pilots, like Darby, who were sitting reserve and not flying. Kathryn saw the stress it took on her friend each month she was out of the airplane.

Kathryn turned the page and glanced at a major flaw—who would be the judge and jury on determining proficiency?

Inspectors had no defined criteria how to investigate pilot training failures and take corrective action. Worse yet, the FAA lacked standardized training for their inspectors on 'how to' evaluate pilots and check airmen.

Check airmen were being monitored by FAA inspectors new to the agency who relied upon prior experience. Unfortunately checkrides and assessment standards varied due to operational differences. Prior experience did not provide inspectors sufficient knowledge to observe check airmen.

The entire system was a mess.

"Have you read enough?" Tom's voice boomed and Kathryn startled.

"What's the gist of this thing?" Inspector Andrews asked. "Looks like we're getting crucified unjustly."

"We're not getting crucified. They're just saying we don't have the proper training," Inspector Barnes said. "Besides—"

"Enough!" Santos snapped. "Obviously we're not doing what is required." He breathed deep and regained his composure before he continued.

"Andrews, when have you conducted a comparison of failure rates between pilot deficiencies? Or Jones, when was the last time you incorporated inspections of remedial training programs into your surveillance plan? Better yet, do you even have a plan?

The group lowered their eyes.

"This document states that we are missing opportunities to improve training and airline safety, and I agree." Tom stood and walked to the window. With hands on his hips, he stared out. The room fell silent. Seconds ticked by. Then he turned and said, "Kathryn, will you please share with the inspectors the problems with tracking?"

Had the group not known she was involved before, they did now. She took a deep breath and glanced around the table.

She cleared her throat. "To start with, one-third of the carriers we visited did not review the training records of pilots entering remedial training programs. During the Regional investigation, the NTSB discovered that the captain failed four FAA certification checks—the last of which occurred sixteen months before the crash, and—"

"Bullshit!" Andrews snapped. "Planes crashed because of your psycho husband."

"Maybe so, but if we were doing our jobs, that captain would have been pulled before he got into that plane," Kathryn shot back. She held his stare and continued.

"Consistent with standard operating practices at the time, Regional hadn't performed a comprehensive search of the airman's full record, and therefore was unaware of the captain's previous failures. We also have no procedures in place to prevent two pilots in remedial training programs from being paired together, and—"

"What about the green-on-green rule?" Andrews said, rolling his eyes.

"*That* rule was put in place to prevent pilots with less than 75 hours in an aircraft type from flying together. But there are no procedures for tracking pilots when they've downgraded because of failures," she said.

"I know what the rule says," Andrews said, rolling his eyes.

"Hear me out," Kathryn said, fighting the urge to smack him. "Pilots with repeated failures and remedial training are absolved from scrutiny after they're bumped back from captain to first officer. Those pilots are removed from the tracking roster and—"

"What does that have to do with Regional?" Andrews scoffed.

"My point exactly," Kathryn said. "The green-on-green-rule doesn't prevent a captain with multiple failures from being paired with a new first officer if he has more than 75 hours flight time."

"Are you guys getting the picture?" Santos said. "We have problems and something needs to be done."

"This is bullshit," Andrews said. "Look at what we have to work with."

"Then we're going to have to work smarter," Kathryn responded. "If we don't, more planes will crash. That triple seven in San Francisco was a sign of things to come."

"That triple seven was a foreign carrier," Andrews said.

"That's enough!" Santos snapped. "This is not a sparring match."

The room silenced, magnifying the roar of blood pounding in Kathryn's head.

Inspector Malcolm Andrews, the principle operating inspector (POI) for Global had been an ass to her since the day she joined the FAA two years earlier. Having been reinstated with time served in the NTSB she stepped over his seniority. There was no way she would turn down her original date of hire and twenty-years seniority. Malcolm Andrews would have done the same.

She fought the urge to bring up his approving Global cancelling their initial training, but this was not the venue for that fight.

"That's enough for today," Santos said, pushing his chair back.

"Read the recommendations. I want you to figure out how the hell we're going to implement this with the resources we've got to work with."

Tom's anger was trumped by responsibility. He was right—they did not have the resources, but they were responsible. She only hoped her recommendations would be enough.

Kathryn had been one of many on the board and instrumental in this project. Finding problems was easy, but the solutions were what counted. The answers to this dilemma had been her focus over the previous year.

Opening the page to her recommendations, she read the first line and stopped short. Her eyes widened. A wave of nausea grew deep in her gut and moved to a tightening in her chest as she turned the page and then another, and another...

CHAPTER 9
TOKYO, JAPAN

DECEMBER 20, 2011

DARBY OPENED HER eyes with a start. Flat on her back, fully clothed, she turned her head left and squinted the time into focus—0745. She had to think for a minute where she was, which was more difficult than normal.

The writing on the wall shouted she was headed into a very long day and an even longer night. She yawned and extended her arms and legs into a deep stretch. She rolled left to the edge of the bed and dropped her feet to the floor. Sitting upright she pressed her palms to her eyes.

The reality of the previous night bounced in her brain. It was one of those 'I drank too much and did I really do that' nights where the pieces drifted into the frontal lobe with the break of daylight.

The only problem was, she only had one beer. She also passed out before she made it out of the room. She had been drunk with fatigue.

Drunk from fatigue. I like it.

She jumped out of bed, pressed start on her hot water pot, pushed the power button on her laptop and then flew nonstop to her bathroom.

Pulling her toothbrush out of her shower kit she stuck it under the water, added toothpaste, stuffed it into her mouth and sat on the toilet. Darby Bradshaw was the master of multi-tasking when it counted.

When done with the necessities she returned to the main room and ripped open a package of instant coffee and dumped it into a cup, then filled the cup with boiling water. She added fake sugar and powdered creamer and then sat at her desk ready to write

FLIGHT FOR SAFETY

An Aviation Blog by Darby Bradshaw
Date: December 20, 2011

Flying Drunk From Fatigue:

Pilots are intimately familiar with being sleep deficit. Flying across time zones and at night messes up circadian rhythms, taking a toll on our bodies. Did you know that lack of sleep impacts reaction time, coordination, and judgment? 17 hours awake is equivalent to an alcohol level of .05.

How many pilots are flying drunk from fatigue? A scary thought.

Studies indicate that with less than 6 hours of sleep we begin to feel stressed, and stress impacts the ability to sleep. When we don't sleep, we also diminish the ability to...

Darby added eleven tips on how to sleep better, and the benefits of melatonin. She was on her second cup of coffee by the time she finished writing and pressed 'post.' She violated more than half of her rules the night before.

She pushed away from her desk and dug through her suitcase, then pulled out her workout clothes. She sat on the bed and fell back. Closing her eyes, she willed herself to the gym.

Her mind drifted to getting called in for violating the chain of command and about the letters…

"Oh shit!" she said, sitting upright.

The reality of the night before hit her like a bad dream.

She rushed to her computer and opened her sent mail.

Oh God. She covered her mouth with a hand. She had not only written, but sent all three letters. She reread the contents and cringed when she read, 'squishing' her holiday spirit. Her word choice could have been better, but other than that, her letter's were fine. Dodging another bullet, she sighed.

She pulled her crew rotation out of her purse and logged onto her company website to see who she was flying with to Singapore.

Tapping keys she accessed the top-secret information in Global.com. The most challenging part of the job, that had once been packing, was now navigating the employees' computer system.

Ahh, here we go. Captain Dick Jones. Darby smiled.

The flight south was always a killer, but Jones was a great guy with lots of time on the plane. Unfortunately his days were numbered too. She closed that page on her computer and opened her email.

Her eyes widened when she saw the director of flying had written, and her mouth fell open as she read his response. The way she saw it, she had two choices—either ignore it or respond.

But as she reread his email her blood pressure climbed. She pushed back from her desk and moved across the room.

Moving away from the weapon was always the safest course of action in times like this. With arms folded she stared at her computer from afar and glared.

"Don't do it Darby," she said, biting her lip.

CHAPTER 10
SEATTLE, WASHINGTON

DECEMBER 19, 2011

KATHRYN OPENED her front door and threw her purse on the chair. How could he have done that?

She was on the team performing the investigation. She had been part of the process, a huge part. She gave hundreds of hours in sacrifice of her family to the safety of the industry. But when it was all said and done with, she was nothing but a pawn.

The assistant deputy used her to gather data. She wrote the recommendation section. Despite what he said, they never planned on using it. They pulled her solutions and added their own—monitor and track failures, and train inspectors.

She was furious. Renewing a check airman's authority every two years would not increase accountability in the system.

Who was tracking and training these instructors? Nobody.

They left out all her suggestions—retain line instructors in the simulator, create avenues for proficiency, redesign requirements for currency, and the biggie—change the footprint of the simulator training for the automated aircraft. They had been in the final draft a month prior. Today they were gone.

Kathryn opened her briefcase and removed the report. She tossed it on the table. "Dang them." She looked at her watch.

The girls would be bouncing in the door at any moment and she had no idea what to make for dinner. She opened the fridge and scowled. Stopping at the grocery store on the way home would have been a good idea, but she was too angry to see anyone.

When the phone rang she closed the door, took a deep breath, and forced a smile on her face so not to bite off an innocent head.

"How'd your meeting go?" Jackie asked.

"It went," Kathryn said opening the freezer, finding nothing but a chill.

"Oh…" Jackie hesitated, "that good, huh?"

"I'm sorry," Kathryn said. She hated being short with her friends. "It's just been one hell of a shitty day."

"For you and me both," Jackie said.

"You okay kiddo?" Kathryn's asked. "Everything alright with you and John?"

Jackie was dating Kathryn's old boss, John McAllister, from the NTSB. He lived on the east coast and the long distance relationship was a challenge.

"John's wonderful. It's just…"

Kathryn closed the freezer and sat at the kitchen table. Jackie was her and Darby's best friend. The kids named them the three Miss-kateers, and there was nothing she would not do for either of them. "Just what, Sweetie?"

"I'm in trouble at work for talking on the phone too much."

Kathryn laughed. "Tell me you're kidding." For the first time that day she smiled.

"You're laughing?" Jackie said with a laugh of her own. "I call the pilots to confirm their schedules before I secure them to make sure there are no family conflicts."

"And they have a problem with that?"

"Apparently, even though I've never had anyone call in sick off my schedule. If someone had done that for Greg..."

Since Greg's death, Jackie was mother, father, and breadwinner. Getting the insurance to pay was a battle still in process. Two years passed and they were still tied up in litigation. To manage being a single mother Jackie gave up her position as a flight attendant and became a training scheduler for Global to be home with Chris every night. Pay cut and all, she survived.

Glancing at the counter Kathryn's eyes landed on a bottle of Shiraz and she poured herself a glass, then sat at the kitchen table.

Kathryn was also a single mother, but she moved into her dream job and received a raise. She glanced at the report. The money meant nothing if they blocked her from doing her job.

"I'm sorry Sweetie, but I think there are as many rats working for the government as Global, and I'm not sure how to deal with them."

"That's a first," Jackie said. "What happened?"

"I'm not sure, but when I get over the feeling of wanting to wring a neck or two, I *will* figure it out." She sighed. "Why don't you and Chris come over for dinner, and we'll order pizza."

They said their good byes and Kathryn sipped her wine and lifted the report. Thank God they had FOQA and ASAP data. At least they could see the results of what the pilots were doing on the line and where errors were being made, despite this piece of shit document and their worthless suggestions.

Shaking her head she tossed it on the table and turned toward the window. The wind howled beyond the pane. December was rolling out like a bear after a long winter's nap—hungry and ready to kill anything in its path. Kathryn knew the feeling.

CHAPTER 11
TOKYO, JAPAN

DECEMBER 20, 2011

THE PHONE RANG interrupting Darby's attempted REM, but she smiled when she heard, "Captain Bwadsha, cwew pick up." As hard as she tried to nap that afternoon, she could not do it. As hard as she wanted to be irritated with the interruption, she could not do that either.

Darby loved Niko, the young woman at the front desk, who despite her encouragement to call her Darby, which came out as Dawby, insisted on keeping her a captain.

Japanese had a difficult time pronouncing the letter r, but Captain Bwadsha had an endearing ring to it. She rolled to her side and looked at the clock, then pulled a pillow over her face. This was not the time to fly, it was time for dinner.

Cutting off all caffeine at 1000 that morning, she worked out for two hours and soaked in a hot bath. Yet, sleep would not come.

She chewed on her lip for a moment and smiled—she had a date with Dick and a beautiful plane to fly to an exotic location. Nap or not, how could life get any better?

She rolled out of bed and headed for the shower.

Hustling her butt, she was ready and downstairs in a flash. A flash being less than thirty minutes. Once in the lobby she looked for her captain. She was tempted to yell, "Anyone seen Dick? You can never find a good one when you need him," but she thought better of it. And there he was—standing in the café in his… *jeans?*

"What's up? Forget your uniform?" she asked as she approached.

"Darby doll," he said, hugging her. "I got rescheduled. They're keeping me here an extra day and sending me back to Seattle tomorrow."

"Bummer. I was looking forward to Singapore with you."

"So you could make me get a masochistic foot torture?"

"It's called reflexology," she said, grinning. "You love it."

"No. I love you. So why don't you call in sick and play hooky with me in Narita."

"In your dreams," Darby said with a grin.

"At my age, sometimes that's all we have left." He kissed her on the cheek and said, "Happy hour Darlin." He turned to leave, but stopped and turned her way. "Watch your back. I heard the Globe-ass boys are after you."

"Word travels fast in this business," she said, with a laugh. Rumors that undoubtedly started with Jack in the Sports Bar.

After dropping off her key at the front desk, she headed toward the crew bus. The sun was setting and the wind bit her nose and ears. A chill found home inside her jacket and she shivered.

"Flight 32?" she asked the young man loading bags. He nodded and bowed. Darby bowed back. He bowed again.

Wondering who technically deserved the last bow, she gave it to him and threw her purse over her shoulder, then said, "Arigatou gozaimasu," meaning thank you very much.

Darby climbed aboard the bus.

"Everyone going to Singapore?" she asked nobody in particular. Twelve female Asian heads bobbed their smiling faces up and down and one white guy waved and she said, "I'm Darby."

"Hey, I'm Jeff, your purser."

"Do you know who the captain is?" she asked.

"Dick Jones."

"Not anymore. They rescheduled him."

"They just never tell me anything," Jeff said. "I hope somebody shows up."

"I'm sure they will." She continued her stroll to the back of the bus. She was not exactly sure why pilots always sat in the back, but there was something comforting about having her back protected.

Darby watched for a captain to come out of the hotel and join them. When the bus pulled out, she knew he had to be at the airport. One thing about Narita, they never left anyone behind.

Once at the airport, she headed toward flight operations with bags in tow. When she opened the crewroom door, she saw him. The four stripes on his shoulders gave him away. Well, that and he was the only pilot sitting alone at a table.

"You must be Darby. I'm Keith," he said, extending a hand as she approached.

"Nice to meet you," Darby said, giving him her hand. He held it a bit too long and she pulled it back, pretending she hadn't noticed. Pilots were off her list. Permanently. Which was a shame because he was kind of cute.

"When did you get this trip?" she asked.

"This morning. I deadheaded in from Seattle."

That explained the red eyes highlighted with dark circles. "Is that legal?"

"I wasn't officially on duty."

"How do you feel?" She asked.

"Fine. Why?"

Her eyebrow raised with a mind of its own.

"I'm okay. I slept the entire way."

"Have you been to Singapore before?"

"No. I'm a first timer."

Not a comforting thought since it had been years since she had flown there. Her inexperience on the plane combined with his never having been there and commuting in the same day was a recipe for disaster. Tonight they would be flying one of the most challenging legs in the system.

"How long have you been on the plane?" She asked.

"Five months," he said with a wink.

Darby raised an eyebrow. Was he joking? She opened her mouth to say something when his phone rang.

"Excuse me," Keith said, as he answered. He walked out of the room and closed the door.

Darby stared at the closed door where his cute butt had just been. She hoped he flew as good as he looked. Then she smiled and shook her head. She was becoming such a pilot.

She focused her attention on the flight plan, and yawned.

Keith returned from his call five minutes later, and Darby glanced up from the paperwork.

"Can I see your flight ops manual? He said.

"Excuse me?"

"I need to see if you're up to date."

Darby leaned back in her chair and folded her arms. "I am." His 'don't fuck with me I'm serious look' won, and she reached into her bag and pulled her manual out and set it on the table.

He opened to the revision page.

"Do you know what you're looking for?" She asked as he thumbed through the other pages. "When I was thirteen I carved out a section of in the middle of my Nancy Drew mystery and hid a pack of cigarettes inside." He continued to check each page. Darby rolled her eyes. When finished, he handed her the manual.

"What now? Want my radio operator's license too?"

"No thanks, but I do want you to tell me the maximum brake temperatures."

Darby narrowed her eyes. "Why? Are you planning on using max brakes for landing in Singapore? It's a pretty long runway."

Keith played stump the dummy for another ten minutes, which got old very fast. Enough was enough.

Darby finally said, "Are you giving me a line check, or do you seriously not know *anything* about this plane?" Then she winked.

Keith's mouth opened, but nothing came out.

The crew sitting at another table burst into laughter. Then someone said, "I was wondering the same thing."

"Yeah, lay off her, buddy."

"Okay, then," Keith said. He gathered the paperwork and stuffed it into an envelope then headed for the door. He turned before he walked out and said, "I'll see *you* at the plane."

When he was gone, one of the pilots said, "Who was that ass?"

"My captain," Darby said. "Or maybe my worst nightmare. I haven't quite figured that out yet."

She stuffed her manual into her bag, and pulled out a gift for each of the pilots in the room and wished them Merry Christmas.

Sucking a deep breath, she headed for the door. This was going to be a longer night than anticipated.

CHAPTER 12
GLOBAL FLIGHT 32

DECEMBER 20, 2011

KEITH WAS SITTING in his seat when Darby arrived to the flight deck. She stuffed her bags into the closet. Tension filled their living space. No better time than now to do a walkaround.

"Can I get you anything before I head outside?" she asked.

Keith turned and gave her the strangest look. "No, I'm good."

Darby took longer than normal for her walkaround. Standing at the base of the stairs she looked up. *Momma said there would be days like this.* She sighed and climbed the stairs.

When she returned to the flight deck Keith was stabbing keys on the MCDU—Multifunction Control and Display Unit, pronounced MacDoo, the airplanes keyboard to the computer.

Apparently he thought if he hit the keys hard enough they would give him what he wanted. Darby contemplated letting him call maintenance and look like an idiot. But she kind of felt sorry for him, and he did a pretty good job of idiot as it was.

"Keith," Darby said, stepping through the doorway.

He jumped then said, "What?"

"When winds automatically upload you need to insert them before you can program anything else."

"Ah shit," he said, pulling a hand over his face. "I knew that too."

Four hours into their flight to Singapore, they started getting significant turbulence. Storms were blooming ahead, but it was Keith who worried her.

"Are you okay?" she asked.

"I'm fine," he said, wiping beads of sweat from his forehead.

He didn't look fine. He had lost most of his suntan within the last few minutes and looked like her alabaster sheets, turning whiter with each mile. The fact that those miles were passing at .82 Mach left her wondering at what point he would become a ghost.

"What's the max turbulent penetration speed?" he asked.

"Do you seriously not know?" Darby said.

"I know, I want to know if you know."

"You need to stop with the fucking questions already," Darby spat. "This flight is exhausting enough as it is. If you don't pay attention to what you're doing you're going to kill us all, and that will really piss me off!"

"Okay, dammit. I forget what it is between the 200 and 300 models, but I think we should be flying it."

"Oh shit! No kidding." She set .78 Mach.

Backlit clouds flashed beyond the glareshield and crept closer, narrowing their window of opportunity to sneak through the storm.

"I think we should go to the right around that cell," Darby said.

"Left is a shorter distance. We'll get through this shit quicker."

"Look at the winds," Darby said. "Flying downwind of that cell will eat us for lunch."

"We'll be fine," Keith said spinning the heading bug.

The A330 barreled forward un-intimidated by the pounding it was taking. Darby reached forward and adjusted the scale on the map to display the ten-mile range, creating a clearer picture of the weather in relation to their path.

She watched the next waypoint on her electronic map approach and picked up the clipboard to confirm they were on course.

The storm grew on all sides of them in equal proportion to her discomfort. She jolted with the plane and grabbed the glareshield.

Clouds grew, rapidly surrounding their Airbus. This system was more expansive than forecasted. Cells were building higher and closer than she was comfortable with.

Up and down Keith turned the radar knob. It was obvious he did not know how to use it. They had an automated system, which made life easier…or was supposed to.

"If you leave the switch in auto, it paints worse than it is. Avoid the red and you're safe." His fingers continued to work the radar. "You don't want to break that little thing off, do you?" she said.

"That's all I fucking need tonight."

Lightning was on all sides of them. The turbulence was so bad she wished she had worn her sports bra. Another jolt and she looked up to the overhead panel. *What the hell?*

"The seatbelt sign is off," she said reaching up and flipping the switch on.

"What the fuck?" He snapped. "That should have been on for the previous twenty minutes."

"I though it was."

"Give a PA," he snapped.

She picked up the handset, "Ladies and gentlemen remain seated with your seatbelts fastened."

Since Captain Overloaded did not think of it, she reached down and turned on the ignition.

Heavy rain was below them, but what was in front screamed warning. Darby's nerves pushed her closer to the edge with each bounce. She was furious allowing herself to be sucked into this trap. She should have been more assertive. They were in the middle of a friggin storm, bouncing at the tops, with buildups going higher on all sides. Lightning flashed out all windows.

"Boom," a deafening bang rang out and shook the plane. Darby jumped. They had been hit by lightning and it sounded like a sledgehammer slamming on the side of the aircraft. The visibility decreased in a flash as rain beat on their windshield. The noise was deafening and she could feel the thunder reverberate in her bones. The plane bounced wildly.

They broke out of the intense rain and a lightshow grander than she had ever seen flashed on all sides of their plane.

They were stuck. The radar painted red across her map on her primary flight display. She saw one little hole they could sneak through. Hopefully it would not close in on them, as this was their only option.

"We need to turn left." When he did not respond she pulled the heading knob and said, "Heading select," and turned the selector to 160 degrees—the best course to get through the crud. "There's a hole this way."

"Yeah. Thanks," he said. "I see that."

They were bouncing like maniacs. Her eyes darted in and out of the flight deck and down to the map. Darby's heart raced. She placed a hand on the glareshield and said, "Hold on Baby," and then reached up and turned off the flight deck lights to get a better picture outside.

Rain streamed up the windshield. *What the hell?* Rain was supposed to fall down, not up. At 450 knots forward motion... *is this even possible?* The outside air temperature was -50C and the total air temperature was -21C. *Liquid water at these temps?* Darby had never seen such a thing. She turned the flight deck lights back on, and then…

Beep. Beep. Beep. Ding. Ding. Ding. The master warning and master caution lights flashed and the airplane cried warning as both the autopilot and autothrust disconnected.

Their airspeed indications dropped to 80 knots.

"Stall! Stall! Stall!" the plane cried.

"We're not stalling," Darby yelled. "Look at our speed." She pressed the data button on the MCDU and then selected GPS data. "Here ya go…We've got a ground speed of 486 knots."

The flight directors had disappeared, and a roar like machine gun fire attacking the plane vibrated the flight deck. Messages displayed rapidly across the ECAM and were being replaced by others faster than she could see what they were.

"Jesus fucking Christ!" Keith yelled. One hand grabbed the thrust and his other grabbed the stick.

"Don't do anything!" Darby yelled over the noise. "Let the plane fly."

Ding.

Darby's eyes flashed back to her PFD. Their pitch was supposed to be at 3 degrees for level flight. They were at 10 degrees and increasing.

"Stop climbing," Darby yelled. The A330 could pitch up from 10 to 12 degrees very rapidly without much effort and a new pilot helping that effort was a mixture for disaster.

"What?"

"Don't climb. Bring the pitch down to three degrees."

Ding.

"But I let go of the stick," Keith yelled. "It shouldn't be climbing."

"It's going where you told it to go," Darby shouted as she

pushed the stick forward. "We have to put it on 3 degree line."

"DUAL INPUT!" a synthetic voice blared over the speakers. Keith was back on the controls—they were both flying the plane so she let go as he began to correct his pitch. She focused on level flight and her hand hovered over the stick until she was sure they had the same goal.

Once level, she moved her hand to the glareshield to hold on, but kept a watchful eye on the pitch attitude.

Ding.

Unlike the Boeing, the A330 trimmed to relieve elevator pressure for whatever pitch attitude the pilot wanted without the pilot's help. It was some g-loading thing and beyond her pay-grade. But when Keith let go of the stick after pulling back, the stick moved to neutral but the nose stayed pointed up because Keith had put it there.

Ding.

This was the first plane Darby flew that the pilots did not trim. It took an effort to pull a Boeing into a stall with cruise power without touching the trim. Not the Airbus in Alternate Law. The A330 was smart, but not smart enough to out think a pilot who was giving it bad commands when the plane was having technical difficulties. Darby kept a watchful eye on all parameters.

"Shit. What the hell's happening?" Keith said, breathing rapidly.

Ding.

"You're in Alternate Law. Just fly what you've got." But he had a death grip on the stick and worked it hard. "Just little pressures to keep her level. Quit jerking the stick like you're whacking off, just fly the plane."

Ding.

"What about our power?" Keith asked. "I think the autothrust is off." The plane bounced and rocked.

Ding.

"Don't rock the wings, you're inducing instability," she said. "Your autothrust *is* off. Don't worry." Her senses were so overloaded that the ding occurring every five seconds turned into background noise that her brain tuned out.

By leaving the thrust levers alone, the power would remain in the last setting. If it were good enough before, it was good enough while they stabilized and one less thing to worry about.

Once he settled down and the rolling motion slowed Darby said, "We're in thrust lock. That's the ding. The plane's holding power for .78 Mach. We're good if you don't climb."

Ding.

Darby reached for the thrust levers. "I think we've had enough warnings for one night. I'll set the power." She pulled the thrust out of the climb detent and set it to 83% N1.

She checked the engine instruments and the MCDU and said, "We're at 83% N1. Our GPS speed is not decreasing. We're maintaining altitude. Just baby her at level flight."

Darby's hand was lightly around the stick with her thumb hovering over the 'take the plane' button, ready to kick him out and take control if he started a climb again. Pitching up at this altitude was a slippery slope she did not want to experience.

The turbulence was moderate to severe. The plane jolted and inadvertently Keith banked. Then his rolling action began again. Back and forth. Each time he rolled farther.

Shit. "I got it," she said. "Give me the stick." She was hoping he would just take his hand off and the plane would stop rolling, but that wish went unanswered.

"I'm fine," he said, but the banking grew worse and he pitched up again.

"The hell you're fine!" He was rolling left. Then right. Then left. 10 degrees one way and then 15 the other and increasing. In Alternate Law they had no protections. She suspected they were in Alternate Two where the roll rate response was about double the normal rate. He could roll her over on her back. And he was climbing again.

Shit. Shit. Shit. Darby pressed the takeover button on her stick. She locked out his stick and took control of the plane. A red arrow illuminated in front of him and pointed her way as a loud synthetic voice broadcasted, "Priority right."

It was career suicide locking out a captain at Global, but at least she would live to do the rug dance. *I will not die in this plane tonight!* The thought of living made overriding the captain that much easier to swallow.

He fought the plane. Each time he moved his stick a green CAPT light illuminated in front of her, telling her to not let go of the takeover button. He did not have a clue that she had taken control. His actions were for nothing.

Darby's heart raced. Sweat dripped into her eye and she brushed it away with the back of her hand.

She pushed the nose down to a level attitude while rolling out of the bank. They were heading directly into the heart of the storm. She moved the stick left to fly between two areas of intensity and then rolled the wings level.

"I got it," she said. He was not aware of what she had done. "Keith!" she yelled. "I got the plane! I'm flying. Relax." He released his hand and committed to being a passenger.

Once stabilized on a good heading she released the stick to neutral and the plane stopped rolling. She kept a gentle hand on the stick. The A330 was a stable plane, always looking to find its center of balance.

Darby did what she could. The rest was up to the Airbus. The turbulence was only light to moderate. The clouds at their altitude and higher were behind them and moving the opposite direction. Their instruments were back.

She reached up and cycled the flight directors off and back on and then engaged Keith's autopilot. She pressed the autothrust button and then pushed the thrust levers back into the climb detent. Power was restored to the Airbus thrust management system.

Everything looked good—on the surface.

CHAPTER 13

SINGAPORE

DECEMBER 21, 2011

THE HOUR clicked over to 0200 when they pulled into the gate. By the time the shutdown checklist was complete Keith moved from justifying to silence. Which was probably a good tactic due to their close proximity.

Darby climbed out of her seat. A wall of ice formed between them. The truth was, she could not blame Keith for what happened, as she was equally responsible.

Once the passengers were off the plane Darby headed down the aisle and into the jetway, leaving Keith behind. The flight attendants were clearly shaken. Thanks to the late hour, everyone had been in their seats, wearing their seatbelts. Despite she and Keith's negligence there were no injuries.

Dragging her bags behind, she stepped outside the terminal. She looked across the parking lot and located their bus, wondering how long the driver would have waited if they had never shown up, and headed that way.

Darby set her bags in front of the open hatch. She sucked a deep breath and closed her eyes, happy to be alive. The thought of dropping to her knees and kissing the ground flashed through her mind. Instead she climbed the stairs.

First on the bus, Darby moved to the very last row and sat in that dark. She wasn't sure if it were the air conditioning or her nerves, but her body began to shake. She wrapped her arms around herself and squeezed.

This has to be a bad dream. She closed her eyes hoping she would awaken in another day and time. Instead, she opened them and Keith stood before her.

"Are you okay?" he asked.

"I don't think 'okay' is going to happen as long as we're flying together."

"Would I'm sorry help?"

With arms folded she raised an eyebrow, bit her lip, and looked away.

"You're not going to cry, are you?"

"Fuck you," she spat. "So what if I do? You damned near killed us! Besides, I'm still a girl and my fucking Victoria Secret underwear proves it!"

"I'd like to see that," he said. "Not that I need proof."

Darby rolled her eyes.

"You didn't deserve the shit I gave you." He slid into the seat beside her, leaving space between them. "If you hadn't been on the plane tonight, I'm…" He took a deep breath then said, "Thank you."

She turned his way and held his stare. Darby spent too many years playing cards to not know the tells of someone bluffing. Maybe he was for real.

"With so little time on the plane, I should have respected your opinion."

"You think?"

"Not often enough."

"Apparently," Darby said. "I don't have any experience on this plane either. All more reason we needed to work together."

"This night should never have happened."

Once the flight attendants were onboard, they began moving toward the hotel. She glanced at her watch—0245.

"What's with all the questions anyway?" she asked.

Seconds clicked by before he answered.

"I guess I was trying to prove I knew more than my first officer."

"Seriously? I was a captain at Coastal until you assholes stapled me to the bottom of the seniority list."

"If it was up to me, it would have been straight seniority. I never thought that was the right thing to do."

She assessed him for a moment then said, "Okay. I'll take that. But what gives with the attitude?"

"Can we chalk it up to being eager?" he asked. She gave him a sideways glance and he added, "Stupid?"

"You're getting warmer."

"How about I was just an ass."

"How about you were a stupid ass," she said, and he laughed.

"We need to write an ASR," he said. "Could we do it together? You may have a clearer picture of what happened."

"I'm sure I do."

This would be their get out of jail free card with the Feds. The company may choose to give them additional training if they viewed it necessary, but the FAA would not violate the pilots, unless they intentionally disregarded a rule, as long as they checked the box for an ASAP report along with their Air Safety Report.

"The good news is," Darby said, "we'll ace our checkrides when they put this scenario in the simulator for recurrent."

"That we will," he said. "Do you want to write it when we get in? Beer's on me. I'd really like to talk about what happened out there. This Airbus is a fucking foreign monster, more than I'd expected. I'd heard guys losing their flight instruments before, but I had no idea what it would be like."

"Three conditions." She turned sideways facing him. "You buy the beer. We do it after a good nap. And you don't submit anything unless I read it and concur, because I'm telling it exactly as it happened."

"I'm counting on it."

"You need to learn this plane," Darby said.

"I didn't realize how much I didn't know until things went wrong," he said, fighting a yawn.

"Imagine what we're going to get coming to the flight line without ground school for the new pilots."

Keith stared for minute, as if this was an enlightenment, and then looked away.

"And don't ever talk about my plane like that again. She's not a monster, she a princess."

He turned her way and laughed. "I wish I could unwind the night. I'm not normally such an ass and a pretty good pilot."

She raised an eyebrow.

"Can we start over?" he asked. "I really am sorry."

"God I wish we had a redo button in life," Darby said. "I would've pushed it a couple weeks ago."

Keith nodded. "Me too." Extending a hand he said, "Let me introduce myself. I'm Keith Stone, and it's very nice to meet you, Darby Bradshaw."

CHAPTER 14
SINGAPORE

DECEMBER 21, 2011

DARBY ROLLED LEFT and squinted at the clock as daylight stabbed through a sliver of curtain. 0830—she slept four hours. She had to get her butt out of bed or the day would be lost, and she would be up all night before her 0300 wake up for the next flight. Besides, she and Keith needed to write their ASR,

She covered her eyes, reliving the details of the previous night. A chill ran through her body and she shuddered. *Don't go there Darby. It's over.* She only hoped.

Throwing back the sheet she dropped her feet to the floor in one movement, then worked her way to the bathroom. She pulled a brush through her hair, and tied her hair into a ponytail. Then pulled on a pair of shorts, sports bra, and a tank top.

First stop coffee, then she would call Keith. Grabbing her purse she headed for the door, but stopped short. She lifted a paper off the floor and read.

"Meet me in the lobby café. I'm buying, K."

Darby rolled her eyes and stuffed the note into her purse.

Once downstairs she headed straight for the café and stood at the entrance scanning the room. When their eyes met, Keith waved. She gritted her teeth. This was the frog she had to eat first.

"Sleep well?" he asked.

"As good as could be expected," she said flatly. He was the last person she wanted to discuss her sleeping habits with, and the sooner they got this done the better. She pulled a chair out and sat.

After a moment of seriously awkward silence he said, "I thought we could write this up on paper first. Figure out what we're going to say, then put it in the computer."

"Sounds good," Darby said, "but I need coffee."

Keith raised a hand and a waiter arrived. Before Darby could open her mouth he said, "My friend would like a coffee with cream and one of those fake sugars. The yellow kind."

Darby raised an eyebrow and he said, "I may be a dick, but I pay attention to details." He returned his attention to the waiter and said, "We'd also like an order of the chocolate Danish, and a fruit platter please."

Once the waiter was gone Keith slid a pad of paper toward her and set a pen on it. She picked up the pen and tapped it on the pad, contemplating how she would write what needed to be said. Then with a grin she pulled the paper close and began to write.

"*It was a dark and stormy night, but Captain Stone missed it because his head was so far up his ass he was blinded by his crap. When he pulled it out, we were in the middle of a storm. He got confused with which stick he was playing with and inadvertently pulled the wrong one....*" Darby glanced up and smiled.

Keith said, "This is going to be good, isn't it." She nodded and chewed on the end of the pen, formulating her thoughts and then continued to write.

Just as she finished her dissertation, the waiter arrived with their food and poured Darby's coffee.

"Thank you," she said to the waiter, and handed the pad to

Keith. "Anything you want to add?"

While he read, she doctored her coffee and then took a sip keeping a watchful eye over the brim. He smiled a couple times and raised an eyebrow once.

When done, he set the pad on the table. "That's pretty close to accurate. I like the part about fornicating with the clouds and ejaculating lightning the best."

"One of my finer lines," she grinned.

He lifted his cup and said, "And I really liked the bus driver section and needing to go back to driver's ed, but you forgot to mention that I pissed myself. "

"Damn it. Give me that paper back," Darby said grabbing the pad from him. "I'll add it right under your lacking all social skills."

Keith laughed. "You know, this is pretty darn good writing," he said looking over her shoulder.

Darby took a bite of Danish and glanced back to see what bimbo caught his attention.

"Excuse me." Keith jumped up and rushed across the room and caught a tub of dishes, teetering on the edge of a table, before it tumbled over. The busboy blushed and bowed as Keith handed him the tub.

Darby licked a chocolate covered finger. When he returned she said, "That was nice."

Keith shrugged it off. "Seriously, we need to talk about what happened. I was an idiot thinking I could take a trip like this after being awake all night. I ate two Tylenol PMs on the flight over hoping I could sleep. I didn't, and it just threw me off. I was worthless." He glanced at the paper. "Worse than worthless."

"Well, maybe you should've taken Ambien. I hear people can eat and have sex on that shit. Maybe it would have helped you fly.

She sipped her coffee and watched him closely.

"I screwed up," he said staring into his cup. "I hate to think what could have happened."

Keith's remorse seemed real, and tension fell from her shoulders. "How many hours were you awake before our flight?"

"Honestly?"

"No. Lie to me," Darby said, stabbing a strawberry. "You're a pilot, it's expected."

Keith grinned and said, "About thirty-six."

"Holy shit!" Darby's mouth dropped open. Keith reached over and touched a finger to her chin and lifted.

What the hell was she supposed to say to that? If flying was not fatiguing enough with ocean crossings, when pilots took it upon themselves to start out behind the eight ball, how the hell could they have a fight against fatigue? Everyone made a stupid decision now and again, but this was ridiculous. But still...

She pulled the pad close, turned the page and began to write. When she was done, she handed him the paper.

"If you're okay with this, then we'll submit it," she said. "Then I have something we're going to do."

Three hours later Darby and Keith were sitting in massage chairs with legs extended and their feet in the hands of expert masseurs, alias foot torturers.

"What the hell is this called?" Keith asked, withering in his chair. "You *like* this shit?"

"Reflexology," Darby said. Men were always worked on harder than the women. But her whispering 'firm' to the guy, and nodding toward Keith, helped to elevated the pain he deserved. "It's really good for you." She grinned.

An hour later they were walking back to the hotel. Well, she walked and Keith waddled.

"Ah, suck it up and be a man," Darby said, laughing. Keith Stone deserved whatever torture she could administer today. This was only the beginning.

"Beer. I need beer, and lots of it," he moaned. This had been his mantra for the previous ten minutes.

When they arrived at the hotel they went directly to the pool. Darby pulled her t-shirt and shorts off, stripping down to her swimsuit. Taunting Keith in her bikini would be his second spanking. Her daily yoga and workout would finally pay off.

Keith pulled his shirt off and plopped his butt at the edge of the pool and stuck his feet into the water, completely ignoring her. Within seconds he lifted a foot and looked at the bottom. Undoubtedly to see if it was bruised.

"You need me to kiss it better?" Darby yelled from her chair.

"There's an idea," he said inspecting the other.

"In your dreams," she countered just as the waiter approached. She ordered two large draft beers and gave him her room number. When he returned with their beer, Keith was on the chair beside her and pulled out his wallet.

"I got it," Darby said. "I think you've paid your dues."

"No way." Keith handed the waiter his credit card. "The captain always pays. I'm not sure when that stopped. On my watch the first officers are not allowed to pull out their money."

"Did you see that jewelry store we passed on the way back?" She asked with a grin.

"Don't press your luck."

Darby laughed. She lifted her beer and said, "Thank you." They touched mugs.

Keith and Darby finished their first beer and then took the second into the pool. An hour later they ordered room service to the hot tub as the sun fell behind the building.

When they were done eating they climbed out of the tub and reached for their towels. Darby stumbled and fell into Keith. He caught her, and they both laughed easily.

"You're going to be cut off young lady."

"Do I have to go to bed early too?" she said wrapping the towel around her waist.

He looked at his watch. "Holy shit! It's six fifteen."

Darby grabbed his wrist and looked at his watch. They had a 0300 wake up. "Where the hell did the day go?"

Wrapped in towels with clothes in hand, they found the elevator. Darby stuck her key card into the slot and pressed the button to their floor.

Keith walked her to her room and when she opened the door he stepped back and said, "Thanks for a great day." He headed down the hall and said over his shoulder, "Go straight to bed. We have a busy day tomorrow."

Darby slept great. Reflexology always helped. She awoke early without the alarm. When she unlocked the door to the gym, Keith was already inside working out.

"Cute butt," she said, passing him as he bent over reaching for some weights.

"Thanks for noticing," he threw back.

Darby rolled her eyes as she climbed on the elliptical trainer.

Three hours later everyone was boarding the bus and Keith stood at the stairs and helped the flight attendants up the steps, introducing himself as he did. They were taking a different crew back to Narita with them, which was probably a good thing.

At the plane they gathered their paperwork, and Darby went outside to do the walkaround. When she returned Keith was in the first class cabin briefing the flight attendants.

"We're planning a smooth flight today. Seven hours and thirty-five minutes. If there's anything you need, just give me a call. Does anyone have any questions?"

Darby stood behind the group and fake bounced, waving her hand excitedly so only Keith could see. Keith grinned and shook his head, then he turned toward the flight deck and Darby followed.

To say the flight went smooth was an understatement. They laughed the entire time sharing stupid stories, and Darby's face hurt from smiling. But it was time to get to work as the airport came into view on their primary flight display.

She pulled up the weather. "Windy in Narita today," she said pressing print. "Fifteen knots, gusting to twenty-five. JAL lost ten knots at 500 feet."

"We'll tell 'em we want the left runway," Keith said, inserting the weather on the performance page. "You ready for a talk?"

Darby pulled out her charts for Narita and followed along as Keith briefed the Venus South Alpha arrival to runway 34 left.

"Gwobal 29, descendo to 7000. Hold over Venus. Expect cleawance twenty minutes past the hour."

She pressed the line select key over Venus in the MCDU and selected hold. She compared the hold in the computer to that on the chart, confirming it was programed correctly.

They were on their fourth turn in the holding pattern. Darby watched the fuel decrease, and each time around she updated

Keith as to what they were landing with. They were at 9800 pounds and about to make another turn.

"We're getting too low for my comfort level," Keith said. "Report minimum fuel and tell them we need to land ASAP."

"Control, Global 29 we've got minimum fuel and need to begin our approach."

"Ahhh. Gwobal 29 continue hold."

"Negative," Keith said to Darby. "We need to land."

"Control, Global 29 needs to start our approach now."

"Ahhh. Gwobal 29 standby."

I've got this," Keith said and keyed the microphone. "Narita, Global 29 is departing holding, heading 020 for Haneda."

"Gwobal 29, diwect Venus, descendo four-thousand. Expect wunway thwee four wight," ATC responded.

Darby rolled her eyes. *Only in Tokyo.* She keyed the microphone. "Due to operational necessity Global 29 needs runway 34 left."

The left runway was 13,000 feet and the right only 8200. With windshear, the long runway was a no brainer and Darby was glad to see she and Keith were on the same page.

When they were cleared for the approach to the left runway, Keith said, "I'm kicking everything off." The autopilot dinged and the autothrust chimed as Keith took control of the plane. "Flight Directors off."

Darby raised an eyebrow as she complied with his command. Maybe this guy does have a set of balls and can fly a jet airliner. Still, she was not letting her guard down.

The plane rocked like a bronco, and he flew a perfect approach to a smooth touchdown.

"Nice job," Darby said. "Didn't know you had it in you."

"Fuck you very much," Keith said with a laugh, as he cleared the runway. "Flaps up, after landing checklist please."

An hour and a half later they were in the lobby of their hotel in shorts and tennis shoes headed for a run in the rice paddies.

Darby did her best to out run him, but the best she could do was keep up. When they finally stopped, she leaned forward, with hands on her knees breathing hard, and said, "Trying to kill me again?"

"Ah, you've got a few more miles in you. But do you mind if we walk back to the hotel?"

She looked up and grinned. "Okay. If we *have* to."

Two hours later they were back at the hotel. "See you in fifteen in the Sports Bar," Keith said. "Don't do that girl shit and be late."

Darby rolled her eyes and walked slowly through the lobby. Once she rounded the corner she kicked it into gear and ran up the stairs and down the hall.

She jumped into the shower, spending less than five minutes in the water. The hell if she would be late after that comment. Instead she would be waiting for him.

She washed her face, added a touch of mascara and some blush, and fluffed her hair. When she stepped into the bar, Keith was already sitting at a table with two beers in front of him.

"Not bad for a girl," he said.

"Some things take time," she said pulling out a chair. Tilting her beer to his she added, "Maybe this speed issue is why you don't have a girlfriend. Don't you know, slow is good?"

He grinned, touching his glass to hers. "I'm thinking sushi in the city. You game?"

They returned to the hotel on the 2200 bus after a long walk in the temple, and the best dinner Darby'd had in a long time. Keith walked her to her room.

"Thanks for a great time," she said.

"You're welcome." He stuffed his hands deep into his pockets. "You know, I could get used to this."

"Me too," she said as she unlocked her door. Glancing left, he was already on the way down the hall toward his room. "Good night," she called.

"Good night," Keith said, over his shoulder with a wave.

At 0600 they were both in the gym. They talked and laughed for an hour on their treadmills running stride for stride. Then they met for breakfast at 0830. Shortly thereafter they climbed aboard the bus headed for the airport. Today's destination—Bangkok.

"How long's the flight?" Darby asked.

Keith pulled out his crew rotation and said, "We're scheduled just under seven. I'm guessing maybe a bit longer with the forecasted headwinds." He folded the paper and stuffed it back into his pocket. "Any ideas for the layover?"

"I got us covered," Darby said grinning.

She was learning many things about Keith, one of which was that he embarrassed easily.

"What are you up to?" he asked, giving her a sideways glance.

"Who me?" Darby said opening her eyes wide and placing a hand to her chest.

CHAPTER 15
FLIGHT 23
NARITA TO HONOLULU

DECEMBER 25, 2011

DARBY AND KEITH were on the tail end of their trip and 400 miles out of Honolulu. The morning was early as the sun rose above the islands welcoming them. The day would be beautiful, just as the previous four had been—with one problem. Darby glanced to her left.

She really liked Keith Stone. Each moment in the plane with him she found herself smiling. Every second on the ground they laughed and shared stories and personal details of their lives. For Darby—all but one. Some things were better kept to herself.

Bangkok was a blast. She took him to a sex show to embarrass him on a totally new level. As it turned out she was the one who was shocked and he whisked her to safety in the form of a nightclub in their hotel. They spent the night sipping Jameson and talking.

On their return to Narita they hopped a bus to Tokyo and took a train to Mount Fuji. Unfortunately they were outside the climbing season so they returned to Narita and ate sushi.

The trip was awesome.

She pulled down the shade and adjusted her seat to avoid the morning blindness.

It was hard to believe they had known each other for only four days. Four days, at seventeen hours per day, was more than enough time to get to know someone. She and Keith were destined to be good friends. Hell…they already were.

It took her a long time to allow Neil to work into her heart and he violated her trust on every level. Darby looked left and smiled, Keith was different.

He glanced up and returned the grin. She shifted her attention forward as the Honolulu airport came into view on her electronic map. Their fun was coming to an end. She leaned right and pulled the book of charts out of her bag.

"They kind of slam dunk us in here," she said. Lifting her coffee cup she sniffed. "Have you been here in the bus yet?"

"We did a few approaches in the simulator. Does that count?"

"In someone's dream," Darby said. "In the sim they position you high on the downwind. Real life they bring you straight in and high. After flying all night it catches you by surprise." She tipped back the remainder of her coffee and stuffed the cup into the garbage bag.

"Like I'm the expert," she said. "I've been here once."

"You want the landing?" he asked.

"I'd love it, but this one's yours. Show me how it's done Boss."

She loved to fly, but it was only fair. She flew both legs to and from Bangkok, and now it was his turn.

"If I grease it on will you carry my bags to my room?" he asked, removing his approach plates. "Kind of like my personal porter?

Darby laughed clicking her shoulder straps into place. "I would love to be your porter chick, but I thought you were going home."

"Damn, that's right. Rain check?"

"Definitely." They stared at each other for a moment and then

Darby said, "You ever going to brief this or just sit on your ass and look cute?"

Keith laughed. "Looks like they're landing eight left. The Booke Eight arrival."

She pulled out the arrival chart and followed along as he briefed the approach. When he was done, Keith asked, "Any questions?"

"Nope. Looks good to me."

It was Christmas day and she would be spending it alone. She thought about the gifts she brought and all the trouble she caused by violating the chain of command. All of that seemed trivial now.

A party for the crews in Honolulu would have been nice, but a good night's sleep sounded better all the time.

"Global 23, reduce speed to two hundred and ten knots," ATC said slapping her back to attention.

Keith dialed back the speed and got off profile as he slowed.

"We're getting a little high," Darby said. Not trying to fly his plane, but she was too tired to go around. "Just like the Boeing I use three to one for planning. It's a good gouge—taking in consideration speed and wind."

"I thought that blue arrow was our descent point."

"Nope. That tells you where you'll hit the path. When ATC slows us up like this, your blue arrow creeps away indicating you're going above profile." Darby pressed the PROG page button, short for progress, on the MCDU. "See this, it's my favorite page. Says you're thirty-four hundred feet high."

"Shit." He pulled the speedbrake lever to full extension, increasing their descent rate.

"As we get back on profile, you'll see how the blue arrow creeps toward us. That's because you're increasing your descent and putting yourself closer to the level off point."

"This makes no sense. You're right…this plane is a woman."

"Told you," she said, with a laugh. "And just don't push the wrong buttons or you'll really piss her off." Darby watched as they moved closer to their path. "Once the blue arrow moves to where you want the plane to capture the path, or level off, stow the speedbrakes."

"If we stow the speedbrakes, won't we just get high again?"

"Nope. The plane's not counting on speedbrakes to make it. When you get there and take them away she doesn't care. She's on her profile based on your altitude and speed."

"Nice," he said as he pushed the speedbrake lever forward.

The winds were gusty but pretty much down the runway. They bounced a bit, but after their first flight, this was nothing. "You want me to activate the approach?" she asked.

"Oh hell. Yeah. Thanks."

Darby laughed. If they forgot to activate the approach the power would go to 250 knots when he selected managed speed. The approach gets a bit sporty when that happens.

They were up all night and flew into the sun. The reality was… fatigue and inexperience did not mix. Keith did a great job, and they had turned into a harmonic team, synchronized in a perfect choreographed play. Thank God for standard operating procedures.

"Global 23, on this heading, cleared for the visual eight left. Contact the tower on 118.1."

Darby responded and then switched to the tower frequency. "Tower, Global 23 is with you on a ten mile final for runway eight left."

"Global 23 you're cleared to land full length runway eight left. Wind zero nine zero at ten. Merry Christmas."

Keith pressed the button for managed speed and called for flaps three and then the gear.

"Make this a good one. I've got to pee and I'm not sure if I can hold it if you pranger her on."

"The pressure's on, baby. Flaps full," he said. "Landing check."

He touched down nicely—even the nose came down and kissed the runway. The best either had done to date. "That was for you, my sweet."

"Nice," Darby said.

They cleared the runway and Darby raised the flaps. She turned the TCAS and radar to off and confirmed the speedbrake lever was stowed. Then she called ground control and got a clearance to taxi into the gate.

"After-landing check complete," Darby said.

The flight deck was silent as they taxied to the gate—as it should be.

They should not have been talking below 10,000 feet either. Only after an accident did someone listen to the chatter on the voice recorder. Reality was that most crews said something—a survival mechanism to confirm everyone was awake for landing.

Tomorrow Darby would fly back to Narita. Keith was done with his pattern, so he could leave early. There was a flight in two hours, and he would be home in time for Christmas dinner.

After the engines were shut down and checklists complete, she hopped up and said, "Be right back."

Her hydration goals included drinking excessive amounts of water to combat the signs of altitude-induced old age. So far it was working, but her bladder complained during a long flight.

When she returned to the flight deck, Keith was mumbling something about Honolulu and being high. "Talking to your imaginary friend?" Darby said.

"Yep," Keith laughed. "My short term memory sucks," he said waving what looked like a pen. "Recorder. Makes it much easier to decipher my notes at the end of the day."

"So spy like," Darby said slipping into her seat. She returned her charts to their books and then stuffed them into the bag.

Keith stood and pulled their suitcases out of the closet as Darby climbed out of her seat.

"Darby," Keith said touching her shoulder.

She looked up and their eyes locked. "Yeah?"

"Thanks again, for everything," he whispered.

"My pleasure," Darby said. "Are you sure Santa didn't send you?"

Keith grinned. "If he did, I'm a believer."

"Me too," she said. "Merry Christmas. I hope we can fly together again."

"We will," he said. He spread his arms wide and she melted into his embrace and he whispered into her ear, "Besides, you owe me a beer."

CHAPTER 16
HONOLULU, HAWAII

DARBY CLIMBED out of the crew van and breathed deep. The scent of the tropics always made her smile, and today was no different. She loved Hawaii and looked forward to island time.

Handing the driver a five-dollar bill she said, "Merry Christmas," and pulled her bags up the ramp and into the lobby.

"Mele Kalikimaka," the woman at the check-in desk said.

"Merry Christmas."

"Where's your crew?" she asked.

"Home for the holidays," Darby said, autographing the sign-in sheet.

"You can't spend Christmas alone."

"No worries. More flights will be coming in, I'm sure I'll find someone to play with me."

The woman laughed and handed Darby her key.

Darby gave her the last gift from her bag. She and Keith had played Santa during their layovers and gave the others away. Done with Santa duties, she headed toward the elevator.

Once in her room, it took her less than three minutes to strip down to her panties and bra. She picked up the phone and called housekeeping to bring her an iron and ironing board.

Darby set her laptop on the desk and pressed the on button. Within minutes her fingers tapped the keys with rapid speed to connect to the Internet. Kathryn had promised to send pictures.

Her smile started slowly and grew wide as the photos came to life.

The kids made her Christmas cards and were holding them in front of the tree she helped to decorate. Then another photo emerged holding the books she had given them—*Circle, Fly Girl* and *The Dragon Empire* for the twins, and *Code Name: Dodger* for Chris.

In another photo, Kat and Jackie were toasting with champagne, and held up a third glass for Darby. Then Jessica was kissing Chris, Jackie's son, on the cheek as Jennifer held mistletoe over his head.

They must have bribed those kids something big to get that photo. Darby laughed. Then tears filled her eyes. She missed them all.

She clicked through more photos, and a tear trickled down her cheek. "I'm such a putz," she said wiping her face with the back of her hand. Maybe being alone on Christmas was not the best idea.

The remainder of her emails were 'Happy Holiday' wishes from friends. Nothing from Neil, which was fine with her.

She shut down her computer and glanced at her watch. A shower and a nap, then she would plot her day. Slipping into the bathroom she turned the faucet to hot and then returned to the bedroom and opened the curtains.

Her seventh-floor room faced the ocean. She glanced down at her matching bra and panties—nothing more than a bikini for the average tourist. She unlocked the door and slid it open. Laughter and the scent of the ocean drifted into her room.

Darby returned to the bathroom, dropping her bra and stepping out of her panties along the way. She climbed into the shower and tipped her face toward the spray. Running fingers through her hair she stifled a yawn.

With heavy eyelids and an achy brain, she looked forward to a long nap in cool, crisp, sheets as the breeze off the ocean caressed her to sleep. Then she heard something and poked her head out the shower curtain.

She should have known the only way to get housekeeping to come was to get in the shower. She climbed out, wrapped a towel around her body, and peeked out the hole. She stared into the face of an ironing board. *Cute.* She unlatched the security lock, stepped behind the door and then opened it wide enough to take the board.

The door pushed in and she stumbled back. Her heart added a few extra beats as she grabbed the door to stop from falling. "Excuse me?"

"Did someone call for an ironing board and iron?" Keith said, standing in a pair of shorts and t-shirt. "Nice look," he said taking her all in—towel, wet hair, and the stupid look she could not wipe off her face.

"You scared the shit out of me."

Keith leaned the ironing board against the wall and set the iron on the dresser. He grinned as he picked up her red bra and twirled it in his fingers. "Nice."

"Holiday spirit," Darby said, closing the door.

"I have a better way to get into the holiday spirit." He reached for her towel and tugged, but she held tight. He raised an eyebrow.

Darby grinned as her heart beat wildly.

"Do you want me to leave? Keith asked.

"God no," Darby said. "I'm just not sure we should screw up whatever this is with sex."

Keith pulled a hand over his face and rubbed his chin, as his eyes locked onto hers. A slow and lazy smile spread across his face and she laughed. What the hell was she thinking?

"Well, you did bring me an ironing board," she said stepping forward and touching his chest.

His heart pounded rapidly beneath the warmth of his t-shirt. "It's been a long time," she said, "you'll have to be patient with me."

Keith touched her cheek brushing a strand of hair back from her face, then brought his lips close to her ear. "It's been a long time for me too."

He wrapped his arms around her and pulled her close.

"I thought you were going home," she said.

"I couldn't leave," he whispered. "I caught a cab and begged the front desk to give me the room next to yours."

Darby laughed and threw her head back. "You didn't have to beg very hard, your name was printed on the sheet *as* the room next to mine. You forgot to cancel it."

"But I would have begged," he said. His lips were a whispers breath from hers.

"I almost told them you wouldn't be using it."

"I'm glad you didn't."

His lips touched hers in a chaste kiss and her body shivered as the charge shot through every cell. The kiss turned into one of fire fueled by passion. She melted into his mouth as he took hers with every bit of intimacy that had grown between them the previous week.

They stayed that way for what felt like forever. When they came up for air he held her tight and they swayed, her body firing on all cylinders.

"You're cold. Let's either get you under the covers or back into that shower."

"Shower," she said, and led the way. The towel fell to the floor and he held her hand as she stepped in.

Keith pulled his shirt over his head, stepped out of his shorts and followed her.

He rubbed a bar of soap between his hands and then placed them onto her chest, moving slowly as he soaped her breasts. His hands slid down her abdomen, not taking his eyes off his work. She shivered beneath his touch. He slid a hand between her legs and the other lathered her back. She melted into his touch.

I will not fall for this guy.

Keith set the soap aside and then slid both hands down her backside and pulled her close.

Darby tilted her head back with a moan as he pulled her in. *This is just sex. It means nothing.*

His mouth found her neck, and her heart sped up. His lips worked their way up to her ear and he nibbled. Both his hands slid down her back and over her ass, and she moaned.

She stood on her tiptoes as his tongue found a home in her mouth. He kissed and sucked as his hands squeezed. Keith stole her breath.

This is only physical.

Her skin sang beneath his touch. His hands slid over her curves as he caressed and became friends with every inch of her body.

A hand found her breast and his mouth followed. He sucked a nipple and gently bit. Shocks of pleasure ran through her body. Another hand squeezed her butt as he pulled her close, sliding his leg between hers.

Her weight settled on his leg and he held her hips, as he slid her up his thigh, pulling her close to his body. He stoked the fire that had been dormant for far too long.

It was all that she could do to breathe, and her body trembled as she came. He held her tight, and rocked her.

Once her breathing slowed he lifted her off his leg, and pressed her against the shower wall. Her feet found the edge of the tub and in a blur of passion they became one.

Time stood still as they moved together under the warm water. Keith carried her to a place she had never imagined. Again and again. He held her hips tightly, pushing himself against her, and whispered, "Oh God, Darby."

'Oh God' carried her to a new level, and they fell together. He held her close until their throbbing slowed and jagged breath calmed, then he pulled back and looked into her eyes. "I think we should get out before we become prunes."

She nodded, unable to catch her breath to speak.

He lifted her out of the shower and shut off the water, then wrapped her in a dry towel. He pulled her close.

They stood there for the longest time. The hug moved all the way to her soul.

"Lets go lie down," he finally said. "We need some sleep."

Taking her hand he walked her to the bed and folded back the sheet and she climbed in.

She put the towel to her hair and dried it the best she could. He picked up a towel off the floor and dried himself, their eyes never parting.

He climbed into bed and turned her, so her back was against his body. He snuggled up close and spooned her. "Get some sleep sweetheart," he whispered, and kissed her neck. "We have all day."

When Darby awoke she glanced at the clock—six hours had passed. Keith was sitting on a chair facing the ocean with his back to her, sipping a scotch. The mini bar had been compromised. She sat up and stretched. He didn't move.

The afternoon sun warmed the room. He was naked other than a towel draped over his lap. Darby glanced in the mirror. The 'go to bed with wet hair' was not the best look, but what the hell.

She stepped behind him and put her hands on his shoulders and he startled ever so slightly.

"Hey sweetie," he said, and placed a hand over hers and squeezed.

Darby rubbed his shoulders slow and deep as she watched the ocean beyond. The swells rose and fell. She knew what held his attention. The waves were hypnotic.

She leaned close, wrapping her arms around him she rubbed his chest with both hands. Her hands had a mind of their own as they slid south under the towel. He was happy to see her and her body stirred.

Leaning forward she kissed him on the neck and licked up toward his ear and nibbled. She reached around him and pulled the towel from his lap and tossed it aside.

"If you take that, I'll get burned in places that won't be pretty." He set his drink on the table, knocking the empty mini to the floor.

"Oh, but it's very pretty," she said, taking him all in. "But you do need protection." She said, climbing onto his lap.

CHAPTER 17

HONOLULU, HAWAII

DARBY AWOKE TO SILENCE with her back nestled into the heat of Keith's body, the clock glowed 0100. His hand draped lazily over her shoulder. The gentle flow of his breath had all but stopped. His finger lightly stroked her arm. She lifted her hand and touched his fingers.

"Sweetie...," he said in a whisper, clasping her hand. "What's the deal with you and Neil?"

She cringed at the sound of Neil's name. That was the last thing Darby had expected Keith to ask in the middle of the night. "We're nothing but friends."

Keith rolled to his back. His arm slid off Darby as their bodies parted. She rolled toward him and leaned on an elbow. The moon, low and full, illuminated concern etched into his face.

He rolled onto his side and faced her. "I've never felt this way, about anyone." He touched her cheek. "The time we spent together was something that I didn't know could exist. But I won't interfere if there's more between the two of you."

"There's nothing," she said. "I trusted him. He defied that trust." Darby hesitated. "He was the first man that I..."

She stared into his eyes and hers moistened. Then she dropped back onto her pillow and covered her face with both hands.

Keith lifted her hands and kissed them. "Talk to me sweetheart."

Darby closed her eyes and took a deep breath. When she opened them, Keith was watching her with no judgment attached. Biting her lip, a million things bounced through her mind. Sucking a breath of courage she sat up and hugged a pillow.

"I was engaged when I was twenty-one." A time when life was perfect. "As corny as this sounds…my soul mate. He gave me my first airplane ride when I was sixteen, and was my flight instructor the summer before he went to work for Eastern." Darby closed her eyes. She was back in the plane in those early days with Brian.

"We've all made stupid career choices," Keith said.

Darby laughed. "That we have. But the only problem was Brian made a far greater mistake with his life."

Keith touched her leg. "What happened?"

Tears filled her eyes and trickled down her face. She wiped them away with a swipe of both hands and returned her arms to the security of the pillow.

"He bought me a first class ticket on his flight to South America. But I got a call…an interview with Coastal Airlines. He told me to go to the interview, that we would have a lifetime of trips together. Then he dropped to a knee."

Darby squeezed the pillow. "He showed me the ring he was going to give to me, but said that I had to wait. That my career was as equally important as his, and he would propose properly when he returned."

"Why didn't you get married?" Keith whispered.

"He never returned." Darby wiped fresh tears from her cheeks. "Remember the Eastern 767 that hit the mountain in Cali in December of '95?"

"Uh, huh…"

"Brian was the first officer."

"Oh babe," Keith said, sitting up. He pulled her into his arms. "I'm so sorry."

"They said it was pilot error. Complacency." Darby's heart broke all over again. "But it was more than that. They trained him to punch buttons…they didn't train him how to fly that jet. His type rating was flown entirely on automation. What could anyone expect?"

Keith rolled to his back and pulled Darby with him. She cried into his chest for the first man she loved who was murdered by a system of complacency fed with a diet of automation.

When she calmed, Keith asked, "When did Neil come into the picture?"

"He was the first person I loved after Brian…but none of it was real." She sniffed and grabbed a tissue and blew her nose. "I found out he was married. He lied to me and that was it. I will never trust him again, but it's hard for me to throw people out of my life. My family has a history of getting mad and they never talk to you again. I've spent a lifetime trying not to do that."

"Sweetie. I'm sorry." Keith hugged her tight and rolled them to their sides facing the moon. "You deserve so much better than all this." He stroked her forehead and snuggled into the nape of her neck.

"Neil was the last person I gave my heart…and my bed to. It's been two years."

Darby awoke to daylight that replaced the moon. This time she was alone. A warm breeze lifted the curtains. Two coffee cups sat silently on the balcony, holding the secrets of what went on at 0400 that morning.

She kicked off the sheet and stretched, then thought about coffee. She glanced at the cups and her mind went back to Keith as she dropped her feet to the floor and sat on the edge of the bed.

Darby moved to her desk and booted up her computer. She signed into the company website and opened her schedule.

Scrolling down the page she tried to figure out whom she would be flying with back to Tokyo. There were far too many names for the short flight. Then she realized why—Bob Hill was on the list.

Bob was a check airman and he had a student—a captain student no less. They reassigned her as a deadhead since this leg only required two pilots. The guys called it dinner and a movie.

Darby linked into her email account—23 messages. She glanced at the coffee maker, but the thought of Starbucks screamed.

She pulled on black shorts, slipped into a pink sports bra, grabbed her sunglasses and purse, and left her room in pursuit of real coffee.

Reaching the ground floor the doors opened and island scents smacked her. She breathed deep and wandered outside. Looking left and then right she darted across the street into Starbucks.

"What can I get for you?" the barista asked.

"An extra-shot, venti, cappuccino. Wet. Thanks."

If she was not going to fly or sleep, at least she could get some writing done. With Keith she never had a chance to work on her training blog.

When she told Keith about *Flight For Safety* and her concern for the classroom being cut, he told her to not worry and enjoy life away from a computer. After she told him about Brian, he said he understood, but something told her he still did not think her blog was a good idea. Maybe it was his saying, "Don't do it Darby." She laughed at this new mantra of her life.

Back in her room she sat at her computer to check her email. Her eyes grew wide when she saw Dick Foster's name. Subject— Apology

Darby, Really no need to apologize. I just wanted to make sure you understood that there are other ways to get answers to your questions than going directly to the CEO.

While I certainly can't presume to speak for Mr. Patrick, or Todd McDermott, or any other member of the executive team, I am confident that they truly believe in having an open door policy and would not be happy with me if I told you never to contact them again.

What I am saying is that you should know better than to waste their time. The sooner you learn the rules at Global, the better off you'll be. We don't go beyond flight ops walls for anything.

I am also asking you to consider the practical side of this. If all 70,000 Global employees decided that Mr. Patrick was the only person who could solve a problem or answer a question, you can imagine how difficult a problem that would pose. An already extremely difficult job would become impossible.

I would certainly agree that Mr. Patrick could have approved this request, but many layers below him could have approved it as well, if you followed the proper chain of command.

If this had come to me from the Seattle chief pilots' office, I would have asked some questions about the number of pilot's we were talking about, how you were going to communicate the party to them and what the availability and cost of a suite was.

Depending on the answers to those questions, I might have approved your request. By the time it got down to me, however, and I sent it to

your chief pilot, there really wasn't much time to act on the request. Had you followed proper procedures, there might have been a Christmas party in Honolulu.

I certainly didn't mean to "squish" your holiday spirit, but rather suggest a different way to express it in the future. Let me know if you have any questions.

Director of Flying, Dick Foster

Darby stared at the words frozen on her screen, then leaned back and folded her arms. Prior to her getting called in, she never heard of Dick Foster. He blew her request so far out of proportion it was teetering on a ridge between ridiculous and absurd. Now he was lecturing her too? This made no sense.

She sipped her coffee and looked over the brim staring at her computer. Her mind whirled, and her foot tapped under the desk. Kathryn's trademark move, but she couldn't help it.

There were so many things she wanted to address with the new airline about training and procedures. But how could she? Who was she supposed to talk to? The bottom of the food chain—Roy? She rolled her eyes. Better yet, did this email dignify a response?

Darby pushed away from her desk, walked across the room and stared at the ocean. She glanced over her shoulder at her computer.

Something did not make sense. The largest airline in the world and the director of flying was schooling her on how busy the CEO was. He should be more concerned with issues like cutting training and canceling ground school, or the inability of dispatch to create a flight plan with a new fuel load.

A warm breeze caressed her face and she closed her eyes.

She wished Keith were with her. He would know how she should respond.

CHAPTER 18
FLIGHT 32
NARITA TO SEATTLE

DECEMBER 28, 2011

DARBY SAT IN THE CAPTAIN'S SEAT as her A330 headed east into the morning sun. She pulled down the glareshield. Her fellow first officer's head was buried in a book.

She picked up the clipboard, glanced at Doug, and then crosschecked their next waypoint. She wrote down the total fuel and time, then returned the clipboard to the glareshield.

The Sports Bar was hopping the night before. Rumors flew that they had found the Pacific Airlines A330 black box. The plane disappeared two years earlier, and everyone had a theory.

Darby closed her eyes. Her mind drifted to Keith. He was lying on the bed as she rubbed oil over his body. Emotion stirred. Her head dropped back as she drifted into his arms. The sun was setting and...

She startled and opened her eyes. She shook her head. *Shit.* The need to wake up shouted loud and clear. The sun was not setting... it was rising, and she was in charge of the plane and needed to be alert—awake at the very least.

Darby picked up her purse, found her compact, and rubbed a smudge of mascara from under her eyes. She pulled a brush through her hair and tied it into a ponytail.

She replaced the compact and stretched in her seat, then patted both cheeks. *Wake up. Wake up. Wake up.* She glanced at Doug, and he was staring her way.

"You okay?" he asked.

"Yep. Trying to stay awake," she said. "So why do you think that A330 crashed?" Hoping a stimulating conversation would keep her awake.

"Hell if I know. The plane probably broke."

"Planes break, but pilots should still be able to fly them."

"Maybe," Doug mumbled returning his attention to his book.

Darby yawned. Soon the world would know why that A330 crashed. General consensus in the Sports Bar was terrorism—there was no way a modern, highly automated plane like the A330 could fall from the sky for anything less.

Flashes of her and Keith's incident in the storm sent chills through her body. She had stuffed the memories deep and ordered another beer, not mentioning the situation to anyone. They would soon see it in the simulator compliments of their ASR.

Darby glanced at the electronic map as the circle of pleasure approached—the time slotted for their break displayed as a green circle. In twenty-five minutes she and Doug would go to the back and Bob, their check airman, and the captain in training would return to do the landing. Today was New Captain's checkride.

At the end of the day, he would be signed off to take command of his own plane. Yesterday was his seventh leg and he landed so hard, they would have to lower the runway elevation on the next set of revisions. Not that Darby hadn't landed hard.

The problem was not the landing, but the lack of discussion as to 'why' he pranged it on.

The A330's nosewheel needed to be flown onto the runway. If the pilot held the stick back to flare, the plane would eventually run out of airspeed, thus losing elevator control and the nose would drop. The new captain dropped his nose by at least two feet, but it had felt like ten. Bob never said anything to him.

Yawning, she opened her bottle of water and took a long drink and then tossed the empty into the garbage bag. She set her watch to Seattle's time zone and sent a request for Seattle's weather. She typed the arrival for runway 16 left into the MCDU and filled out the performance page.

Shivering, she reached to the overhead and turned up the heat and asked, "You want the bunk or the seat when we go back?"

"Bunk for sure, thanks."

"Enjoy it while you can, those days are numbered."

The company was removing all bunks and soon pilots would take their crew rest in the business section. Their union, ALPO, the Airline Pilot's Organization, said they 'fought' to keep them, but that had been a ruse.

"Hell, everyone is making such a big deal about the bunks going away," Doug said. "Global's been flying with guys sleeping in a seat for years."

"Yeah, but they were three day trips. Out and backs. There's a hell of a lot more fatigue on a ten or twelve-day trip with multiple ocean crossings. You're in a hotel room for what...nine nights max in the eleven days? Our patterns are different from anything they've experienced at Global. Cumulative fatigue cannot be erased."

"Maybe so, but I'm sure you flew many flights single crew up to twelve hours on the 747."

"I did," she said. "And then we learned what fatigue can do. Progress moved us forward. This bunkectomy just took a huge step back."

"I hadn't thought about it like that."

"The non-safety team hadn't either."

The crewrest optimization committee should have been under the direction of the central air safety chairman, not random pilots appointed by the ALPO master executive counsel. The loss of the bunks was a direct hit to safety. They needed somebody with human factors and safety related technical expertise to fight the battle to keep them.

Darby reached up and pressed the crew call button to the forward bunk.

"Uh… yeah?" A voice mumbled over the speaker.

"It's that time," Darby said, and the phone went dead.

CHAPTER 19
OKLAHOMA CITY, OKLAHOMA

DECEMBER 28, 2011

DICK FOSTER GLANCED at his watch and then stuck his hands deep into his pockets as he looked toward the Bricktown Canal. He had twenty minutes before he was supposed to meet Wyatt and Clark, the men who were making his career move faster than he ever expected.

Captain George Wyatt, the director of flight operations, and Captain Rich Clark, the manager, brought him into their circle of trust. They gave him a position that most pilots would kill for.

He was officially one of the elite at Global Air Lines as the head of all chief pilots—he was the director of flying. Who cared if he was a first officer, this was position he not only deserved, but earned.

Everything was perfect except for that damned Darby Bradshaw. *That fucking little bitch.* Something told him they were heading into a storm with that one. He would be damned if he would allow her to speak to him as she did.

This was his airline. Nobody, especially some Coastal bitch, would make him a fool. He would teach her respect if it were the last thing he did. He opened his eyes and squinted into the rising sun and sucked a deep breath.

He planned on working for Global prior to beginning his military career. He always wanted a piece of this airline and the Air Force was the fast track to his dreams. He made the right connections in purgatory and kissed enough ass in the service that he was guaranteed a position.

The road to be hired, at what is now the world's largest airline, was paved in sacrifice.

When he was hired by Global three years earlier he parked his ass in flight operations and did whatever it took to be noticed. Life was all about connections and playing the game.

He played better than most. The director of flying was a coup that nobody deserved more than he.

Dick was on reserve, so living in the office was easy. It only took three years of eating shit to be advanced to the director of flying. At best he had hoped for an assistant chief pilot position.

He glanced toward the ballpark and then looked over his shoulder. He lifted his wrist—fifteen minutes. He would be early and have the guys' coffee ready for them when they arrived. He turned and jogged toward Starbucks.

Dick pulled open the door and stepped up to the counter and heard Clark laugh. He turned, then glanced at his watch and looked up. Wyatt and Clark were sitting at a table.

He wandered over. "Good morning, Gentlemen. Did I have the time wrong?"

"Good morning," Wyatt said. "No, you're fine."

"Go grab your coffee," Clark said.

Dick returned to the counter and ordered a Venti French roast. He glanced over his shoulder and nodded at Wyatt who was watching him. He returned his attention to the counter and paid the chick serving him and dropped a quarter in her tip jar.

With coffee in hand, he returned to the table.

"Gentlemen, thank you for joining me this morning," Wyatt said. "Sorry for the drama of an early morning meeting, but I wanted to keep this out of the office." He lowered his voice. "We have a problem with one of our bush pilots."

Dick pulled his chair closer to the table and leaned in.

"I don't think Bradshaw's going to be a problem," Clark said. "She'll step into line."

"Her meeting with the assistant chief pilot didn't seem to help." Wyatt took a sip and looked over the brim at Clark. "Under no circumstances will *any* pilot take *anything* beyond flight ops walls. Those Coastal pilots need to learn the rules."

"She wrote innocuous letters," Clark said. "That's nothing. She'll be fine."

"I understand your response had a little backlash," Wyatt said to Dick. Their eyes locked.

This was why he had been told to bring copies of the letters.

"She's a bimbo," Dick said. "It's nothing that I can't take care of." Women did not belong in the cockpit and Darby Bradshaw was a perfect example of why not.

"I hope so," Wyatt added.

"What happened?" Clark asked, looking between them.

Wyatt stared at Dick and gave a head nod toward Clark. "Show him."

Dick pulled copies of his emails from his shirt pocket, unfolded them, and handed them to Clark.

Clark's smile grew as he read, and he broke out in laughter by the time he finished. He extended the letters toward Wyatt, who sat with his arms folded and shook his head.

"Sassy little thing," Clark said. "Looks like that girl needs a spanking. If I wasn't previously occupied, I wouldn't mind stepping up to the plate to take care of that one."

Dick laughed. "Well, I'm just the guy to give it to her. The spanking that is."

"Good." Wyatt looked between them and said, "This is the last thing we need right now." He lifted his cup and sipped, then asked, "What about that blog. Can we shut it down?"

"I don't think so," Clark said. "She's not violating any rules. More or less it's positive for the pilot group. Besides far too many pilots and flight attendants have blogs these days. It might just keep her out of our hair."

"What are your thoughts?" Wyatt asked Dick.

"I agree with Rich. I don't think it'll be a problem," he lied.

That bitch and her blog *were* a problem for him. It was good. One more reason he wanted to take her down. He knew exactly what she was doing and where she wanted to go. It would be a cold day in hell if she would ever be part of his Global management team.

"She flew with Stone last week," Wyatt said. "Armstrong's got her under his thumb. Hopefully they'll take care of it."

"When did Stone get hired in training?" Dick asked.

"A few months ago," Wyatt said.

Dick was not sure what he thought of that.

"Those Cobras are turning into a bit of a challenge," Clark said draining the last of his coffee. "But nothing we can't handle." He crushed the cup in one hand, and dropped it on the table.

"Cobras?" Dick asked.

"Coastal Pilots," Wyatt answered. "They're willing to strike at anything."

"Nothing a lesson or two won't fix," Clark said. "Besides the south owns the union. They couldn't strike if they wanted to."

"What are we going to do with Bradshaw?" Wyatt asked.

"To start with, I'm pulling her in for a formal sit down with the chief pilot and her union rep for the tone of her email," Dick offered. "We'll scare the shit out of her. She'll behave going forward. If not, I'll work on plan B."

"I hope plan A works," Wyatt said. He placed his palms on the table and looked between them. "Thank you for coming gentlemen."

Clark stood and Dick followed, but Wyatt remained seated.

"I'll see you both next year," Wyatt said. "Happy New Year."

When Clark and Foster left the coffee shop, Wyatt stood. He left their cups on the table and walked toward the window and watched the boys walk toward E. Reno Avenue. Once they were out of sight, he pulled his phone out of his pocket and pressed speed dial.

"How'd it go?"

"Good," Wyatt said, "but I'm not sure if we can force her to stop writing that blog."

"Are we going to have a problem with her?"

"I don't think so," Wyatt said placing a hand on his hip. "Time will tell, but I think we'll cage the beast before the year is out."

CHAPTER 20
FLIGHT 32
NARITA TO SEATTLE

DECEMBER 28, 2011

W ITH ONLY TWO HOURS remaining, Darby's prophecy came true—there would be no sleeping in the business class seat with the last meal service in progress. Unfortunately, this was the wave of the future.

She excused herself and climbed over the passenger on her left and found her way to the back of the plane. She grabbed a cup of coffee and chatted with the flight attendants about the holidays.

When Brenda and Jane exchanged a look, Darby's eyebrow raised and she said, "What?"

"I heard you got called into the chief pilot's office for emailing Mr. Patrick," Brenda said. "Is that true?"

"Guilty as charged."

"I flew with Jack," Jane said. "It's hard to keep stuff like this quiet,"

"Yep, I'm a bad one." Keeping rumors quiet on the flight line was next to impossible.

"This is bullshit," Brenda snapped.

Darby shrugged. "Maybe so, but now I better get back up front and babysit the boys. It's never a good thing to leave two captains unsupervised for too long."

Brenda and Jane laughed. Darby glanced at her watch and said, "We're about ninety minutes out."

She wandered to the front of the plane and called the flight deck via the intercom. "You guys need anything? I'm coming up."

Seconds later the door opened.

"You're early," New Captain said from the left seat.

"I like to watch," Darby said.

"Me too, Baby," New Captain said.

Darby rolled her eyes. She liked being up front for the takeoffs and landings to take notes. Especially with a training captain.

As the new captain and Bob discussed scuba diving, Darby reviewed the arrival and approach plates and then punched in a request for the current weather.

Time flew and within no time ATC broke into the equation. "Global 32, descend and maintain flight level two four zero."

"Global 32, leaving three nine zero, for two four zero," Bob responded.

New Captain dialed 24000 into the altitude selector and pulled, putting the plane into an open descent. "Get us the weather for Seattle," he said to Darby.

"Printing it now."

"Good. Then kiss them good-bye for me," he added.

After the weather spit out of the printer, she read it and then picked up the PA. "Good morning ladies and gentlemen, from the flight deck, this is the captain speaking."

"Captain?" Bob scoffed. New Captain gave her a sideways glare. She was not making brownie points.

Darby released the talk button and shrugged. "Sorry. Good habits die hard." She pressed the switch and continued. "From the flight deck, we've just begun our initial descent into Seattle Tacoma's International Airport. A beautiful day today. Winds are light, skies clear, and the current temperature is 47 degrees.

"If you'd like to set your watches to the local time, it's six-thirty a.m. We'll have you on the ground and at the gate in about 30 minutes for an on-time arrival. On behalf of the entire flight crew and our wonderful flight attendants serving you today, we hope you've enjoyed your excellent service. Thank you for flying Global Air Lines."

"Global 32, contact arrival on 119.2," ATC said.

Bob acknowledged the clearance and then contacted approach control.

"Global 32, descend and maintain one seven thousand, cleared direct Newberg, direct Olympia, Olympia seven arrival. Altimeter three zero one one," approach control responded.

New Captain dialed 17000 on the flight control unit, and pulled for a continued descent. They were already in open descent, so he did not need to pull the knob again. *Everyone started someplace.*

This was New Captain's line check. His final ride to determine if he was safe to take passengers on his own.

He told them three times the day before, he was a 'Boeing 777 captain' and Darby was sure that his Boeing experience made him an expert on the Airbus. She swallowed a grin—if an instructor heard what a pilot did on another plane once, they had heard it a thousand times. Who cared? This was a different animal.

Crossing over the Newberg VOR the plane turned to a course of 341 toward the Olympia VOR.

He had 97 miles to lose 4000 feet so a managed descent would have been a better option. Learning to fly this plane with efficiency would come with time. A three-to-one profile got you close on all planes. Automation was a killer of brain cells and skill.

They descended to 17,000 feet and trudged along for what seemed like forever. Darby glanced at the fuel. The company was still over fueling, so while he wasted gas they could fly a few extra approaches and still go to an alternate.

"Are we good to twelve thousand?" New Captain asked.

"Negative."

"Get me lower."

"Seattle, Global 32 requesting lower," Bob said.

"Global 32, descend to twelve thousand, via the Olympia Seven Arrival."

"You're good down to twelve." Bob reached up and dialed in 12,000 feet on the flight control unit.

Darby raised an eyebrow. *What's he doing?* The autopilot was on. Dialing altitudes and pushing buttons was not Bob's job, he was the pilot monitoring. New Captain was supposed to be flying.

Once over the Olympia VOR, the plane turned to a heading of 022 degrees on the arrival.

"Descent and approach check." New Captain pulled for selected speed and dialed it back to 250 knots. "Activate the approach."

Bob complied, then read the descent and approach checklists and New Captain responded.

Over FOURT intersection New Captain reached up and spun the heading to 340 degrees and pulled for heading select.

They were on downwind at 12,000 feet and there was only one plane in front of them. A flight profile that once was low was now very high and they were headed for a slam-dunk.

"Global 32 descend and maintain six thousand. You're number two for 16 center."

"See if you can get me the left," New Captain said. Bob placed the request.

Darby glanced out the window and then at the mileage and shifted in her seat. She had yet to see a go-around in this plane and she was about to experience just that.

"They've got you a little high. They could turn you in at any time," Bob said.

New Captain dialed his speed back to 220 knots and called, "Flaps one."

"Flaps one doesn't really do anything for you," Bob said.

"Global 32, turn right heading of zero seven five, base leg for 16 left," ATC said.

"Right heading zero seven five, for Global 32," Bob replied.

"Good. We got the long runway." New Captain spun the heading bug still unaware that he was very high on the approach. "That's what we've got programmed. Right?"

"Yeah," Bob said.

New Captain dialed the speed back to Vapp. "Flaps two."

Bob reached up and dialed the speed bug up to 170 knots. "You don't want to slow up here. This plane won't slow down and go down. You'll need speedbrakes, flaps and—"

"On the triple-seven we couldn't use flaps and speedbrakes," New Captain said, and Darby rolled her eyes.

"You can on this plane," Bob said.

New Captain pulled the speedbrake handle full aft, but forgot about the gear. Which would be a great help right about now, and she hoped they would get on it sooner than later.

"Global 32, do you have the runway in sight?" ATC asked.

New Captain said, "Tell them no."

"Negative. Global 32 would like the ILS."

"Global 32, four miles from KARFO, turn right heading one

four zero, maintain four thousand until intercepting the localizer, cleared ILS 16 left approach. Contact tower over KARFO."

New Captain turned the heading bug. He dialed 4000 feet into the flight control unit and pulled for open descent.

Bob reached up and selected...*Oh shit.*

He intended to select approach but pressed altitude hold instead. For an already high plane, he might have just screwed the pooch on this one. *Why the heck is he flying New Captain's plane anyway?*

"Why's it leveling?" New Captain yelled. He clicked off the autopilot and pushed the nose over and dove the plane for the glide slope. They were two dots high.

"Shit," Bob said, pulling the altitude knob to put the airplane into open descent and pressed the approach button, then engaged the second autopilot.

Darby's eyes darted between the altimeter, speed, and the two captains. Her heart rate shifted to max power. They were high and fast and two captains were flying the plane at the same time. This was a molotov cocktail in the making.

"Tower Global 32 heavy is with you over KARFO," Bob said, and pulled flaps three without New Captain asking for them, still flying New Captain's plane.

"Global 32, cleared to land runway 16 left. Wind one four zero at ten," ATC said. "You got the full length if you need it."

"Cleared to land, 16 left Global 32," Bob responded extending the landing gear without being asked. "Best rate of descent is one hundred and seventy knots, flaps three, full speedbrakes and gear down."

"Flaps two," New Captain said glancing at the flap indication. "Oh wait...flaps three." He pressed the managed speed button.

Bob placed the flaps to three.

"Flaps full," New Captain said.

Bob moved the flap handled into position. As they captured the glide slope signal Darby glanced down to write a note on the best rate of descent—170 knots, gear down, flaps three, and full speedbrakes.

"Terrain. Terrain," the plane screamed warning and Darby's head popped up as her heart slammed against the wall of her chest.

The pitch attitude was higher than normal and the power was increasing toward takeoff thrust as they sank into the ground. The terrain warning warned them of impending impact.

Time froze, as did both captains. They glanced right and left from their respective seats and then out the forward window. No reaction. No response. The plane's nose pitched up in attempt to climb back to and hold the glide slope—but from Darby's view the Airbus was bellying into the ground.

Time shifted to slow motion, but everything happened quickly and then Darby saw the problem.

"Speedbrakes!" she yelled.

New Captain shoved the speedbrake handle forward and the plane appeared to jump back onto the glideslope. Within seconds they stabilize with a normal pitched attitude for approach, but they were way too close to the dirt for comfort.

They had dove toward the glideslope, flew through it, then pitched up to capture it. Their high rate of descent so close to the ground triggered the terrain warning.

To make matters worse, they left the speedbrakes out. With gear out, full flaps, speedbrakes extended, and the excessive rate toward the ground followed by a pitch up attitude, the plane was performance challenged.

Bob said, "Gear down, flaps full, speedbrakes armed, landing check complete."

He recited the landing checklist from memory and New Captain did not respond. But Darby confirmed everything was done. Her heart pounded wildly in her throat.

They landed hard and missed all intersections, but stopped at the end of the runway.

"Global, clear the runway to the right."

"Why the hell do they want us to go to the right?" New Captain snapped.

"NOTAMS said there was construction," Darby said. "You can't taxi left from the last intersection."

NOTAMS—Notices to Airmen, were notes for their flight and something he should have read prior to departure, and prior to the arrival. New Captain grunted as they cleared the runway. He had blown past all his useable exits to the left.

Bob called ground and told them they were clear of the runway. After receiving their taxi clearance, both captains did their respective after landing flows. Ground control was on the number one radio and Bob dialed in ramp control on number two. Two radios. Two controllers. She was not sure who was on what.

"Ramp, Global Three Two," Bob said.

"At Global, we have the third pilot call ramp," New Captain said.

New Captain was a Global original and Bob had been a Coastal pilot. Procedures of who did what and when drifted in like a fog bank that would eventually lift, but now created a wall impacting safety.

"What if there are only two pilots?" Bob asked and missed ramp's return call.

"But there are three," New Captain argued. "Get us a gate Darby."

"Ramp, Global 32 is on the ground," Darby said. "Do you have a gate for us?"

"We have a gate—S1!" New Captain, yelled. "I wanted you to tell them we're here."

She bit her tongue. New Captain yelled at her for one reason only—he screwed up the approach and had failed his line check. This was what they termed a cluster-fuck, and she had never experienced a more dicked-up anything in her life.

"Global 32, where are you?" the ramp controller asked.

"Ramp, Global 32 is on taxiway Tango," Darby said. "We're about to cross Juliet."

"Can't see you, sweetheart. Give us a call when you get to spot eighty-eight."

"Will do," Darby said. Bob knew better than to call the ramp that far out.

After they crossed the active runway, New Captain said, "shut down the right engine."

Bob opened the crossbleed valve, and then pulled the engine master switch to off.

Darby glanced at the taxi chart. They were going to make two left turns—first into the ramp and then into parking. Shutting down the right engine was stupid, but at least they were on the ground.

Her mind flew back to final approach as the ground came up to meet them. She closed her eyes and tried to shake free of the image. Her heart beat like she'd had three triple shot venti cappuccinos in a twenty-minute period.

She never felt death was imminent in a plane before today. Not even with Keith on their first flight. But then she had been in the seat with an element of control. Sitting in the jumpseat watching the ground come at her was something she *never* wanted to experience again.

She opened her eyes and followed their taxi route on the chart wondering what to do after they blocked in. Should she leave during the debrief or stay? Failing someone was never an easy thing.

They were cleared into the ramp at spot 88 and then to the gate. Their aircraft was still in motion, so the first left turn with the right engine shut down was not a problem. When they stopped short of the gate at a 90 degree angle, with another left turn ahead, that was another issue.

The structural limitations on the gear included no differential braking for turns at speeds below 20 knots. Not to mention with the inside wheel fully stopped. This would be like trying to pivot turn a dump truck standing still. They would need to restart the right engine, or shutdown the left and get pulled in with the tug.

When the ground crew waved them in, New Captain pushed up the thrust on the inboard engine and stepped on the left brake. He pushed more power and worked the nose wheel eeking out a turn. Pivot. Pivot. Pivot. Darby cringed. *What the hell?*

Bob said nothing.

They pulled into the gate and shut down the left engine. The captains performed the shutdown and securing checklists. The flight deck was eerily quiet, other than standard responses.

This is not going to be good.

When all checklists were complete, Darby unbuckled her belt and stood. But before she could maneuver out of the flight deck Bob extended his hand to New Captain and said, "Nice job. Welcome to the plane. You better hurry, so you don't miss your commuter flight."

CHAPTER 21
SEATTLE, WASHINGTON

DECEMBER 28, 2011

AFTER CLEARING CUSTOMS, Darby rushed to the train that would take her to the main terminal. Her stomach rolled into a ball of nerves as she relived what happened on their approach.

How the hell could he have passed that guy?

The train pulled into view and the doors opened. Darby was in forward motion toward them when her name rang out.

Without turning, she moved quickly and stepped onto the train hoping the doors would slam shut and she could get as far away from reality as possible. Wishful thinking stopped short, as did the doors. A foot stuck through the opening and the check airman pressed inside.

Darby gave him a tight-lipped smile. The kind that was forced, confirming she was not happy. More than unhappy, she was pissed. If she had a smile for, 'you're an f-ing idiot' she would have given him that one instead.

"Any plans for the New Year?" he asked.

"No." She adjusted her purse and crossed her arms. Her mind whirled with a zillion things she wanted to say, but held them down like lava ready to explode. And then a thought occurred to her. "Should I fill out an ASR?"

"I'll take care of it," he snapped.

"We're all supposed to fill them out," she said. "Aren't we?" Darby liked and respected Bob. She could not understand his motivation for passing such poor performance.

"I *said* I would take care of it." His smile disappeared and eyes glared warning. His glacial tone sent a chill through her body.

She turned away and stared out the window as they flew through the tunnel.

When the doors opened Darby bolted as quickly as she had arrived. She walked past the elevator that lead up to flight operations and headed for the crew bus.

She stepped onto the escalator, pulling her bags behind. Half the way up she took a deep breath and glanced back. The check airman stood at the bottom of the escalator with hands on hips, staring her way.

Looking past him, not allowing their eyes to meet, she ran a hand through her hair and casually turned away. When her back was to him she placed a hand to her chest in an attempt to calm her heart.

Visions of the ground coming her way attacked her again. Then the burning shell of the plane that crashed in San Francisco flashed before her. If these guys had disconnected their autothrust the results would have ended in a fireball on top of a major freeway. Her body shook.

Trying to clear her mind she closed her eyes, but that made the images all the more real. She opened them just as the top stair sucked under her foot. She stumbled off the escalator, steadied herself and then walked past the coffee shop—a first.

She found her way up the next escalator, hustled across the overpass, and down the escalator to the bus stop. She parked her bags, sat on top of her suitcase, and waited for the crew bus.

Glancing at her watch she drummed her fingers on her leg. Then pulled her phone from her purse and typed a text message to Kathryn—*We almost crashed today. You won't believe what happened.* Her fingers zipped the words out and she pressed send.

Moments later a message followed—*Welcome home. 'Almost' is the better alternative. Dinner tonight. Talk then?*

See you tonight. Darby pressed send.

"What are you doing? Writing about me?"

Darby startled and looked up. Bob stood to her right, towering over her.

"In your dreams," she said. She wanted to tell him that he was a dumb-fuck on so many levels. Instead she put her sunglasses on and asked, "So what happened back there?"

A rhetorical question. Airplane mismanagement and two pilots flying was the issue. When two pilots flew the same plane nobody was in control. He also should have allowed the new guy to screw up and go around if he had to. They had enough fuel.

"I flew with this guy for eight days and he's been doing a great job. I'm emailing him notes on everything that happened. He's going to be fine." His voice was a rapid-fire, non-convincing string of empty words. The only person he fooled was himself.

De-brief by email? That was about as effective as getting pregnant during phone sex. There was no way to know if the student received and understood the message sent without a discussion.

Darby would never have signed him off, but that was not her call now that she was a junior first officer in a captain's world. She also would not have flown his plane and would have allowed him to go around. Maybe he would have been fine if Bob had not got involved. Maybe his go-around would have proven he could make decisions and fly—that he was safe.

They should have executed a missed approach with such a destabilized, dicked-up approach. The visual of the San Francisco flight came to mind again. They too had been behind the airplane, slow, and nobody responded.

If she had not seen the speedbrake lever extended, she was not so sure what would have happened. If and when the two captains got their heads out of their butts and executed a missed approach, could they have done it? Chances were the results would have been the same as Brian's flight in Colombia.

The bus arrived and she climbed aboard. Bob stood off to the side and watched with arms folded.

Once she was settled inside, she pulled out her phone to listen to her messages. Bob turned and walked away.

Kathryn—"Welcome back. Dinner at six. We all miss you."

Jackie—"Hope you had a great trip! See you tonight."

Neil—"Hey Doll, plans for New Years? Saving my dance card for you."

Membership Card Services—"This is the last chance to take…" Delete.

And then there was Keith—"Welcome home, Sweetheart. Wish I were in your arms right now. I wanted to spend New Year's Eve with you, but scheduling called. Heading back to Asia. Meet me in Tokyo on the 31st and we can bring in the New Year together. I miss you."

Darby smiled for the first time that morning. She was about to return his call until she saw the name on her phone.

CHAPTER 22

DECEMBER 28, 2011

Darby arrived at Kathryn's house shortly after five and parked alongside Jackie's car. She smiled at the fairyland outside her window. The zillion white lights would shine through the New Year and then the take-down party would begin.

She climbed out of her car and closed the door, thankful for the families inside this house. As exhausted as she was, it had been far too long since they'd had a girls' night without the kids. There was no way she would miss this party, despite the urge to cover her head and hide until 2012. Darby sucked a deep breath, placed a smile on her face, and headed for the door.

Before she reached the front steps snow began to fall—heaven sending her a message. If only she knew what that message was. She knocked once and then entered her safety net. Kathryn and Jackie were setting the kitchen table when she sauntered in.

"Darby!" Jackie yelled. "Where's the tequila?"

Jackie was feeling no pain and Darby was way behind this party.

"Tequila?" Darby put her hands on her hips. "I'm afraid if I had half a shot tonight, my party would be over before it started."

Jackie's sobering face was priceless. Darby winked at Kathryn and pulled her purse off her shoulder. She reached into her bag and removed a fifth of Patrón.

"It wouldn't be the holidays without truth or dare," Darby said.

Jackie took the bottle and held it high over her head. "Score!"

Darby laughed. She was glad to see Jackie let loose.

Kathryn set a stack of plates on the table and then hugged Darby a bit longer than normal. "I want to hear what happened this morning."

"I'm not sure you do," Darby said. "Where'd you send the girls?"

"They're at my house with John," Jackie said.

"What?" Darby's eyes widened as she feigned shock. "John McAllister is babysitting?"

Jackie smiled bright. "He came to town to spend New Year's with me, and said he'd love to stay home with the kids. In his words, 'You ladies need a break'."

Jackie set the bottle on the counter. "First of the year he's on temporary assignment to Seattle."

"Do you have that boy whipped or what?" Darby said with a laugh. "Good for you." Kathryn handed her a glass of merlot.

Darby took a sip and her mind drifted to their approach into Seattle. She stared into her glass, twisting the stem between her fingers, as visions of the ground came her way.

"What happened on your flight today?" Kathryn asked.

Darby startled, splashing wine over the edge of her glass.

Jackie rushed over with a towel. "Where were you?"

"Sorry," Darby said. "I drifted to the twilight zone. Where's that bottle of tequila anyway?"

"Not yet," Kathryn said, pulling a plate of Brie with raspberry sauce from the oven. She stuck a box of whole-wheat crackers under her arm, grabbed the bottle of wine and said, "Living room. Tequila can wait. Darby has the floor."

"This sounds ominous," Jackie said as they followed Kathryn. "What happened?"

"A new captain was getting line-checked today, and damn near killed us. But I think it may have been the check airman's fault. "

Kathryn's brows raised.

Darby sat on the couch and stared into the blood red liquid. She took a long sip, sighed, and then told the ladies what happened on their flight.

Once done she hesitated, sucked into the weight of the room, and added, "It was what they did when that terrain warning went off that really bothers me." Darby looked into her glass, fighting the images.

"What'd they do?" Kathryn asked.

"They didn't do anything."

Darby set her glass on the table and stood. She walked to the window and watched flakes fall and then turned toward her friends.

"They sat on their asses in disbelief, and did absolutely nothing. At the very minimum they should've figured out the speedbrakes were out and managed their airplane. What they should have done was aborted the approach and gone around."

"That's not a good response when you're a pilot," Jackie said.

"No shit." Darby folded her arms and drummed her red nails on her sleeves. "And definitely not a good reaction if you're a check airman."

She returned to the couch and lowered her voice. "I should have yelled, 'go around', but it had all happened so quickly." She bit her lip and added, "I kept seeing the picture of that triple seven burning in San Francisco."

Silence hung heavy between them. Then Kathryn said, "He'll get more training. Everything will be fine."

"But all the sims are full," Jackie said and then waved her hand. "Forget I said that. I'll figure out how to fit him in."

Darby opened her mouth, then closed it. She stood and headed for the kitchen with one focus in mind—tequila. Not that the added drama was needed for the reality of what happened, but Kathryn would need a chaser for what Darby was about to say next.

She returned with the bottle in hand. Jackie had gone to the bathroom, but Darby did not wait for her to return. "He didn't down him."

Kathryn's eyes open wide. "What?"

"You heard me." Darby folded her arms with the bottle of Patrón wrapped inside and gave her the 'I'm not kidding' look. Their eyes locked and Kathryn's face sobered.

They both knew that Darby just put Kathryn in a precarious position. She set the bottle on the coffee table and sat. "Sorry for dumping this on you."

If Kathryn did anything because Darby told her, friends or not, Darby would lose her job. Despite the 'so called' squealer laws, a pilot never went to the FAA for anything if they valued their career. Even if the FAA was your best friend.

Darby hated to put Kathryn in this position, but the entire situation unnerved her.

"Shit," Kathryn said leaning back and folding her arms, her foot bouncing. She closed her eyes for a moment, then opened them and asked, "Are you sure it was that bad?"

"Positive. On the ground they missed the last taxiway, frequencies got screwed up, and when they shutdown one of the engines trying to get into the gate they exceeded all sorts of limitations."

"And he passed him?" Kathryn asked, furrowing her brow.

"Shook his hand and said, 'good job'."

"No way," Jackie said, from the doorway. "Did you talk to the check airman? Maybe there was more to it."

"Tried to avoid him, but he followed me to the crew bus." She rolled her eyes. "We chatted."

Kathryn leaned forward and moved the tequila to the side table and topped off Darby's wine glass. "Did you file an ASR?"

"When I asked him about that, he said, 'I'll take care of it,' and dismissed me. I told him we were all supposed to submit one. He repeated, 'I said I'd take care of it!' Really pissed like, and that was it."

Darby spread Brie across a cracker and then stuck it into her mouth. She had not realized how hungry she was until her stomach grumbled. Or maybe her body functions were returning to normal after letting some pressure off by talking about this.

"You've got 24-hours after coming home from an international flight to submit the report," Kathryn said.

"I know, but the problem is, when we fill these things out, we're all supposed to be on the same page. I have no clue what, if anything he wrote." Darby breathed deep. "It's my word against two captains, and let's just say I have the cards stacked against me right now."

"But they'd bring him back to training," Jackie said.

"No. They won't." Darby reached for the tequila. She ripped the plastic off the lid with her teeth.

"You have to submit that ASR," Kathryn said. "That's the only way they'll create a training scenario."

"You think?" Darby stood and grabbed three shot glasses from a cabinet over the bar, and brought them to the coffee table. "They're supposed to. This afternoon I called Brock Townsend, my initial instructor, to ask him what to do. He said that a non-pilot manager is now randomly selecting events for our LOEs and they're not using the ASR data anymore." This meant that her and Keith's event would not be used either. Their lesson would be lost in a useless system.

"That's not how it's supposed to work," Kathryn said. "The most significant part of AQP is to use that data in training."

"I know." Darby reached for the tequilla. "But 'supposed to' and 'reality' aren't on the same page in this new world in which we live. Hell, they aren't even in the same book."

Jackie sighed and went to the kitchen for limes, and Kathryn lowered her voice and said, "I'm not sure what to do with this. This guy shouldn't be flying, and that check airmen shouldn't be checking."

"I couldn't agree with you more," Darby said. "But the check airman said he was going to email the new captain notes on what went wrong. He also said that he did a great job the entire trip. I only saw two legs."

"I want to pull his checking status."

"You can't!" Darby snapped. Then she gave Kat her best 'I'm sorry, pleading' look. "I wish you could, but we both know what would happen." Darby filled the shot glasses. "My career would be over and I'd be working at Starbucks. Not that the career shift wouldn't fulfill my daily coffee fix, but—"

"They can't fire you for talking to the FAA about this," Jackie said, returning with the limes.

"They'd find something else to get me on. Trust me, my career would be over. There was a training instructor that wrote letters about safety issues. They kicked him out of training and in seven months they've given him six line checks."

"That's harassment," Jackie said curling up on the couch.

"They call it managing the problem." Darby sighed. "Ladies,

it's time to liven up this party. Tell me something good. Anything."

Jackie and Kathryn exchanged a look. Kathryn grinned and Jackie hit her leg with the back of her hand. Darby licked and salted her hand waiting for the punch line to the physical drama.

"Tell her," Kathryn said.

"I got called in for talking on the phone too much."

"Calling 1-900-BABE again?" Darby asked.

"No. But there's an idea." Jackie licked her hand, sprinkled it with salt, and held up her shot glass. "My boss is an idiot."

"My boss is an idiot, too." Darby said touching her glass to Jackie's. "Wait. Who is my boss?"

Kathryn held her glass to her friends. "We can throw my boss into the pot too."

"To all the idiot bosses above and below, look out stomach here we go!" Darby said, and they tossed back their shots.

Jackie made her face she saved only for good tequila and then said, "Good one Darb."

"I do my best." Darby grinned and sucked her lime.

"It gets better." Kathryn set her glass on the table. "That report you helped me with, the assistant inspector general didn't use any of my recommendations."

"Are you serious?" Darby said. "No way." Kathryn worked long and hard on that program. She also had more on the ball than all the inspectors at the FAA combined. How could they not listen to her?

"Lets just say that the last twelve months of work, and hundreds of hours I spent into the night were for nothing. I've been used, lied to, and manipulated."

"And you're not even married," Darby said. "Okay, this is by far the most depressing party I have ever been to."

"Want to do a little dance for us?" Jackie asked, with a laugh. "I brought dollar bills."

"A ten-day trip. Near death. No sleep in Honolulu because I was up all night having the best sex of my life..." Darby grinned. "I'm afraid if I danced tonight, you'd both have to mop me up off the floor."

"Sex?" Kathryn choked. "Neil came to Honolulu?" she closed her eyes and shook her head.

"You forgave him!" Jackie squealed. "I'm sooo glad."

"Neil? Oh God. You both should know better than that."

CHAPTER 23
KATHRYN'S HOUSE

DECEMBER 29, 2011

DARBY AWOKE TO the smell of coffee and the sizzle of bacon. The night before they stopped at one shot of tequila. The second bottle of wine was opened and carried them through a leisurely dinner where Darby told them about Keith Stone.

Jackie said she would check company records to confirm he was single, and Kathryn planned to search his background via the FAA computer system. She did not tell them that she already had conducted a search of her own.

Darby suspected Keith was for real, and this might be the beginning to a great relationship.

She rubbed her eyes and rolled out of bed. She stood and stretched, then padded to the bathroom and pulled a brush through her hair. Pulling on Kathryn's robe she wandered downstairs.

"Can I move into this bed-and-breakfast full-time?" she asked stepping into the kitchen. She pulled out a chair and sat beside Jackie.

"Good morning," Kathryn said and put a cup of black coffee in front of her. Within moments the microwave beeped and she poured hot cream into Darby's mug.

Darby ripped the top of a yellow packet and dumped the

contents into her coffee.

"You know that stuff is bad for you," Jackie said.

Jackie was always trying to get Darby to stop putting artificial things into her body. She was right about the chemicals, at least, but comfort food trumped right.

"How'd you sleep?" Kathryn asked filling Darby's glass with orange juice.

"Good." The truth was, she would not sleep more than four consecutive hours for the better part of the week compliments of the trip. "I forgot to tell you guys something," Darby said, slowly stirring her coffee. "I get to visit the chief pilot's office again. They want me back for another meeting."

"What'd you do this time, buy flowers for a flight attendant?" Kathryn said, dropping bread into the toaster.

Darby laughed. "Close. Dick Foster didn't like the tone of my email."

"What email?" Jackie asked.

"I wrote letters of apology to the guys that I violated. Foster wrote back scolding me. But he also said if I had any questions to email him, so I did. I asked him who I was supposed to talk to about natural hormones and vitamin therapy so insurance would pay for it."

"You didn't," Kathryn said, choking on a laugh.

"I did. Then he gave me an email address to a guy in HR, who told me to buy my vitamins at Wal-Mart."

"No way!" Jackie said. "Don't they know that they're not tested and most of them don't do anything for you?"

Darby grinned, and her purse began to ring. Kathryn handed it to her and she dug through and pulled out her phone. She smiled and answered, but her smile faded as she listened.

"What's up?" Kathryn asked after Darby set the phone down.

"Me. Tomorrow. With a report of 1200 to Amsterdam…a six day trip."

"You're going to miss New Years Eve!" Jackie said, like this was a surprise and Darby laughed.

"I fly holidays, so I better make the best of it." Darby's heart sank. "For a moment I thought there might be a scheduling God sending me to Asia."

"Can I ask you something without you getting mad?" Kathryn said, as she put the bacon on a paper towel.

"Who me get upset?" Darby said with eyes wide, placing a hand to her chest.

Kathryn sat beside her. "I think it's shitty they called you in for emailing Mr. Patrick. Forcing you to write those letters was stupid, and Foster's letter was condescending as hell with the lecture and all, but it wasn't that bad. What's really bothering you with this?"

Darby brought her cup to her lips and sipped. She had wondered that too. The truth was, it was the combination of everything.

"I guess, it's not as much the chain of command, it's just they never told us about it. I would have followed it had I known. At Coastal we just went to whomever could get the job done. Then this Foster guy lectures me about protocol. He never introduced himself to the pilot group and I'd never heard of him before, and—"

"He needs a lesson in management," Jackie said.

"No kidding." Darby stood and snatched a piece of bacon. "But the strange thing is, his telling me that I'm not allowed to go outside their walls for 'anything', where Mr. Patrick encourages an open door. Something's just weird," she said taking a bite of her bacon. "Why would he waste the time to write? Not to mention, calling me in. Something's up."

"How'd the other guys respond to your apology?" Kathryn asked.

"Captains Wyatt and Clark were pretty cool about it. They just said it was not a big deal and to go to my chief pilot for anything in the future."

"Foster bringing you in for the tone of an email is ridiculous," Kathryn said perplexed.

"On a scale of one to ten, about a twenty on the stupid meter." Darby leaned against the counter. She hesitated and sighed. "But maybe I deserved this one."

"What'd you say?" Kathryn and Jackie asked at the same time.

"I might have mentioned that Mr. Patrick and I had a history of emailing so why would this be any different, and I told him all policies had to be written to be enforced."

"What's wrong with that?" Jackie asked.

"Nothing. It might be the part where I said I was never in the military and had no knowledge of how the chain of command worked, and that my best friends managed families and worked too, far more efficiently than the military, and maybe a get it done attitude might be the better plan."

"Tell me you didn't," Kathryn said.

"The only thing I'm going to tell you is—never email while you're fatigued, missing Christmas and emotional, topped off with a super-sized beer chaser and an accidental Tylenol PM combo."

Darby opened the fridge and found a can of whipped cream and covered the top of her coffee, "And definitely don't write when you're pissed."

CHAPTER 24

AMSTERDAM, NETHERLANDS

DECEMBER 31, 2011

DARBY WALKED INTO THE LOBBY of the Amsterdam hotel. There were over twenty pilots and even more flight attendants milling about. Some just arrived, while others were checking out. She glanced up the ramp willing herself strength to make the trek.

The flight to Amsterdam was smooth. She took first break but could not sleep, so she spent the night contemplating life as they flew into the darkness until they met the sun on the other side of the ocean. The captain took the landing.

They did the typical bag drag to the bus and she dozed on the thirty-minute drive to the hotel.

Darby sucked a deep breath and pulled her suitcase up the ramp wondering about the legality of flying from one ocean to the other side of the world one day apart. She pushed that thought from her mind—scheduling sent her, they knew what they were doing. She just had never experienced jet lag like this before.

At the top of the ramp a group of pilots stood together talking. A captain said something to the others, nodded her way, and everyone turned and looked. She parked her luggage and headed their way.

As she approached the group someone said, "Are you Darby Bradshaw?"

"The one and only," she said with a grin and a slight bow.

"Watch your back. I heard Foster's on the hunt for you."

"Seriously?" Darby's eyes widened. They had to be mistaken.

"Who's Foster?" a captain asked.

"Our director of flying," Darby said.

"Why's he hunting you?"

"Could be a number of things…chain of command violation, the tone of an email. Or maybe because he's a dick," Darby said, wiggling her little finger, "and a small one at that."

Everyone laughed, and a first officer said, "Watch out, they hand out line checks like candy."

"I will, thanks." Darby turned and headed toward the check-in counter.

The merger had gone smoothly—from the surface anyway. But an undercurrent was pulling strong. A select few Coastal pilots hit rocks as they were dunked and dragged by Global originals. On the surface it all looked pretty, but the feelings were something else, and every once in awhile someone was sucked into the undertow.

Picking up her key the words "hunting you," tossed in her brain. She had to remind herself that most everything on the line was blown out of proportion. But still…that comment was a little unnerving. What did she ever do to Foster?

She climbed into the elevator and within minutes the doors opened on her floor. She stepped out and followed the hallway to her room. Once inside and settled, she turned on her computer and commented on five new responses to her recent post, then shifted to her email.

Scanning the list, one message caught her eye. It was from one of the girls in their pilot girls' group.

Darby grinned as she read—*Hey ladies, last week I signed my name at the podium before the captain. He said, "At Global, the captain always signs first." Then I said, "Oh, I thought it was ladies first." He didn't think I was funny. The rest of the trip was less than spectacular. Especially when he...*

There were not many women pilots at Global, most having come from Coastal, but they stuck together. They shared stories and challenges with the new airline and provided support.

They came together for the same reason ISA+21, the commercial women's pilot group, was formed when the first women were hired at the major airlines. The time when women were not accepted in the flight deck. Darby thought those days were gone, but she was beginning to wonder.

Darby selected reply all to the email and typed—*So ladies, guess what happened to me...*

CHAPTER 25
CHIEF PILOT'S OFFICE,
SEATTLE, WASHINGTON

JANUARY 12, 2012

DARBY WALKED INTO a small room just off flight operations and fought to slow her heart rate. Despite Keith's insistence everything would be fine, she was not so sure.

It took a week after her return to find a day that her union representative, the chief pilot, and his assistant chief pilot were all available for Darby's 'come to Jesus' meeting.

Keith called her that morning and they talked for two hours while he waited for his commuter flight. He told her not to worry, and listen to what they had to say. It would all go away. He would come see her in four days. What came next brought a smile to her face then, and now.

She enjoyed the memory for a moment and then forced the smile off her face to match the intensity of the situation. Shifting her weight from one foot to the other she waited for her union representative, Walt Dodd, to get off the phone.

Dodd held copies of all her emails and talked on his cell with his back to her. When he was done, he stuck his phone into his pocket and turned toward her.

"Putting this shit in writing about your health could be used against you," he said.

"How?" she asked, raising an eyebrow.

"They could pull you off line for a medical."

"You mean I could give up the 'dream' and go home with disability insurance?"

Dodd laughed. "You know, that doesn't sound like such a bad idea." He hesitated, and then said, "Ah hell, let's go hear what the boys have to say."

Darby and Captain Dodd left the room and walked down the hall and into flight operations, then past the flight planning window and all heads turned.

Chief Pilot Odell stepped out of his office, poked his head into Roy's office and said, "You ready to go?"

Then, as a four-person pod, they moved past the window again, into the hall, and down to a conference room where they each took a seat around a large oak table.

They were either making a show of their action to the other pilots as a warning, or to humiliate her. Both of which worked.

Once they were settled in the room, the chief pilot spoke first.

"Before we go any further, I'm obligated to ask you...do you have any health issues that make you unable to fly?"

"As long as I don't take the drugs that our insurance covers," Darby said. "The current drugs allowed on our plan are not the safest and most effective course of action."

Insurance covered osteoporosis drugs that made bones brittle, and the only hormone therapy available was known to cause breast cancer. Sickness was a huge business. With Green Life Healthcare, rates skyrocketed and benefits went down. They paid far too much money for coverage that left out alternative healthcare options.

Darby did not intend taking on this fight, it just slipped out in the heat of pissed off. They allowed women to fly, but they did not take into account their unique health issues.

"Writing this could cost you your medical," Odell said.

"If telling the truth that our medical insurance only pays for drugs that will make us unsafe to fly is the cause to pull me from the flight line, doesn't that say something?"

"How do they make you unsafe?" Roy asked with a scoff.

"That damn osteoporosis crap makes your bones brittle. Femurs snap without warning. How safe would that be on short final in gusty conditions?"

"This email you sent to Wes Sullivan, director of H.R., was inappropriate." The chief pilot said.

"He should know better—especially in his position. To suggest that Wal-Mart vitamins are the solution to serious medical issues due to price is ludicrous." Darby folded her arms. "Is this why we're here? For some insurance issue?"

Too many of her friends had taken early retirement for issues that could have been solved with proactive, natural healthcare. Maybe this was the time to bring it on.

"Dick Foster asked me to rein you for all your emails," Odell said. "He doesn't like your tone."

"If I hadn't been told to send apology letters in the first place," Darby said, her voice steady, "then we wouldn't be here."

"I didn't tell you to write anyone an apology," Roy said.

"Then why did you send me their email addresses?"

"I appreciate that you wanted to do something nice for the crews," Odell said, avoiding the issue of who said what to whom. "But Global is a different world than we're used to. I've known you for a long time and I don't want to see you in trouble. All I'm saying is back off. I also want you to reconsider that blog you're writing."

"Why waste your time with all this writing anyway?" Dodd asked. "You need to give it up and drink more beer."

They all chuckled—everyone but Darby.

Odell picked up another sheet of paper and said, "These emails about the delays and fuel burn, or anything else you might think you know...I'm telling you there is *nothing* that you could write that they don't already know."

"You're telling me that management pilots flying desks, know more than the pilots flying planes?" Darby snapped. "There is something seriously wrong with that statement."

"Bradshaw," Dodd said, "think about what *you're* saying. You're a first officer on reserve and rarely fly. You're also a woman in a man's world."

"In case you haven't noticed we're living in the 21st century," she snapped.

Dodd and Odell exchanged a look, and Dodd laughed.

"We may be living in the 21st century," Odell said, "But we work at Global."

What the hell is that supposed to mean?

"What about her getting line check?" Dodd asked.

"That's a rumor," Odell said. "She's not going to get a line checked,"

"What about that guy who received a line check every month for writing about safety and substandard procedures?" Darby asked.

"That was a different case," Odell said.

"How so?" Dodd asked.

Instead of answering the chief pilot picked up a stack of papers and scanned them. Apparently that subject was closed.

Darby wanted this over. "Tell me the rules and I'll follow them."

"You email this office for everything," Odell said.

"Do you guys know why I wrote to the CEO?" Blank faces told her the answer to that question.

"He was the one person who could get this done the quickest," Dodd finally said.

"And the problem with that was?" Darby asked, raising an eyebrow.

"The problem is that we have a chain of command," Odell said. "You start at the bottom."

"And how would I know that?" Darby asked.

"Because I'm telling you," Odell said.

"Companies are required by law to communicate their policies to employees," Darby countered. "Besides, Mr. Patrick had an open door policy at Coastal, and we used it. If the same CEO is running Global, why the change?"

"God dammit Darby!" Odell snapped. "Don't you get it? Patrick has nothing to do with running flight operations at Global. Wyatt, Clark and Foster own us. They say start at the bottom, you ask how low."

Darby's eyes widened. She hesitated a heartbeat and said, "What about the warning that Foster is hunting me?"

"You brought that on yourself by telling people about this situation," Odell said.

"Are you kidding me?" Darby spat.

"A captain called into operations saying that he would support you. Vouch for you as a person and a pilot, and thought it was horrible that you'd been disciplined for trying to do something nice for the crews."

"When did you get that call?" Darby asked.

Odell looked at his notes and said, "December 23rd. What difference does that make?"

"None," she said.

"Did you email thirty women about this, too?" Odell asked.

"Thirty three if want an exact number," Darby said. "How'd you know?"

"One of the ladies forwarded your email to her chief pilot in New York."

Darby shook her head in dismay at the violation of trust all the way around. Global was the airline built on trust and integrity—yeah right.

"If you have problems with anyone hassling you," Roy said, "you contact this office. We don't allow that."

Darby began to laugh. There were so many things she wanted to say to that, but thought better of it.

CHAPTER 26
SEATTLE, WASHINGTON

JANUARY 12, 2012

KEITH STONE WAS irritated as hell. He wanted to be in Seattle, but not this way. He pulled his bags from the overhead compartment and began his journey downstream with the other passengers. *Armstrong could have waited to drop the axe.*

When he landed in New York nine hours earlier he called Darby at 0400 her time. Even though he could not be there in person, he wanted to relieve her stress. He did his job well and kissed her back to sleep the best way he could.

He then waited two hours for his commuter flight. He was on a plane headed for Arizona when his phone rang. Ten minutes later he would have missed the call.

Captain Burt Armstrong, the fleet training captain, said, "Get here ASAP. We have a problem." Keith rushed off the plane and onto the next flight to Seattle. He got stuck in a middle seat and listened to babies cry for the entire trip.

There was only one thing that Armstrong would not discuss on the phone—Keith was being kicked out of training because of the ASR that he and Darby had submitted. He deserved it, but Armstrongs's immediacy was a bit theatrical.

Breathing deep he waited for the people in front of him to

move. One would think after a six hour flight they'd want to get off this bird as quickly as he did.

Darby was a far better Airbus pilot than Keith. He was not sure why he did not tell her that he was an instructor after they got to know each other. Embarrassment came to mind. He gave instructors a bad name—those who can't do, teach.

The truth was, he did not want to tell her why he had been out there in the first place. He learned, first hand, why everyone loved her. Then it was too late.

After they'd slept together, there was no way he could tell her any of it. That woman moved him in ways he never thought possible. He needed to see her again.

Once off the plane, he walked quickly through the Seattle terminal, up the escalator, across the overpass, and down to the buses. He waited for the Alamo Shuttle. After his meeting he would go to Darby and tell her the truth.

The drive to the training center took twelve minutes from the rental facility. Keith parked, and walked to the back of the building. He scanned his ID and entered.

He took the elevator to the third floor and followed the hallway to the training offices. The office doors were closed and the building quiet. When he arrived at Armstrong's door he took a deep breath and knocked, then opened it.

"Thanks for coming," Armstrong said, moving around his desk with a hand extended.

"Not a problem," Keith said, shaking it firmly. "I'm kind of surprised at the morgue out there."

"One cube at a time, soon they'll all be gone," Armstrong said with a smile. He returned to his desk. "Sit, please."

"Have a nice Christmas?" Keith asked, delaying the inevitable.

"I did." Armstrong folded his arms and leaned back in his chair. "Do you know why you're here?"

"I can only guess." Darby flashed through his mind, followed by flashbacks of his screwed up flight.

The director laughed. "Of course you can." He rubbed his chin. "There was a reason we pushed you out to Tokyo so quickly before Christmas. That Bradshaw woman needed to be put in her place."

Armstrong slid his chair back and stood. He walked to the door, opened it and looked out. Then closed it. "Coastal pilots need to be taught the rules, especially that Bradshaw woman." He turned and said, "You've put me in quite a spot."

"Excuse me, sir?"

"What the hell were you doing? You were supposed to write her up. Instead you got involved in something that was none of your damn business." Armstrong returned to his chair and slid a sheet of paper across his desk—a copy of an email.

Reference: Captain Stone called the Seattle chief pilot. The email was from the director of flying, Dick Foster, who clearly indicated his displeasure. *This is about Darby, and not the ASR?*

Keith sighed. The battle continued with Foster. One day he hoped Dick would realize they were on the same team.

"You told me to check her manuals and write her up if she did anything wrong. I had no idea that this had anything to do with her emailing Patrick. You'd said she was weak."

The writing on the wall hit his brain hard, as if he had run into it head first with his eyes wide open. This had nothing to do with Darby's performance in the plane and everything to do with the political arena. She pissed someone off. Not a good thing, especially if you were a woman at Global.

What the hell did she do? And to whom?

"The less you knew about that, the better, but what the hell were you thinking?"

"I guess…I wasn't," Keith said scratching the back of his head. "She was pretty upset about the entire deal. Sorry that she wrote Patrick. I don't think it'll happen again. That fucking little drama queen sitting in the assistant chief pilot's position should never have told her to send those apologies."

"I couldn't agree more. The ensuing emails have caused quite a stir, and your phone call caused a shit storm." Armstrong sat heavily in his chair.

"I thought if the Seattle office laid off her, she'd blend back into the flight line peacefully. She's an excellent pilot and a good kid."

"Ah hell. You fucked her didn't you?"

Keith tried not to turn the many shades of red he felt. "I'm just saying, that she's not going to cause you or anyone problems."

Armstrong leaned forward. "She *has* caused me problems. I don't need Foster's shit…or any of those guys in flight ops on my ass," he said slapping his desk. "I was told to start a file on her. Not create a fucking fan club."

"Sorry, sir." Had he known the facts he would not have made the call, but he also would not stuff her file. Keith was not sure if Armstrong knew that, but the less said the better.

"They've got her over in the office right now. Foster ordered Odell to reign her in." Armstrong grinned. "That office is the last of the Coastal management pilots and we've got them in our pockets."

"You sure they'll come in line?"

"Hell yes. They're a bunch of whores. That chief pilot will do anything we say. He's counting his stock options as we speak."

Frank Dawson, the director of training, and Armstrong would

eventually push all Coastal pilots out of the schoolhouse. The training center moving to Oklahoma City helped that action. Flight operations had their own agenda.

"What do you want me to do?" Keith asked.

"Keep your mouth shut and don't say anything positive about a Coastal pilot again," he said. "They *are* the enemy. Until we beat their fucking asses into submission, I don't want you to forget which side you're on."

His and Keith's eyes locked. "You were also supposed to convince Bradshaw to stop writing that blog."

Keith fought the laugh that grabbed his gut. *'Make' Darby do something?* He searched for the words to tell Armstrong that, as hard as he tried, convincing her to stop the blog was impossible. The stakes were too high.

Armstrong leaned back, folding his arms behind his head, and smiled. "I'm sure I can mitigate damages. I also don't think after today Darby Bradshaw will be a problem."

"What about Foster?"

"Don't worry about him, I've already covered that. He's a little boy with big dreams stamping his feet for control. Nothing but an annoyance." Armstrong stood. "You're going to be an asset to the department. We'll just let this transgression slide."

Keith stood and said, "Thank you, sir."

The rain shifted from a drizzle to a downpour by the time Keith walked out of the training center. His wipers worked full speed as he sat at a light prior to the highway that headed back to the airport.

He wanted to see Darby, but maybe it would be better to slip out of town and not let her know he'd been there. If he saw her, how the hell could he hide what they just discussed? What would he tell her? She would know something was up.

Keith drummed his fingers on the steering wheel.

"Ah fuck." He hit the blinker, cranked the steering wheel and turned left.

Fifteen minutes later he was pulling into her driveway. He shut off his car and stared at the windows waiting for her to pop into view.

He spent many hours on the Internet learning everything he could about her. What car she drove, where she lived, and how much she paid for her house. There was nothing of public record that he did not know.

Keith climbed out of his car and Seattle's wrath soaked him. He wiped a hand across his face, then headed up the path. He knocked on the door and within minutes she pulled it open.

Her face shifted from one of fury to instant surprise and then to joy within a matter of seconds—the many colors of Darby.

"What? Oh my God! What are you doing here?"

"Taking a shower," he said, looking toward the sky.

Darby laughed as she grabbed his arm and pulled him inside. "My God, you're soaked. Let's get you out of those wet things."

"I can't think of a better idea," he said, kicking the door closed.

CHAPTER 27

DARBY PULLED KEITH CLOSE, placed her lips on his, and melted into the warmth of his mouth. She was transported from hell to heaven within a matter of minutes. His hands moved to the sides of her face, then one shifted to the back of her head and his fingers slid through her hair. The other found its way to her back and he pulled her close.

Time did not exist. They kissed as lovers lost in the silence of her home. Keith released her mouth to a wave of gentle kisses that he trickled down her neck. She tilted her head back and the power of his touch ran deep into her soul.

His lips moved up her neck and nibbled her ear. Her hands found their way to his belt and she fumbled as she unbuckled it. He moaned as her fingers moved to the clasp on his pants and then the zipper.

He pulled back just enough to lift her sweater over her head and tossed it aside. He slid his hands inside her bra, lifting her breasts above black lace. Her nipples hardened—he kissed the left and then the right. He pulled back and his hands moved to the front of her pants and he pulled the zipper open.

At the same time she yanked on his tie, then pulled it over his head and tossed it. His hands were on her hips and lips on her mouth as he backed her through the entryway while her fingers worked hungrily at buttons on his shirt.

She maneuvered them into the living room and bumped into the couch. He gave her a gentle nudge and she fell back over the armrest, landing in the softness of the cushions. She grinned as he devoured her body with his eyes. He grabbed her pant legs and pulled until they were off her body and dropped them on the table. Then pulled his shirt off and tossed it.

He removed his pants and then stepped out of his shorts. He reached down and touched her cheek. She could not remove her eyes from his. Keith slid his hand onto her chest. Her heart beat wildly beneath his touch.

Then he joined her on the couch.

Their pleasure came hard and fast. She couldn't hold back and neither could he. They came together and rolled onto the floor. She landed on top of him and began to laugh. Catching his breath he joined her laughter.

His heart pounded strong. They lay that way for a long time. Then Keith said, "Sweetie, we need to talk."

Darby froze. We need to talk was never a good way to start any conversation. She pushed away from him and looked into his eyes. There it was—guilt.

"Whatever it is, you sure as hell better not be married," she said climbing off him.

"No. Nothing like that." He scrambled to his feet as Darby left the room. "Where are you going?"

She returned with a couple robes and handed him one. She slipped into the other, then turned the fireplace on. She sat on the edge hearth, thankful for warmth with the flip of a switch.

"Pink?" he said, giving her a sideways look.

"The best I could do," she said folding her arms. Despite the warmth of the fire, a chill crawled up her spine.

"What's going on?" she asked.

Keith pulled the tie around his waist and swung the end.

Darby laughed. "I think that might be your color."

Tussled hair, bare legs and splash of hairy chest peeking out. He was definitely adorable. Somehow whatever he had to say felt less dooming in pink and Darby sighed.

"If you tell anyone, I'll have to kill you."

"Depending on what you have to say, I might have to kill you first," she said. "What's your pleasure, coffee or wine?"

"Wine if you'll join me."

They moved to the kitchen and he sat at the table while she opened the wine. "How did you know where I lived?"

"I looked you up on the FAA website."

"We can find pilot's addresses? That's a scary thought."

"You need to be a licensed pilot to access the database. Besides, if you can't trust a pilot, who can you trust?"

Darby raised an eyebrow and then poured their wine. "I was wondering the same thing," she said handing Keith his glass.

"To truth," she said tilting her glass as she sat beside him

"Truth," Keith said tipping his her way. Then he took a long drink. "This is delicious. What is it?"

"Las Madres merlot," Darby said handing him the bottle.

He looked at the label and set the bottle on the table. "Nice. Speaking of which, how'd your meeting go?"

Darby laughed. "Whatever it is you have to say, must be daunting—delay, delay, delay."

Keith grinned. "I'm serious, what they'd say?"

"Okay...the meeting first. In one word—interesting. More or less I was told to keep my mouth shut, get on my knees for Wyatt,

Clark, and Foster and kiss their ass. Oh, wait...maybe it was kiss my own ass. I can't remember. But they were overly concerned about my health and something tells me they don't want me to write my blog."

Keith laughed. "So it's over?"

"I'm not sure, but at least I know the rules."

"Are you going to follow them?"

Darby sipped her wine and grinned. "I don't know. Probably. But so far I've got bad girl status with Global."

"I really like the bad girl part of you, but I would just let this all die a natural death. The pilots at Global are military and—"

"So I've heard. And guess what? They have penises too!"

Keith laughed. "They have their ways and a pecking order." Darby raised an eyebrow and Keith grinned shaking his head. "Nobody asks questions when given an order, or speaks to anyone other than their immediate supervisor. Never question orders."

"Then they need to put that in their operations manual."

"Over Patrick's dead body," Keith said. "Corporate philosophy touts an open door policy."

Darby sighed. "Makes perfect sense to me. Not."

"The guys in flight operations think we're in a war."

"With the Coastal pilots?"

"You guys are wild cards. You say and think what you believe. There are some management pilots who feel threatened."

"Because we email the CEO?" Darby said filling her glass.

"More than that. Coastal pilots had a hell of a lot of say on procedures, training, etc. and—"

"That's a bad thing?"

"Not bad, just a threat to management pilots. Most of them are desk jockeys." He sipped his wine then said, "They don't have the flying experience that management pilots at Coastal had. Hell, most of them have very few hours."

"So they're losing sight of safety because of their egos? Not to mention a great group of instructors who are exiting because of that stupidity." Darby felt like she stepped back twenty years in her career. "And what about them canceling ground school?"

"I know," Keith said, raising a hand.

"It's a pile of bullshit," Darby said. "Speaking of which, what's so important you have to tell me?"

Keith sipped his wine, then set down his glass. "I work for the training department."

"What?" she said, dumbfounded. Her mind flew in a million different directions, then her emotions caught her by surprise. She began to laugh. She laughed so hard, her laughter turned to tears. "I'm sorry," she said with her best attempt to regain composure.

"Of all the reactions, this is the last I'd expected."

"I thought you were going to tell me you were gay or something," she said wiping a tear. "Why didn't you say anything?"

"It's the pink, isn't it?" He lifted her hand and kissed it. "Maybe I was trying to impress you? Then you ended up saving my ass. I thought I'd go away and you'd never have to know that the training department hired incompetent pilots."

"Impress me?" Darby grinned. "I could say many things about your performance, but that would've been my last guess."

Keith squeezed her hand. "There's a reason I'm single," he said.

"Incompetent with women too?"

"Apparently so."

Darby leaned forward and kissed him on his lips, then whispered, "You're not incompetent. Let's just say inexperienced. But…" She sat upright and narrowed her eyes. "What were you going do if I showed up in the simulator and you were there? Did you think I wasn't going to find out?"

"I hadn't expected this," he said, touching her cheek. "I thought we'd fly together and go different directions. Hell, we're not even in the same base. Besides, I do line training not sim and I figured if you found out later you'd assume I'd just been hired."

"How long have you been an instructor?"

"A few months."

"And you've been on the plane for five?"

"Give or take,"Keith said.

She bit her lip. Then a wave of embarrassment flushed over her and she said, "So you know Neil?"

"I met him the morning before I left for Tokyo at an instructor meeting. It was nothing more than nice to meet you type of thing."

Darby stared into his eyes. She so wanted to believe him.

"I didn't know how you felt about him, and I didn't want to interfere." Keith kissed the back of her hand, then turned it and opened it one finger at a time. She did not realized she was holding her hand in a fist. He placed his lips inside her palm and kissed. *Oh my God.* This was not a fair way to have a conversation.

"Neil's just a friend." She shivered with the touch of his lips.

"I had to be sure." Keith trailed kisses up her arm and then moved to her neck and whispered, "I'm glad you changed your mind...on the pilot thing."

"Trust is really important to me," she said.

"I hope you know you can trust me."

"I do," she whispered. She closed her eyes and laid her head on his shoulder, and he rubbed her back. "Do you want to take a soak in my hot tub?" she murmured under the heat of his hand.

"I'd like that."

CHAPTER 28
SEATTLE, WASHINGTON

FEBRUARY 20, 2012

CAPTAIN BURT ARMSTRONG, the A330 fleet training captain, drummed his fingers on his desk as he scanned Bradshaw's latest post. This was anything but good. He glared at the screen. Each word infuriated him more than the last.

He pulled his cell phone out and pressed speed dial. The phone was answered on the first ring.

"Did you see Bradshaw's post today?" Armstrong asked.

"I did, and if it's accurate, it's damn good writing."

Hell if he knew its accuracy. He was a Boeing pilot. He didn't need to know the workings of the Airbus. He had people. But he would be damned as to how the hell she heard about that event.

"We don't need her airing dirty laundry," Armstrong said.

Laughter broke through the phone. "Maybe you need to teach your kids how to fly Fifi."

Fuck you. This was anything other than a laughing matter. "I need your help. She's yours eleven months out of the year. We get her for a few days at best. You need to do something."

"What's the deal with this one...she shut you down?"

Armstrong's mind whirled. He was not prepared for the question of why, and 'yes' would have been the easiest answer.

"She's not an instructor," Armstrong finally said. "Anything she says on that blog is representative of Global. She screws it up, we take the heat."

"Have you got someone who could review her work before it goes live? This might be just what you guys need."

"We don't have time to play on the Internet with a blog," Armstrong said. "It's juvenile, and not the way the largest airline in the world trains pilots."

"Apparently, from the fiasco at Kennedy, some of your pilots aren't trained. You're lucky they were able to stop."

"There are always that ten percent who screw up," Armstrong said. "Who the hell does she think she is writing about this?"

"We're watching, and when we find something we'll—"

"Silence her," Armstrong said. "Sooner than later."

He said goodbye, disconnected the call and set his phone down. He read her post one more time and shook his head.

Those fucking pilots who couldn't land their plane at Kennedy forgot to activate the approach, and did not have a clue what was happening. They were afraid to disconnect the automation and fly. Exactly what Darby wrote about in her blog.

This was anything but good. There was one thing he knew for sure, they did not need flight incidents hitting the airways. Especially now. *How could pilots be afraid to fly their planes?*

Drumming his fingers on his desk he wondered if Stone told her. He couldn't be that stupid. Then it occurred to him—Neil Jordan. He and Bradshaw had a past.

But how the hell did Jordan hear about this?

His orders for all parties involved was silence. His orders were always followed. He closed his eyes, and sighed. What if that plane had gone off the runway? *Maybe we've gone too far.*

CHAPTER 29
SEATTLE, WASHINGTON

APRIL 2, 2012

THREE MONTHS PASSED and Darby had not seen the inside of her airplane. She was officially twelve days away from going non-current and there was no flying in sight. Line holders were parking their trips on reserve lines, opening up their schedules so they could pick up open time and then taking back their lines to get high time.

What that meant was some pilots flew over 100 hours each month, and others, like Darby, were not flying at all. Manipulation of the computer system, where line-holders flew and reserve pilots did not, lined many pockets in green, and left others non proficient.

Sitting in front of her computer, Darby opened the post she worked on earlier that morning.

Flight For Safety
April 02, 2012
Automation Versus Manual Flight

When I took my 757 type rating check, I was told to use the automation. This checkride was conducted "managing" the auto-flight system.

When we were done I told the FAA examiner, "This was the

easiest checkride I've ever taken. Mandating automation will come back and haunt us. Pilots needed to know how to fly. We should not only continue to train pilots how to fly, but should test those flying skills in the simulator without the automation and encourage them to hand fly on the line."

He chuckled and said, "The reliability of these planes is high and the probability of failure is unlikely, there won't be a problem."

I said, "Never say never," and then told him my friend was dead after he hit a mountain with a perfectly good airplane because he was taught to program, not how to fly the jet.

Seventeen years later, guess what the FAA is recommending in the SAFO—Safety Alert for Airline Operations? Pilots should fly their planes and not rely on the automation.

Unfortunately, this previous year we witnessed a plane crash in San Francisco because the pilots did just that—disconnect the automation—and could not manage the approach. Is the past coming back to haunt us?

Fly Safe! DB

Darby pressed publish then closed the lid on her computer. *Flight For Safety* was her only connection to the sky, her plane, and the pilot community. It also was turning into her personal therapist.

Across the street, her neighbors were piling the kids into their Suburban. Darby pulled her attention from them and glanced toward the sky, then back to the mess on her kitchen table.

She was preparing for recurrent training. This was her first recurrent check on the A330 and she was studying her butt off to prepare. She was confident she would not embarrass herself, but those little hairs on the back of her neck stood at attention.

Sliding her chair back, she closed her eyes and took a deep breath. She reached her arms toward the sky then bent over her legs and stretched. Opening her eyes, chipped red toenails stared her way. *You'd think I'd have time for a pedicure.*

The reality was between studying, blogging, and spending every spare moment with Keith or her friends, she didn't have time for much of anything else. Except for an occasional nightmare.

The ground coming to meet her plane attacked her regularly, but when Keith held her through the night she was able to stuff the nightmares deep into the bowels of her mind.

Darby's phone rang and Neil's name flashed across the screen. She pressed ignore, needing to stay focused on her day.

When Neil heard about her relationship with Keith, he was pissed and said, "Don't trust him Darby. He spends too much time in the director's office." *Like Neil should talk about trust.*

She sighed. Her nine-month recurrent training checkride was at 1900 and she would not be late, despite what she had been told the night before. She stepped to the counter and poured herself another cup of coffee.

She was told to show up fifteen minutes before her checkride. Her simulator partner last night said, "You're gonna have it easy." Something she was not so sure of.

The brief was a significant part of the check. Darby returned to her kitchen table and sat in front of her systems manual, with coffee in hand, and continued to read where she left off.

If the student put in the headwork, they normally did fine in the sim, even if they had not been flying.

Tonight she was supposed to get an oral, have a walkaround review, and an emergency equipment test. There was no way an instructor could manage all that in fifteen-minutes. They were supposed to have a ninety-minute brief. Something stunk.

Chapter 30
FAA Headquarters
Seattle, Washington

April 2, 2012

KATHRYN SAT OUTSIDE Jack Walton's office, her foot bouncing. She had been trying to schedule a meeting with the assistant inspector general for three months with no luck. Today her luck changed.

Her boss, Tom Santos, told her that he would speak to Jack on her behalf, but he never did.

It was time she stepped over the chain of command and go directly to the source—the assistant inspector general. Tom said, "Good luck. Let me know how that goes for you."

Unfortunately, whenever she tried to get a hold of him he was always busy or out of his office. But today was different.

She parked herself in his waiting area while keeping a watchful eye out the window on his car.

Kathryn and his secretary, Doris, became friends over the previous three months. It was Doris who called Kathryn and told her today would be good. She was planning on giving him all day if she had to.

"Mr. Walton will see you now," Doris said. They exchanged a conspirator's smile and Kathryn glanced at her watch. All day turned out to be less than three hours.

She stood and followed Doris to his office.

"Kathryn," Jack said moving around his desk and extending his hand. "It's wonderful to see you again. I can't thank you enough for the tremendous work you did on the audit. We couldn't have done it without you." They shook firmly. "What can I do for you?"

Kathryn sat with a deep breath and crossed her legs. "It's good to see you too. I've been trying to find you for almost three months."

"You know how this damn bureaucracy keeps me hopping," he said with a wave.

"Yes, I do, and that's why I'm going to get straight to the point."

"Please." He folded his arms and grinned. "I enjoy a good point now and then."

"What the hell did you do with my recommendations?"

Jack's right eye twitched. She worked closely with this man for over twelve months and knew the meaning of every twitch and color. She touched a nerve.

"There's no need to use profanity."

"You and I both know that hell is not profanity, it's the place we work." Kathryn placed the report on his desk. "I worked damned hard for you and this department. For you to throw my work out the window…I deserve an explanation."

"You can't win everything," he said, narrowing his eyes.

"Win? This is not about me winning. This is about fixing a hole in our system and doing something right. We've spent hundreds of thousands of dollars over the last year and for what? This?" She waved at the report on his desk.

"What's wrong with the report?" He leaned back, folding his arms. "We did what needed to be done."

"These recommendations barely tickle the surface of the problems and they don't address the real issue—training. My kids could have written this."

"Maybe I'll be forced to put them on the payroll too," he said under his breath.

"*Excuse me?*" The reality of her stepping on toes was surfacing in each corner of the bureaucratic walls. She'd had no idea how deep the resentment flowed.

"I'm sorry," he said. "That was uncalled for, but you were shoved down our throats and—"

"Shoved down your throats? Are you serious?"

"I couldn't be more serious." He pushed back from his desk and stood. "You step over people with twenty years seniority because your husband was a nut job. That doesn't give you the experience to be working in this office."

If it had not been for Kathryn, Bill's chaos would have gone global. The potential deaths were far too great to count. Yet fighting with the assistant inspector general was not a ring she wanted to step into. Not yet.

With hands on hips he stared at her, and she held his gaze. Her heart beat wildly in her throat.

"That's your opinion," Kathryn said. "There's something going on here, and I'm going to find out."

"That there is," he said. "It's called bureaucracy. Welcome to the FAA."

"But the recommendations in this report are not sufficient." She said pulling a hand through her hair. "Where did mine go? Why did you pull them?"

He walked around his desk and sat beside her. "I appreciate your investigative abilities. You did a fantastic job finding the holes in the

FAA's processes. You surprised me, actually. A pleasant surprise."

His smile returned, but his brows knit together as he spoke. "But gathering data on a fact finding mission versus having the experience to make suggestions that are relevant are two different stories. I'm sorry, but you need more experience."

"I started with the NTSB some twenty–two years ago," Kathryn said. "When did your employment with the government begin?"

"My time in office is irrelevant. I was given the task of supplying recommendations. I did my job thanks to your data." He reached out and placed a hand on her shoulder and squeezed. "We both did our jobs."

"The report doesn't suggest anything of substance." She pulled from his hand as she stood and walked three steps away and turned.

"Substance? What substance did you expect?"

"You read my recommendations. The problem lies in training within the airlines. Your solutions revolve around tracking."

"Track properly, you'll find the holes in training."

"If you find them…then what? Pilots will slip through the cracks. We can't watch everything. Why not build a boat that doesn't leak instead of using resources to find the holes?"

"With the current recommendations nobody will slip through the cracks."

"Your recommendations are only as good as the carriers' honesty, or the honesty of the instructors," Kathryn said. "Besides, just because an instructor gets line checked every two years does not make him a good instructor. Who's doing the checking? Who's doing his training? Better yet, are the pilots learning everything they need to know to be safe?"

Darby's flight with the check airman in Seattle mirrored the plane that crashed short of the runway at San Francisco. How many more flights, with pilots who were trained to fly automation, were being taken care of by the hand of God? Luck would soon run out on that equation.

Kathryn took a couple steps toward Jack. She picked up the report off his desk. "I'm not saying everything in here is bad. Training FAA inspectors on AQP is essential, but training pilots is *more* important. Are they getting quality training? Are companies using the AQP program correctly? Are we an agency that monitors then reacts, or should we create programs that demand safety and quality training programs?"

"This is a good first step," he said. "We're doing what's been asked of us. We'll be able to identify problems at the airlines with what we've got in place."

Kathryn shook her head in dismay. Tracking and monitoring were essential, but that was only part of it. The frosting on the cake—the pretty stuff.

"We need substance and this isn't it." Kathryn placed her hands on her hips. How could she back down when lives were at stake?

"We've made huge strides, young lady. I'm done with this conversation." He stood and pushed past her returning to the chair behind his desk.

"Frosting a cardboard box does not make it a cake," Kathryn said. "It may look pretty on the outside, but soon the weight of that frosting will soak into the box and implode. You watch. If we don't do something sooner than later, you'll see more planes hit the ground."

CHAPTER 31
RECURRENT TRAINING

APRIL 2, 2012

DARBY SAT AT the briefing table reviewing her notes. Despite the fact that today would be easier than yesterday's session, the added tension of playing the waiting game toyed with her nerves. Glancing at her watch, she yawned.

She had been waiting an hour and twenty-two minutes, but who was counting. The instructor was seriously showing up 15-minutes before her session was to begin. Who would have thought?

When the door swung open Darby jumped and in walked Captain Glen Smith.

"Hey Glen, what are you doing here?"

Glen was a 747 Captain she had flown with at Coastal when she was first hired. But tonight she was scheduled to have an instructor fly in the left seat, not another line pilot.

"I didn't do very well the other night," he said pulling out a chair. "I needed a couple more sessions. Guess I'm ready to go now."

More training was not uncommon on this plane, but if anyone needed a pre-brief it was a captain who needed more time.

"Sorry to hear that," Darby said. "Should be fairly easy tonight."

"I hope so."

The door opened and in rushed the check airman, Alan Jones,

exactly twelve minutes before they were scheduled to be in the simulator.

Jones stepped past her and sat across the table and rummaged through paperwork. When they introduced themselves to him he nodded and made some noise of acknowledgement, but was in another world.

When the paper shuffling ended he asked, "Any comments or questions before we go down?"

"I've been on the plane for less than a year," Darby said. "This is my first recurrent and I haven't flown in about three months, but—"

"So you're making excuses already?" Jones asked sarcastically.

"No. I'm telling you my experience."

"I need your licenses," Jones said.

When he finished checking their medical certificates and licenses he returned them. "This is going to be exactly like a real flight. Do everything you would in the plane." His attention was focused on Glen as he spoke. "After we're done with the check, you'll still need to get your RNP approaches in so we'll zap you to Palm Springs and take care of that.

"Then we'll do some en-route work—an engine failure with a drift-down at altitude. I'll have you fly it," he said to Glen. "That part will be training. If you mess it up, and everyone does, we'll just talk about it. Any questions?"

"I have one," Darby said.

His mini-brief was clearly for the captain, but he looked her direction and raised both eyebrows. She took that as a go-ahead.

"The paperwork says we have a cost index of 30, but the flight plan has us cruising at a Mach .82. Is it possible to get .82 with a cost index that low?"

A cost index was a number that indicated the relative cost of time versus fuel—a number they put into the computer that told the plane how fast to fly. The higher the number, the faster the plane flew. Did it fly at .82 Mach with a 30? She did not have enough experience to know.

He stared at her for a moment and said, "Why wouldn't it?"

She shrugged. "Then why do the guys on the line put in a cost index of 100 to get Mach .82?"

"How the hell would you know what the guys do on the line? You never fly," he said sarcastically.

Darby's eyes widened She knew pilots who walked out for far less. Her gut said, 'end it here' but her brain said, 'just get your training done.' If she sucked it up she could go away for another nine months.

Once in the simulator Darby climbed into her seat and said to Jones, "Will you let me know if I miss anything on my preflight? It's been a long time and I'd really appreciate it."

"I'm not here," he snapped. Then turned toward the instructor's station and began programming.

Darby rolled her eyes and began her preflight. *What's his problem?*

Glen decided to fly the session, so she focused her attention on the overhead panel and the internal preflight. When finished, Glen was still fumbling with inserting the flight plan. Darby decided to help him out and fill in the flight data and get the weather.

When she went to type in the request, the number 3 ACARS displayed—NO COM. In the simplest terms, ACARS was the computer used for digital communications, and theirs was not working.

"Can I get the ATIS?" she asked Jones. The ATIS was the weather for the airport. Normally simulator instructors just tossed it up on a piece of paper—a non-event even on a checkride.

"I'm not here," Jones said.

"Then I need maintenance, because we've got a bad radio," Darby said. She didn't care if he was having a bad day, he should have checked the attitude outside the simulator.

"I said I'm not here. Don't you know how to get the ATIS?"

What a jerk. Darby located the frequency on a chart, and dialed it in to listen to the report on the radio, like she did when it was unavailable in digital format. Within moments the airport conditions broadcasted over the flight deck speakers.

As she wrote down the information, Jones—who 'wasn't there'— said, "I didn't even know this feature worked in here. Never had to use it before."

Darby closed her eyes and took a deep breath. *Keep your mouth shut and just get through this.* The fact her license was on the line tickled the back of her brain.

She and her captain started the engines, ran all checklists, and taxied into position.

Each time she glanced back, Jones was texting on his cell phone. Darby spent too many years with Kathryn's kids to not know what was going on behind her back.

Heck, she had done the same thing a time or two. But never when there was a captain who failed training or a pilot who had not flown for three months and asked for assistance. He owed them more than this.

The captain pressed the thrust levers forward. Darby said, "Thrust is set." As the speed increased and they accelerated down the runway she made her standard call-outs. "Eighty knots. One hundred knots. V1. VR."

The captain pulled the stick back and pitched the plane up into the flight director.

"Positive rate," Darby said. When the captain did not respond she said, "Gear up."

"Uh...oh yeah, gear up," he said.

She raised the gear handle and then all hell broke loose. Red warning lights flashed. Instruments went black. Chimes dinged.

Darby's eyes immediately focused on airspeed and then pitch— both good. Then the captain yelled, "You got it," and let go of the stick. "Tell ATC we have an emergency."

"I got it," she said. The plane stayed pointed where he put it when he released the stick, but Darby took control and continued to fly the departure.

She engaged the autopilot and then called ATC. "Trainer One has had an electrical emergency and we'll be requesting radar vectors back to the runway."

"Trainer One climb to two-thousand feet. When able, turn right to a heading of zero three zero, you can expect radar vectors to ILS three zero left."

Darby repeated the clearance, glancing at the captain as she spun the heading bug to 030.

Glen pulled out the QRM—Quick Reference Manual, the book of how to handle the malfunctions, and held it in his lap.

He stared at the ECAM—the computer screen that currently displayed numerous messages and the steps to be accomplished prior to going to the book.

Darby looked from the screen to the captain and fought the urge to laugh. The look on his face was priceless. He had no clue where to begin, or what the problem was.

He then said, "I got the plane," and tossed the QRM into her lap, taking control of the A330 that was technically flying on the autopilot.

"You've got the airplane," Darby said catching the book. "We're turning to a heading of zero three zero, and cleared to—"

"What the hell do you have the QRM out for? Don't you know you're supposed to do the procedure first!" Jones yelled.

"Yes, I'm about to do that," Darby said.

The 'I've had enough of this shit,' part of her brain growled. But the 'suck it up' girl pressed on. The thought of stopping the session flashed through her mind, but all she needed to do was make it work. Get along and graduate. She could do *anything* for four hours.

"Trainer One, turn right to a heading of one two zero," Jones said, playing air traffic control.

Glen repeated the clearance while Darby read the messages on the ECAM and performed the steps as she worked through the procedure. Once all the steps were complete she reviewed the status page on the ECAM and then went to the checklist in the QRM to follow up what she and the plane just accomplished together.

"CAT-two and CAT-three approaches are not authorized," she said. "Do we have the weather minimums for a CAT-one?"

"Yes," Glen responded.

CAT I, CAT II, and CAT III approaches allowed different landing minimums depending upon equipment and certification of the plane. As equipment failed, the weather had to be better. A perfect airplane could fly itself to an autoland with zero visibility on a CAT III approach. Today, due to their failure, they were limited to a CAT I.

Darby filled out the performance page in the computer for

their approach and then typed in the minimums. "Do you want me to activate the approach?"

"Yeah, that'd be good," Glen said.

"We also need to do the overweight landing checklist."

"We're not overweight," Glen said.

"Yes, we are."

"Don't you two know how to read?" Jones snapped as he shoved his body between them and pointed at the placard that displayed the aircraft weights.

Of course Darby could read, but she did not have to. She knew the weights. She knew every friggin limitation because she studied and memorized them all. He would have known that if he showed up on time and gave them the required oral.

"Uh…let's do the overweight landing checklist," Glen said.

Brilliant idea. Darby located and read the procedure.

The checklist said to use managed speed while configuring. In managed speed the plane displayed the final approach speed for landing, and the autothrust maintained minimum maneuvering speed for the given flap setting. In selected speed the pilot manually dialed the speed back for their given flaps setting.

Glen remained in selected speed.

"You're supposed to use managed speed," she said returning the book to the side pocket.

"Trainer One turn right to a heading of two two zero."

Darby confirmed the clearance and Glen dialed in the heading. He was still in selected speed so Darby pulled the QRM out of the side pocket again and re-read the line about when the managed speed was required. "Glen, you're supposed to—"

"Trainer One turn right to a heading of two seven zero," Jones said. "On this heading you're cleared for the intercept, cleared for the approach to ILS 30 left. Contact the tower over JALUN."

Darby repeated the clearance and then said, "You're supposed to be using managed speed."

"Okay, okay," Glen said.

Within seconds Jones was between them. "Why the hell aren't you two using managed speed?"

Glen selected managed speed. Then he pressed recall on the ECAM. 'CAT 2 only' popped up, and he said, "We're supposed to do a CAT two approach."

"No we're not."

"But it say's CAT two only."

"I know what it says, but that's not what it means. I'll explain when we get on the ground." The localizer came alive, as did the glideslope. "Course is active. Glide-slope is alive."

"I think you're wrong," he said.

Once they were stable, she reached down to get her QRM to read the statement that CAT II and CAT III approaches were not authorized.

Due to their electrical failure the plane could not fly a CAT III approach, thus it displayed CAT 2 Only—meaning it knew it could not do a category three. But the company further restricted the approach to a category one, and that was discussed in the manual.

She flipped pages and located the statement when Jones yelled, "Why the hell are you doing a CAT two approach?"

Darby jumped.

Having had about enough of his shit she said, "We're not doing a Cat two approach." Then she looked at the PFD display and saw the minimums for a CAT II had been set to 933 feet.

"What the hell?"

"I changed it," Glen said.

Darby retyped the minimums to 1023 feet. She contacted the tower. "Trainer One is over JALUN for landing."

"Trainer One cleared to land runway three zero left."

Darby read the landing checklist then said, "You won't have the number one reverser. You'll also need manual speedbrakes."

"Thanks," Glen said.

After they touched down, the spoilers did not come out as prescribed and Darby called, "No spoilers!"

Glen's hand moved from the thrust levers to the speedbrake handle—the lever that extended the spoilers.

Spoilers were as important as brakes for stopping a heavy jet, thus the term speedbrakes. Full up they allowed the weight of the plane to settle on the landing gear so the brakes and tires would be more effective. They did not arm them due to the malfunction. Not a big deal. Glen just needed to pull the handle.

The autobrakes kicked off. Not sure if it was by accident or intentional Darby called, "Auto-brakes off."

Then she looked at the spoilers and still nothing came out.

"No spoilers!" she shouted again. When he did nothing she slid her hand under his, knocking his away, and pulled the handle back.

Darby breathed deep as Glen battled to stop his plane traveling down the ten-thousand-foot runway—more than half of which was behind them.

CHAPTER 32

THEY STOPPED THE PLANE on the runway, but Darby's heart continued to fly. If it had not been trapped inside her chest, it would have landed three miles farther down the runway and off the other end.

"It wasn't pretty," Jones said, "but I'm going to pass you."

Darby was pissed. Their performance should not have been a passing event. What happened in this training event was exactly what killed passengers—conflict, lack of understanding, and the inability to communicate.

Okay, maybe not kill them…but a captain who throws his hands up and says, "You got it!" because he didn't know what 'it' was, was not someone she wanted at the helm of her ship.

To make matters worse, Darby never witnessed, or experienced, such a nasty piece of a shit-assed, god-damned, friggin, simulator session in her life.

She wanted a retake.

"Why the hell didn't you get those speedbrakes out Bradshaw? You're supposed to be his backup," Jones snapped.

"I yelled the second I didn't see them come out. He put his hand on the lever." Jones turned his back to her. "How was I supposed to know he wasn't going to pull it?"

At least they were done with the checkride.

"We're going to Palm Springs to do our RNP approaches," Jones said as he punched buttons on the instructor station.

RNP was the abbreviation for Required Navigation Performance. The system used GPS, global positioning systems, to bring the plane down to lower landing minimums that allowed for curved paths to get around terrain, noise sensitive areas, or tall buildings. Pilots needed to be trained to the new standards.

Darby did her approaches the day prior during her training and was surprised Glen did not complete his, especially with the additional time.

"Are you going to reposition the MCDU," Darby asked, "Or do you want me to re-program the new position?"

"You're going to have to stop asking so many questions," Jones said, "or people will think you don't know what you're doing."

She moved from upset to max pissed. Turning her back to him she mashed buttons and programmed the computer for the approach. She knew how to do it. She just didn't know if she needed the extra step like the night before.

Darby stabbed the keyboard. Glen's mouth hung open as he watched her fingers dance. When she was done she folded her arms.

Jones repositioned the simulator and then moved up close to talk Glen through the approach.

Darby read the checklist when Glen called for it. Other than that, she said nothing. Her mind was no longer on what they were doing, but what they had done. One of the single most dangerous things a pilot could do in a plane was focus on the runway behind them, and she was doing just that.

It took everything to hold her tongue. All she wanted to do was get the hell out of the simulator. But after Glen's approaches they had one procedure remaining—an engine failure at altitude with a track turn off.

When a jet lost an engine at altitude it could fly, but normally not at its cruising altitude where the air was too thin. So the plane needed to drift to an altitude where it could perform.

Unfortunately the invisible traffic lanes below were filled with aircraft, and the crippled plane would come down on top of them. Thus a procedure was created to fly off the airway as the plane descended.

Darby memorized the drift-down handout, written by check airman Brock Townsend, but she would just be watching the demonstration.

Glen landed after his final RNP approach and Jones returned to the instructor station to reposition them over an ocean.

"Okay," Jones said, "Bradshaw, I want you to fly this."

The hairs on the back of her neck no longer stood, they marched. He was up to something. Glen was supposed to fly this segment.

"Where are we?" Darby asked.

"You tell me where you are," Jones said.

"Do you have a chart?"

Being zapped somewhere over an ocean was not something they did often in a plane—they normally flew there. So knowing where she was in relation to an airport would tell her which direction she would fly after the engine failure.

"Oh God," he said digging in his bag. He pulled out a chart and threw it at her. Darby ducked, but caught it in the air.

She unfolded the chart. *Fuck you Jones.*

Darby pressed the button for the position monitor page on the MCDU, then selected the number 1 IRS position and checked the coordinates and glanced at her heading. She then checked her position on the chart.

They were heading west over the Pacific, and Anchorage was a little more than four hundred miles off her right butt-check. She knew which way she would turn and where they were headed.

She selected VOR on her Flight Control Unit and picked up Anchorage. "Okay, I'm good to go."

"Where's Anchorage?" Jones asked mockingly.

Darby read the airport coordinates. "61° 10.4" N, 149° 59.9" W." Two could play his game.

"Show me with your hand."

Darby extended her left arm toward him and raised a finger, then swung her arm wide and across the front of her body, and pointed past her right shoulder in the direction of Anchorage. The finger she used was the pointer, as much as she wanted to give him another choice.

"Fine," he said.

When the engine failed, Darby pushed the thrust levers to the max continuous thrust position, disconnected the auto thrust, spun the heading bug 180 degrees to the right and began the turn.

As the airplane slowed, she maintained her altitude and dialed the speed bug to the green dot speed—the speed that provided the best lift-to-drag ratio when the airplane was in a clean, gear and flaps up configuration. Slowing to this speed enabled them to get as far off the centerline of the track as possible before they descended, avoiding potential traffic.

She reached up to the overhead panel and turned on the aircraft's exterior lights. Holding her altitude as the speed slowed she pressed the PERF button on the MCDU to determine the drift-down altitude. She then dialed 28,000 feet into the flight control unit.

As the speed reached green dot she pulled for open descent, all the while Jones was trying to teach Glen the proper procedure for shutting down the engine and how to use the checklist correctly. She took a deep breath and focused on flying.

Once Darby was established on the offset, she set cruise power and turned the heading bug direct to the Anchorage airport.

Despite Jones having briefed Glen that he would do something wrong on this procedure, Darby was glad he had nothing to say to her about her performance. She practiced this procedure a hundred times in her mind.

After the simulator came down she gathered her things and followed Glen and Jones to the debriefing room.

Thankful to be done, she was disappointed that they did not received a better evaluation. Hell, she had not received an evaluation at all. Jones owed them his attention if nothing else.

Jones cleared his throat and said, "I've decided to put you both on special tracking."

"*What?*" Darby's mouth dropped. "Did I fail something?"

"No. But at Global it's the instructor's prerogative to special track if we think it appropriate."

Glen laughed. "Don't worry Darb, I've been on special tracking for over a year."

"Failing always requires tracking."

"It's nothing," Jones said leaning back in his chair. "They do this all the time. Besides, I would think someone who *never* flies would want an extra day in the simulator."

What was she supposed to say to that?

CHAPTER 33

DARBY WALKED ACROSS the lobby of the training center, her emotions all over the place. Jones screwed with her on a completely new level, and then he had the nerve to special track her.

She should have stood up to him. She should have stopped the session when he made that first comment about her making excuses. What she should have done was insert her foot up his ass, but he was not worth ruining a pair of perfectly good shoes.

He was right about one thing—she did want the simulator time. Especially since Christmas and New Year's were her only flights in the previous nine months.

She pressed the palm of her hand into the door and flew into the parking lot. This was not the way to get more time. "Dammit," she said pulling the keys out of her pocket as she stormed toward her car.

Once inside her car, she closed her eyes and the video of the training fiasco began. There were far too many opportunities that screamed for her to stop the session.

He should have busted her for not standing up to his sorry ass. That was her only mistake. That and not walking out.

A pilot needed to know when to stop the chain of events before they turned into an accident. Granted this was only training, and in a simulator, but she should have put a stop to his bullshit before it got started. Darby deserved better than this. Hell, passengers deserved better than this.

"Fuck you, Jones," she said slapping her steering wheel. She tilted her head back against the headrest. "Darby, you're a gutless wimp," she chided herself. Why hadn't she stood up to him?

She glanced at her watch and then dialed Jackie. It rang three times and the answering machine picked up.

"It's me, Darby. I just had a session with an idiot instructor. I want to get another evaluation before I fly. Call me." Just as she ended the call her phone rang.

"How'd training go?" Keith asked. "I saw you were with Jones."

"Oh, it went." Darby sighed. "Wasn't pretty."

"That good huh?"

"Can you say, 'cluster fuck'?"

Keith laughed. "Babe, I'm sorry. He's one of the biggest dicks we've got, if not the biggest."

"I don't care about the size of his penis," Darby said, "but he sure in hell shouldn't be an instructor."

"You passed, didn't you?"

"Yeah, but that ass put me on special tracking."

"What happened?"

Darby told Keith the night's events from Jones showing up 15 minutes before the session and his lack of attention because of his texting, as well as his sarcastic comments.

"Sorry sweets," he said. "But I'm glad you didn't walk out."

"Why?" Darby closed her eyes and waited for another Global lesson.

"Might as well slap Armstrong's wife on her ass. Same impact."

"So much to learn in this new world."

"Yeah, well...just try to keep a low profile," Keith said. "On a better note, did you vote for the CP?"

The CP was the contract proposal between the union and the company. Unfortunately the union was shoving it down the pilot's throats in some mysterious rush. Not a good tactic in any book.

"Yep, and I voted no," she said still thinking about what she wished she'd said to Jones.

"Why? We're getting a great raise."

"Just enough pay to blind our senses. Management thinks pilots can be bought." Darby pulled her seatbelt across her body and stuffed it into the clip. This was not a conversation she wanted to get into now.

"Well...most of us can," Keith said with a laugh. "But what's wrong with the contract?"

Darby chuckled too, and then said, "You really want to know?"

"Enlighten me."

"Work rules and safety are not for sale. Never trade contractual improvements. And we should never negotiate for aircraft—if the company needs them, they'll buy them."

CHAPTER 34

SEATTLE, WASHINGTON

APRIL 3, 2012

DARBY AWOKE EARLY the next morning. She sat at her computer wanting to write about what happened the previous night in the simulator, but instead, took the safer course of action and attacked her email.

Messages from union leaders concerning the contract proposal filled her inbox. This would be the first union agreement after the merger. Attitudes flared. Union leaders battled union leaders. Opinions were like assholes, everybody had one.

Darby shook her head in dismay. She wondered what happened to unity and safety—the foundation that their aviation brotherhood was built on.

Despite Bill Jacobs having been the instrument of hundreds of lives lost, he was also dead right concerning the problems within the current union cadre. If only he'd had a better way to make his point than killing people.

She pushed back from the table and walked to the counter and refilled her coffee cup, then added a splash of vanilla syrup.

Bringing the cup to her lips she thought about her checkride. What aggravated her, on top of getting a screw job in the simulator, was her not standing up to Jones. She should have stopped the simulator session, despite what Keith thought. Instead she allowed him to walk all over her. She returned to her chair and set her cup beside her computer.

Darby continued to read the debate on the contract. She shook her head and sighed. Her union should focus on work rules, training, and safety issues. Somehow ALPO was feeling like an appropriate name for something that had gone to the dogs.

She startle when her phone rang.

"I'm sorry," Jackie said when Darby answered. "I had no idea you'd been scheduled with Jones."He's one of the biggest jerks we've got in the department."

"So I've heard," Darby said wandering to her living room.

"You need to report him."

"I know," Darby sighed. "But it's not that simple."

"He's got so many complaints against him as it is, I'm surprised he's still working in training."

"He's a rat that deserves to be ratted out, but Keith said to let it slide. I have to trust him on this one," Darby said curling up on her couch.

"So…" Jackie said. "I kind of told the manager of training what happened."

"Please tell me you didn't," Darby closed her eyes. *Shit.*

"He's a good guy. He's one of the few still concerned with quality training and—"

"It's just, I've been lying low since Neidermeyer, alias Dickless Foster, has been hunting me," Darby said pulling a pillow onto her lap.

"Please don't make light of this. If you crashed a plane because you didn't get your training, and I didn't say anything, I'd never forgive myself."

"Point taken." Darby's phone beeped and she said, "I've got another call. I'll call you later." Switching calls she answered.

"Darby Bradshaw?" a voice said and she acknowledged. "This is the A330, Fleet Training Captain, Burt Armstrong. I heard there was a misunderstanding in the simulator last night, and you weren't happy with your training."

"I'd be hard pressed to call what happened last night training."

"What was the problem?"

"Well…" Darby said. Trying to decide how tactful she would be.

"Okay then," Armstrong said. "Just what I suspected—"

"The term problem puts it mildly," she said. With zero tact, she went for the direct approach and told him everything.

"Sounds like the perfect storm."

"I wish the session was video taped," Darby said.

When AQP came into play instructors were required to video all sessions. Not to reprimand the instructor, but for human factors awareness for the crews to see their own behavior. She would have to ask Kathryn what happened with that requirement.

"I'm sure he was unfamiliar with the process. This is a new scenario for the year."

"It's been new for three months," Darby said, "and I'm not sure how an instructor can expect to show up 12 minutes prior to a session and give an oral, brief, and do the paperwork."

Darby closed her eyes and counted to five. Armstrong had no intention of doing anything about this.

"You do know what was in that oral, don't you?" he asked.

"Limitations, systems questions and the walk around video."

"Nothing that was a big deal—"

"It's a big deal to me," Darby said. "I'm not flying and the only thing I can do is the book stuff. I've been an instructor and know how it is. I also know that we can determine a lot by how well the student is prepared."

"I'm sure he was just having a bad day."

"Of course! That explains why he was texting."

"We've got a problem with many of the instructors texting in the simulator," he said. "And—"

"I don't have a problem with someone texting. I have a problem with someone texting when he's supposed to be assessing a captain who needed extra training, and a first officer new to the plane who hadn't flown in three months."

"I'm sorry you weren't happy with your training," Armstrong said. "This is a customer service business and we want everyone to leave happy."

Darby rolled her eyes. "I don't care if I'm happy. I want to leave knowing I learned something. I want to leave knowing that I'm not going to go out and kill a planeload of people."

"We want that too," he said with a laugh.

"Nothing about that session was right."

"We often have differences of opinion in the simulator."

"Difference of opinion?" Darby counted again, but she did not make it past three. "Sir, with all due respect, this was anything but a difference of opinion."

"I'm sure he's got his side too."

"When you talk to him, ask him what grade he put in the computer for the oral and walkaround I didn't receive."

Falsifying FAA documents was a major violation for all parties involved, instructor and company.

This time she counted to see how long it would take for him to respond to that slap in the face. She was up to five when he spoke.

"I'm going to look into this further," he said with a chill to his voice. "Until then, what can we do to make this right?"

"I want to come back to the simulator today or tomorrow and have another check so I know that I'm safe. "

"I'm sorry, we can't do that," he said. "We don't have the simulator availability. They've already got you in the system to come back in three months. But I'll tell you what I'll do. Email me and let me know when you're coming in, I'll see to it that the session is yours. Anything you want."

"It would be nice to hand fly and get some crosswind landings."

"Okay then, send me that email and we'll make it happen."

They said their goodbyes and Darby shivered. They did not have time to assess if she were safe? Yet they were willing to put her on a plane. There was something seriously wrong with that on so many flight levels.

She wanted to tell him there would be two hours available after any of Jones's sessions, but thought better of it.

CHAPTER 35
GLOBAL FLIGHT 92
SHANGHAI, CHINA

MAY 16, 2012

FLIGHT 92 WAS INBOUND to Pudong Airport, Shanghai. Chad had been flying the A330 for two years, but China was a first. Everything appeared straight forward—as straight forward as a woman's logic. Somewhat like the Airbus.

Meters were easy in the A330. Press the metric button on the flight control unit and the metric altitude displayed in addition to the altitude in feet. Charts enabled them to confirm their altitude in feet with the metric numbers, but this made things a bit busy and took all the more attention, overusing brain cells.

He was not sure how the guys in the old days managed without automation. Combining hand flying with the language, it was surprising more planes were not lost.

Communications sounded like a bad song—whaa ha bah wahhh. It drove him nuts and gave him a headache. His brain spent too much time trying to decipher the noise and move it into intelligent data, making focus difficult.

There were many planes in the area. He could see them on his electronic map and hear the pilots talking. But he had no clue where they were going or what they were saying. His head ached and the pain grew worse by the minute.

Air traffic control was hard enough to understand with their broken English. And then there was his captain. He'd only been on the plane for a year, hardly enough time to know the intricacies of the Airbus. Chad felt as if he were flying single pilot.

"Grobal Nine Thwo, thurn right heading thwee thwo seven. Descend six hundwed methers."

The ATC controller's accent was strong and Chad hoped the communication barriers would be caught with a read back.

His captain replied to the clearance while Chad turned the heading selector and then spun down his altitude to 600 meters. He glanced at his approach plate and crosschecked the altitude clearance in feet—1968. He pulled the knob for an open descent.

They were being vectored in close and there was nothing about this approach that he felt comfortable with. At least it was his leg. Then again, being the second set of eyes for the captain might have been the better option.

The visibility was down to minimums at the airport and the hour was approaching midnight. At the current rate every available brain cell was being used. The flight was short, but the trip had been long—nine days and counting. Chad was exhausted and all his attention was focused on what he was doing.

"Flaps one," Chad called and then, "flaps two." He dialed the speed back.

ATC gave them vectors and then cleared them for the ILS to runway 35.

Chad pressed the approach button and then selected the second autopilot. "Gear down. Flaps three," he called.

The captain lowered the gear and moved the flap handle.

They were intercepting both the course and glideslope just

outside the outer marker.

Chad did not feel comfortable being vectored in this tight. He would have much rather had a nice ten-mile final, but what was he to do? "Flaps full, landing check."

The captain read the checklist and then said, "I'm going to clean the map up for you."

They were half a dot from capturing the glideslope in the crud. Not the time or place to do anything but focus on the approach.

Cleaning up the map meant nothing more than removing unnecessary waypoints. The points were clutter. But approaching the outer marker while intercepting the final approach course and glideslope, during instrument conditions, while in China airspace, nobody should be messing with the box.

Chad focused on flying the plane. Then his electronic map flashed and with a blink of an eye the green line connecting his plane to the runway was gone. All he saw was another green line that darted left from the outer marker.

"What happened to my map?"

His eyes flashed to the top line of the PFD confirming the glideslope was armed and that the course captured.

"Oh shit. Sorry. I'll fix it for you," the captain said.

"No! I've got the localizer and glide-slope. *Don't* do anything. I'm fine, we're about to capture the—"

Ding. Ding. Ding.

Fine was short lived. Bells rang and lights flashed at the same time the plane was capturing the glideslope—or supposed to. There was nothing for the plane to capture. The captain removed their approach and they flew through the glideslope.

"Fuck!" the captain yelled frantically stabbing buttons. His version of 'fix it' meant to take out the approach and reinsert it with a finger dance in the middle.

Within seconds Chad's data was back, but they had gone high at a critical moment.

Traveling at 142 knots forward, a million thoughts flew through his mind all at once. Data stormed his brain—did the captain still have the missed approach inserted correctly? Did Chad remember what it was? Who was departing off the other end? Where were all those planes on his electronic map headed? Should he miss the approach or continue?

He knew what he had to do.

Without delay he pushed the nose forward while pulling the speedbrake lever full aft. He reengaged the autopilot, dialed vertical speed of 1200 feet per minute, selected approach and engaged the second autopilot. He watched the ground closure rate and mentally prepared for a missed if they could not get stabilized.

"Confirm we're cleared to land," Chad yelled.

"Tower, is Global 92 cleared to land."

"Grobal Nine Thwo, cleared thwo land runway thwee five. Wind zero thwee zero at then."

Capturing the glideslope he selected managed speed. As they slowed he configured the plane then pushed the speedbrake handle forward and moved it to the armed position. They completed the landing checklist and seconds later they hit minimums and Chad saw the runway.

He took a deep breath and clicked off the autopilot. Pulling the thrust levers back to match the current power setting he pressed the button under his left thumb, disconnecting the autothrust.

"What'n the hell happened?" the captain asked as the airplane said, "100" indicating they were one-hundred-feet off the runway.

Chad ignored him.

"Fifty," the plane called. He pulled the thrust levers aft and touched the stick giving it the slightest of tickling that it was about to go to work.

"Thirty."

Chad gently pulled back on the stick, arresting the descent rate.

"Retard, retard," the plane called and Chad pulled the thrust levers to idle. Within seconds the plane touched down. He flew the nose to the runway and then grabbed a handful of reverse levers and pulled.

There may have only been two levers, but he hung onto them as if they were the captain's neck.

When they cleared the runway Chad said, "What happened? You fucking killed the approach! You should have had your head outside, not up your ass trying to fix things. It's like a limp dick, don't fuck with it!"

"But it shouldn't have done that," the captain said. "Should it?"

"It did exactly what you told it to do," Chad snapped. "If you don't know what you're doing, don't fucking touch the buttons."

CHAPTER 36
SEATTLE, WASHINGTON

JUNE 25, 2012

STANDING AT HER front door, Darby wished Keith good luck and told him to have fun. He was off to a corporate golf game followed by an eight day trip. She waved as he drove away.

It was hard to believe it was six months since she'd flown a plane, and three months since her simulator fiasco. Unfortunately her confidence diminished with each day she sat around waiting.

Tonight she would visit the simulator for her 90-day recency. Glancing at the sink and then her computer, she decided the dishes could wait. She opened up her laptop, and powered it up.

Three months earlier Darby began the process to buy a trip. Something they did at Coastal where a pilot stayed home and another pilot flew their trip. No extra pay was involved, just a good deal for everyone. Company included.

An overworked pilot stayed home with pay, a reserve pilot gained experience, and if they got their landings, the company saved money by not bringing them into the simulator.

Roy, the assistant chief pilot, said the Seattle pilots needed to stop manipulating their schedules to avoid flying, and denied her.

She was pissed at the accusation, but blew it off and tried to get a session in the simulator. Only there was never any time. Her next move was to write a resolution to the union, enabling pilots that did not feel proficient to call scheduling and book a flight.

She had no doubt this resolution would solve the problem. Darby stood and refilled her coffee cup, then returned to her table and logged onto her gmail account. Today she would find out when she could plan a trip.

Dodd's email had arrived as promised and she read. Her mouth fell open and temper ignited. Grabbing her cell phone she dialed his number.

"Walt it's Darby. What the hell is going on with our union? Why would they care about my resolution if it were optional to fly? It's not like they would be forced to. And calling the chief pilot's office to make it happen is a bunch of crap. I've been trying to buy a trip for three friggin months and—"

"Calm down."

"I am calm. I'm pissed. Huge difference."

"Roy said they'll buy a trip, on a case by case basis."

"I have proof saying otherwise."

Darby pulled open the fridge and removed a pitcher of iced tea and set it on the counter. "He doesn't make the rules," she said pulling a glass from the cupboard.

"It wasn't just Roy. The pilots didn't want this either."

She sat heavily on a barstool. "Why not?"

"You didn't hear it from me, but Global pilots think that if they write a resolution that implies their pilots might not be proficient, that wouldn't look good for them."

"Seriously?" Darby dropped her forehead on the counter. Not once, but twice. If only she could pound some sense into all of them.

"It's a democratic system. If the majority don't agree it's over."

"There's something majorly wrong with a management pilot

at a union meeting, downplaying an idea for safety," Darby said filling her glass, "as well as pilots' egos overpowering safety."

"You should've been at the meeting," Dodd said.

"If I ever imagined this would be the outcome, I would have. I've got a dozen emails requesting a trip buy. Phone calls trying to get into the simulator. Emails to management saying I don't feel proficient."

Darby sat at her table, and sighed. "What if, when I finally go out and fly, I have an accident. What would the media do with this paper trail and management not doing a damn thing about it?"

She raised her glass and sipped, a chill ran through her body just thinking about the possibility.

"We kind of hope that'll happen."

Choking on her tea, she sprayed the table. "Excuse me?"

"I don't mean that we want you to crash. But the point is, nothing will ever get fixed until a plane goes down for lack of proficiency."

Darby was not sure if she should laugh or cry at his statement. Instead, she said goodbye, grabbed a towel and cleaned up the mess, then logged onto the company website to see who would be her instructor.

She located her schedule. "No f-ing way!" Picking up her phone she pressed speed dial. Jackie answered on the first ring.

"I'm scheduled to fly with Jones tonight. What's the deal?"

"No you're not."

"It's on the schedule."

"Then somebody changed it. I'll call you right back."

She wanted to confront Jones and put this behind her. More importantly, she needed someone who would give her a good ride and get her up to speed.

Darby scrolled through the schedule to see what other sessions were available. Within minutes her phone came alive.

"I called the manager of training," Jackie said. "You're not to go in the simulator with Jones. We've rescheduled you for tomorrow at two."

"I'm looking at the simulator schedule," Darby said. "Why don't you swap instructors and let Jones go with the student in the other simulator and let me have the other instructor?"

"We looked at that too, but the other student's been having problems and they don't want to put him with Jones."

Darby rolled her eyes. "Do you see a problem here?"

"You're preaching to the choir. It's a huge problem. But I've been taking a bunch of shit for anything I say." Her voice cracked.

"Kiddo, are you okay?"

"No. I think they're moving me off the Airbus and putting me on the MD-80."

"How about dinner tonight?" Darby said. "I'll cook. That should cheer you up."

Jackie laughed. "You cook? I'd love to see that, but I'm busy."

"How about after my session tomorrow night?"

"That works for me. I'll call Kat and tell her to bring that pink stomach stuff."

"Ha, ha," Darby said rolling her eyes with a grin. "I'll let that comment slide if you answer me one thing."

"Anything."

"I've got bounces tomorrow and that simulator tracking thing in a month. Why in the heck don't we just combine the two events? Especially since the simulators are always full and there's no time to let anyone fly?"

Jackie sighed. "Because, my friend, that would make sense."

CHAPTER 37
RAINIER GOLF AND COUNTRY CLUB
SEATTLE, WASHINGTON

JUNE 25, 2012

KEITH GLANCED AROUND the Rainier clubhouse feeling like he was about to take a checkride on a plane he had never flown. But as Darby always said, "There's a first time for everything."

His nerves were not only because of whom he would be playing with, but the fear that he would suck big time. Then he learned they were playing best ball. He could handle that. Their scores would be a group effort and if he tanked a shot or two, nobody would notice.

This was a game with the president, chief executive officer, vice president and top managers from every department, including all fleet training captains. The game was touted as a 'team building' exercise.

Even the top union counsel members would be playing. Keith nodded at Walt Dodd, the Seattle captain rep and then noticed the coffee bar to his right. Just what Darby prescribed for most everything.

In the few months since they had been playing house, she turned him into an addict. He smiled at the thought of Darby. It was she who he was addicted to. But for now black coffee would be his pleasure and he headed that way.

Global Air Lines was known in the industry to have the best working relationship with their employees. Better than any other airline. Keith was convinced that Global's stock prices reflected that relationship.

They were weeks away from voting on the Contract Proposal. Management needed the contract signed sooner than later, but it was up to the membership to give it a thumbs up or down and not to be discussed on the golf course. He suspected those rules were meant to be broken.

He poured a coffee then wandered to the check-in table to see who his teammates were. Running a finger down the list of players he located his name. He was on a foursome with the A330 fleet training captain, Burt Armstrong, the vice president of the airline, Todd McDermott, and the head of Seattle union counsel, Walt Dodd. *Nice.*

Keith's career was pointed in the right direction. It would not be long until he found himself moving into a management position being paid twice as much as those flying. He could care less if he ever strapped on a plane again, there were more important things he needed to do.

Flying was a means to an end. He loved the layovers, but sitting on his ass for hours was not for him. He belonged in an office where he could make a difference.

It might take a couple years, but a management position with all the benefits was within his reach if he kept his mouth shut and did what he was told. How the hell Dick Foster made director of flying so soon unnerved him.

Keith was not far behind. He'd had good training in the military with the 'shut up-suck up' game. He had one problem—Darby.

He had fallen in love with her, and she would be the death of his of career. For now, all he had to do was play the game and try to not allow his two worlds to overlap more than they already did. In time everything would work out.

"Stone," Armstrong called as he approached. "Good to see you," he said with an outstretched hand.

"Good morning," Keith said shaking his hand.

"Beautiful day," Armstrong said.

"The best." Keith glanced around the room and located the other half of their team standing at the pastry bar, laughing. "They any good?" Keith asked nodding their way.

"They are," Armstrong said. "But don't let any of this intimidate you. By the end of the day, you'll see we all pull on our pants the same way."

A bell rang and an announcement came over the loud speaker. "Please locate your teams. We will be starting in ten minutes."

The vice president and the union rep were still laughing as they approached.

"This must be that fine instructor we've heard so much about," Vice President Todd McDermott said.

"Keith Stone," Keith said extending his hand. "Nice to meet you, sir."

"None of that sir crap," McDermott said, shaking Keith's hand. "We're all playing on the same course. Please, call me Todd."

"Just don't play better than him," Walt said to Keith. "Good to see you again."

"Ahhh, Captain Dodd," McDermott placed a hand on Walt's shoulder, "*Letting* me play better than you again?"

Walt grinned and winked at Keith.

This was the beginning of a very good day.

Keith was honored to have been chosen to participate. The director of training, Frank Dawson, was supposed to have this spot, but occasionally he picked one of the instructors to take his place. This year he chose Keith.

Everyone in flight operations and training knew he was dating Darby and he thought it would be to his demise. She definitely pushed some buttons.

Instead of being upset that Keith was dating her, Armstrong said, "Good move Stone. Keep your friends close but your enemies in bed."

When Armstrong asked him if she was a good screw Keith shrugged. That brought a laugh and kept him from having to say anything. If only he avoided her from the very beginning, but now he doubted he could live without her. He sure as hell did not want to.

Armstrong expected Keith to control Darby. *Yeah right.* He smiled at the futility of that thought. While he could not keep her from writing the blog, he helped to make it innocuous which kept Armstrong off his ass. Except when he was on a trip.

Darby had a way of popping something on line that always upset Armstrong. What was Keith supposed to do? He actually thought it was funny, but feigned concern for Armstrong's benefit.

Dodd cleared his throat. "Looks like we have company," he whispered to Keith. "Three o'clock."

Keith turned his head as the CEO, Lawrence Patrick, approached.

"Gentlemen, how are we doing today?" Mr. Patrick asked with a broad smile.

"Good," Armstrong responded.

"Who's this fine young man?" Mr. Patrick said.

"Keith Stone." Keith extended his hand and shook Mr. Patrick's.

"Nice to see you again," Armstrong said to Mr. Patrick.

"Gentleman are you ready to play?" Mr. Patrick asked.

"If you're asking if I'm ready to kick your ass," McDermott said, "the answer is yes."

Mr. Patrick's eyes narrowed. "I would expect nothing less, but you can kick my ass from another team."

"By whose authority?" McDermott asked, placing his hands on his hips, his tone shifting to ice.

Keith glanced between the two of them. This was anything but good. The thought of taking five steps back crossed his mind.

"By the authority of me," Mr. Patrick said. "You don't mind, do you Todd? I just want to talk to my boys. Find out how the road shows are going for the proposal. You know, get a feel for the heartbeat of the company."

"I'm not telling you anything," Captain Dodd said. "Unless you're ready to sweeten the deal we discussed."

"Excuse me?" Mr. Patrick said. "Since when does the union openly take bribes?"

Keith's mouth fell open. *Was Walt Dodd serious?* Keith shifted his attention back to the CEO. Time stood still like one of those nightmares where everything moved slow motion, where he could not move or scream. He inched back, not sure he wanted to be in this game.

Captain Armstrong elbowed Keith. "Welcome to the team." All faces stared his way and the group broke into laughter, and Keith blushed.

"Don't worry, Keith," Mr. Patrick said. "We always mess around with the new guy. But Todd, I'm serious. Do you mind if I swap places with you? I need to discuss a few training issues with Burt."

"Not at all," McDermott said. He turned and walked toward his new team.

CHAPTER 38

DARBY SAT ON THE PATIO of her favorite coffee shop and watched people rush by. She sipped her brew and then closed her eyes lifting her face to the sun as she visualized landing her plane.

100 feet look down the runway. 50 feet think about moving the stick to neutral. 30 feet slowly bring the nose to level and pull the thrust to idle per command. Touchdown. Fly the nose to the runway. Remember reverse thrust. A very mechanical process, but so easy to screw up if you let your head get in the way with a crosswind.

In five hours she would be back in the seat. Unfortunately, it would only be in the simulator. She tried for more than half a year to get a flight to no avail. She was nervous about her bounces, which was ridiculous.

She opened her eyes and winked at the guy who was staring at her. He blushed and looked away.

It amazed Darby how that session with Jones took a huge chunk of her confidence. As the days passed her mind played games with her and she began to doubt her ability.

Her frustration was more than his being an asshole. He beat her up in a way that nobody could understand unless they lived through it. Something the early women fliers experienced. The only difference was, today Jones was the exception and not the rule.

Darby wanted to know she was safe. She did not need someone to tell her she could fly—she needed to see it for herself. Six months was far too long to be out of a plane.

A ringing phone broke into her thoughts. She looked around and the sitting area was empty, then she glanced down. The vibration should have been the first clue that it was hers, as her phone was nestled into her sports bra.

By the time she pulled it out, she missed the call. The number was local, but unknown. She pressed the voicemail button and sipped her cappuccino while the message played.

"Darby, this is Jason Hinkens. I'll be in the sim with you this afternoon. I wanted to give you a heads up that I'll be getting my check airman recertification while giving you your recency. I'll be in the other simulator, running a bit late, but Captain Doherty should be around somewhere and we'll start as soon as I'm done debriefing the other crew."

She restuffed her phone and tipped her cup to finish her coffee. Putting on her sunglasses she sighed.

Two check airman for bounces, this is a first.

Darby arrived to the briefing room fifteen minutes early and there was a pilot sitting at the computer.

"Hi, I'm Darby. Are you in sim four at two?"

"I am," he said, standing. He extended his hand. "Doherty. I'll be watching Jason conduct the ride. This is his recertification to be a check airman. He'll be in the seat with you and I'll work the instructor station, but he'll be running the session."

"Do you think I could go down and practice a preflight? It's been a few months since I've been in the simulator." No way in hell she was going to tell him how long since she had flown. *No excuses.*

"Sure." He shuffled through a stack of papers. "You can program this," he said handing her a flight plan.

Darby took the paperwork and headed down the stairs and into the simulator. She scanned the instructor's station and found the external power button and pressed on. Climbing into her seat she reached overhead and powered up the airplane.

She started at the top left of the overhead panel and began her flow, carefully turning on all the appropriate switches to configure the plane for flight. By the time she was finished she felt confident that she had put everything into the correct position. Then she programmed the MCDU, the airplane's computer and brain, as she typed in the coordinates off the flight plan.

By the time she finished, both check airmen were entering the simulator. Jason introduced himself and climbed into the captain seat.

"I'm fairly certain the overhead is perfect, but I have a question about inserting step altitudes."

Jason glanced at the computer, then knit his brows. "How did you program this flight plan?" he asked.

"I just typed the coordinates in sequence."

"Do you remember when you were first trained how you went to the via page?"

It had been a year since she manually loaded a flight plan into the computer, but the lightbulb went full bright.

She began punching buttons and programmed the flight plan the correct way while Doherty programmed the simulator from his station. Jason watched her, and when she was done he said, "Good."

Doherty stepped forward and asked, "You two ready to go?" He repositioned them to the centerline of runway 24 right in

Minneapolis.

"Yep," Darby answered.

"We'll do a visual pattern to get comfortable with the simulator," Jason said. "When you're ready to fly, we'll go."

"Ready," Darby said and pressed the thrust levers forward. When the power was set she removed her hand.

"Eighty knots, one hundred knots, thrust normal," Jason called. "V1. VR." Darby rotated and he said, "Positive rate."

"Gear up," Darby called. She climbed to two thousand feet and engaged the autopilot. She turned the heading bug to follow the clearance Doherty provided for a downwind vector. "Activate the approach please," she said. "Flaps one."

"Trainer One, turn right heading one five zero."

Darby spun the heading bug to her base leg. "Flaps two."

"Trainer One, if the airport's in sight, you're cleared to land," Doherty said.

She clicked off the autopilot and called, "Gear down, flaps three," as she rolled onto final. "Flaps full, landing check."

All checklists complete, she was cleared to land and put the plane on the runway centerline.

"Nice job," Jason said. "But I noticed when you flared you dipped your left wing."

Doherty stepped forward. "Show me how you flare."

She rested her arm on the armrest, held the stick and tilted her hand back for the flare."

"Exactly what I thought," Doherty said. "Jason, this is something to keep an eye on. We teach students how to flare with the armrest for stability, but when they pull back the pilots hands naturally tilts inward."

"I hadn't noticed that before," Jason said.

The next pattern they flew without the automation. Darby missed flying and she could not remove the grin that took hold.

Her vision was narrow and the process of scanning more of an effort than she remembered. That was the price she paid for not flying, and the reason pilots needed experience—to be able to fly without effort and leave brain cells available when emergencies occurred.

The next departure they gave her an engine failure. After they landed, Doherty said, "I've seen enough," and the simulator came off motion.

Darby walked to the parking lot, her step much lighter than it had been in many months. Normally bounces were a rush in and a rush out. This time she got to do it all.

Climbing into her car she powered up her cell phone and saw that she missed a call from Kathryn. They shifted dinner to Kathryn's house because she wanted one less thing for Darby to worry about.

She listened to the message hoping their plans were still a go.

"I hope your session went great," Kathryn said. "Don't forget the wine. You're going to need it tonight. You won't believe what's on the news."

CHAPTER 39

DARBY OPENED the front door. "Knock, knock," she said. "Anybody home?" She wandered into the kitchen toward the laughter, but nobody was there. She set a bottle of Merlot on the counter and followed the voices into the family room. She stood in the doorway with her hands on her hips and smiled at the sight before her.

"Aunt Darby!" Jennifer yelled and ran into her arms and whispered, "Jessica's flirting with Chris."

"I can see that," Darby said. "She's doing a pretty good job, too."

"Oh God," Jennifer said, releasing Darby. She placed her hands on her hips and rolled her eyes. "She *is* just like you."

"So are you my little darling," Darby said, patting her butt. "Where's your Mom?"

"Backyard. We're barbequing."

"Awesome," she said. "See you in a few."

Darby returned to the kitchen and tossed her purse on the counter. She picked up the wine and headed toward the backyard. She opened the sliding glass door to the scent of grilling steak.

"Hey guys, something smells delicious and I'm starving."

Kathryn took the bottle from Darby and gave her a hug. Jackie looked up with tears streaming down her face.

"Oh my God," Darby said pulling from Kathryn and moving toward Jackie. "What happened?"

Jackie handed Darby a newspaper.

"Pacific Airlines 574," Kathryn said. "They have the black box."

Jackie wiped tears with the back of her hand. "I'm sorry guys, I don't know what's wrong with me." She sniffed. "It's just that…I know how those families feel."

Kathryn stood behind Jackie and gave her a squeeze. "I know, Sweetie." The truth was, they all did.

"It has to be sabotage," Jackie said between sobs. "Doesn't it? There's no other reason."

"I don't know," Kathryn said shaking her head.

Darby sat at the table and unfolded the *Times*.

Nobody was surprised when they had found parts of the plane drifting at sea, but pulling the black box from the ocean was nothing short of amazing.

Pacific Airlines and Airbus Industries spent millions of dollars locating the Airbus for one reason only—liability. Lawsuits were filling courtrooms against everyone involved. Darby shook her head and focused on the *Seattle Times* report.

Pacific Airlines Flight 574, an Airbus A330, crashed over the Pacific Ocean on December 14, 2009. The black box has been retrieved. The plane climbed after the autopilot was disengaged, stalled, and remained stalled during its three-and-a-half-minute descent into the Pacific Ocean.

The inputs made by the pilot flying were mainly nose-up. The initial report indicates potential pilot error. Generally, pilots would push the nose down to recover from a stall, not pull.

The report indicates that the autopilot and autothrust disengaged at the start of the incident, but it did not say why. Pacific Airlines pointed to equipment failure and to faulty airspeed probes.

Darby sat heavily and a shiver crawled down her back as she continued to read.

In a statement Pacific Air Lines said, "It appears that the flight deck crew was monitoring the changing weather conditions and thus altered their flight path. The initial problem was the failure of the speed probes, which led to the disconnection of the autopilot and the loss of the associated piloting protection systems.

All data collected must now be analyzed. It will only be at the end of this complex task, which requires patience and precision, that the CAA will be able to establish the causes that led to the disaster."

Airbus said, "The preliminary information released by the CAA today is consistent with facts published in the preliminary and interim reports. Their work constitutes a significant step towards the identification of the complete chain of events that led to the tragic accident of Pacific Airlines flight 574 in December 2009."

The few lines of the transcript they chose to include was not enough for a full evaluation, but enough to know there was equipment failure and the plane went into Alternate Law. Her heart broke for the families involved, especially the pilots.

She looked up and said, "I can't believe it." She set the *Times* face down on the table, her heart ached.

"Me either," Kathryn said, handing Darby a glass of wine. "To think they pulled that black box out of the ocean is nothing short of amazing."

"Oh, I knew they'd bring it up," Darby said. "With what's at stake, all parties involved would die in search of answers. What I can't believe is the pilots crashed this plane."

Kathryn's hand moved to her mouth. "No. They wouldn't."

"The pilots stalled that plane," Darby said. "I don't know why—"

"On purpose?" Jackie snapped. "It can't be. Not again."

"I don't think they crashed on purpose. I think they didn't know how to fly their plane."

Darby thought about her flight with Keith over the same route. What would have happened if he continued to pull back on the stick and they stalled? If they had, they would have done a stall recovery. Why didn't these pilots?

"They didn't know how to fly?" Kathryn asked with confusion narrowing her eyes. "How's that possible?"

"Oh, it's possible," Darby said. "This is also the accident that Walt Dodd said we needed to deal with the proficiency issue."

Unfortunately the crash in San Francisco, despite both pilots managing to crash a perfectly good plane, went to the back page of all the papers. It crashed on U.S. soil, but was a foreign carrier.

That crash should have been the accident they needed to prove that pilots were losing their skills. But if she were right, this A330 crash was more than pilot error. These pilots did not know how to fly. Now they had two accidents to prove her point.

"The paper said the autopilot disconnected," Jackie said, wiping her eyes. "Why would it do that?"

"They lost their instruments when it went into Alternate Law." The more she thought about it, this was exactly what happened to she and Keith. "But they still should have been able to fly."

"The concept of control laws changing during a crisis gives me a huge concern," Kathryn said. "Especially if the crew didn't realize what law they were in or that flying parameters had changed."

Jackie blew her nose and said, "What do you mean laws?"

"Laws are not a big deal," Darby said. "They're just levels of protection. Airbus built in those protections so pilots can't screw up and fly their planes beyond unsafe parameters and stall."

"But the paper said they stalled." Jackie said.

"When the plane went into Alternate Law, they lost those protections and were able to stall," Darby said, trying to keep the frustration out of her voice.

"The problem is that pilots today allow their planes to do all the flying, and they go for years just programing the computer. They forget how to fly, or never had a good foundation. When something breaks and the autopilot disconnects, they don't remember how to fly."

"You haven't been flying," Kathryn said.

"I know, and it scares the hell out of me."

"Whatever happened, I hope it's not terrorism," Jackie said, blowing her nose.

"Well…" Darby said. "What's scarier—terrorism, or your pilots not knowing how to fly their planes?"

Kathryn breathed deep and shook her head. "Do you seriously think these pilots didn't know how to fly when they lost their automation in that storm?"

"On face value, yes," Darby said nodding. "But they've only reported a fraction of the transcript. There are huge holes in what we're reading here. Something doesn't fit and we could be waiting for a long time to get the full story."

"But the families need to know," Jackie said.

"I was concerned about automation destroying proficiency of our flight crews," Kathryn said, slipping into a chair between Darby and Jackie. "I never imagined it could take down a plane."

"Me either, and most everyone flies with the automation all the time," Darby said. "Then there are the rest of us that never fly because of the reserve schedule. Nothing is good about any of this."

"Greg said Coastal wanted them to fly with the automation."

"They did," Darby confirmed. "They thought it would increase fuel savings." When Jackie narrowed her eyes, Darby added, "The plane is far more efficient than the pilot. Well, if it's managed properly. Trust me, even with automation pilots can waste fuel because they don't know how to manage their planes."

Kathryn stood and put the steaks on a platter then covered it with foil. "We saw this coming. The takeover of automation and pilots losing their flying skills. We need to do something to make them click it off and fly their planes to keep sharp."

"It's not just the pilot's fault," Darby said. "Tell me, when are we supposed to hand fly? The FAA's approved a system requiring pilots to use automation within RVSM airspace and RNP approaches, etc."

"We've created a monster," Kathryn said with a sigh.

"Not to mention, automation is the safest way to fly an approach after a twenty-hour day, landing on the otherside of the world on the backside of the clock," Darby said. "We need all the help we can get."

"Pilot's still need to know how to fly," Kathryn said.

"They do, and I'm not sure what the answer is." Darby sipped her wine, wondering how this accident would play out.

"Why don't you write a blog about it" Jackie said. "I mean you're on the plane and could explain what happened from a system perspective."

"That's an excellent idea," Kathryn said. "The drivel that comes out in the newspaper is usually for theatrics. You could tell it the way it really is."

"And you could explain about the laws and such," Jackie said. "We can't let this accident be buried." She uncovered the bowl of potato salad and stuck a spoon in the center. "Too many people died. You know they'll try to cover it up."

"I'm not going to allow it to get buried," Kathryn said, "and finding the black box couldn't have come at a better time."

Jackie raised an eyebrow.

"I've been working on a proposal with Darby's help. After their wiping out my recommendation on the safety audit, I decided to take one of my ideas and create a training program. Darby's right, this is the ammunition we needed."

Darby stood and opened the sliding glass door and yelled, "Jess, Jen, Chris…you have three minutes or I'm eating your share."

"Oh my God, I totally forgot to ask you how your ride went," Jackie said.

Darby smiled. "Couldn't have been better."

"I knew it," Kathryn said. "I didn't think they were out to get you." She tilted her glass toward Darby.

"Oh don't count on that," Darby grinned and lifted her glass. "But tonight, two points for the fly girl." They all clinked their glasses together. "Just remember one thing," she added. "You're not paranoid if they really are out to get you."

"Who's out to get you?" Jennifer asked, pushing past Jessica in the doorway.

"The good old boys club at Global," Darby said. "But not to worry, I don't knock down easily."

"That's right," Jessica said. "Real pilots never give up control."

CHAPTER 40
SEATTLE, WASHINGTON

JUNE 27, 2012

SCREAMS FROM THE CABIN awoke Darby and she squinted at her clock. 0200 shined bright in her otherwise black bedroom. She reached across the bed for Keith. He was on his trip, but reaching out to touch him became an unconscious reflex that she did with every nightmare.

Grabbing a pillow she rolled to her side and begged for sleep, but the sandman would not come. She could not shutoff the noise in her brain. She rolled to her back and pulled the pillow over her face as Airbus Laws bounced in her head. *So many deaths.*

She lifted the pillow and glanced at the clock. 45 minutes passed since she first opened her eyes. She rolled to her side again and Bear stared her in the face. "Grrrrr," she said and stuffed him under the pillow. She swung her feet to the floor and rubbed her eyes.

Darby left the window open, the brisk night air felt good. She slipped into her robe and pulled the belt tight as she wandered downstairs, and made a pot of coffee. With a steaming mug in hand she climbed the stairs and set her coffee on the desk, then closed the window.

She sat in front of her computer and pulled up the portion of the transcript the *Times* published. She wished they printed more. *What are they not saying? More importantly, why?*

After logging into *Flight For Safety* she selected 'New Post' and began to type.

Flight For Safety
June 27, 2012
Pacific Airlines 574: What Really Happened?

Two years ago, December 14, 2009, an Airbus A330 was swallowed by the Pacific Ocean never to be found. So we thought. Each day that followed left more inquiring minds to believe we might never know what really happened to Pacific Airlines Flight 574. Then they brought her to shore with answers in tow. Unfortunately leaving much more speculation as to why a perfectly good airplane was swallowed by the ocean.

With the report we know what happened—the plane crashed. But do we know why? This post is not to discredit the pilots, the company, or the airplane, but to learn from this event so accidents like this will never happen again.

By the time Darby finished with her post, she explained Airbus Laws, specifically Alternate Law. She wrote how the trim worked, about thrust lock, and discussed the pilot's excessive banking and their induced instability. She did her best to convey the noise level and over stimulation of warnings she experienced in this same situation.

The pilots never performed ECAM procedures, they were lost at the concept of basic aerodynamics and stalled. 228 people died. But how could they blame the pilots? They only knew as much as they were taught. They too were victims of the system.

Darby went downstairs to refill her coffee cup. Something bothered her about the article she was about to post. It was good, but it wasn't enough to just tell people what went wrong.

This accident would undoubtedly be a blame game for years. What they needed to do is make sure that this never happened again. But how? She knew exactly what she needed to add.

Darby returned upstairs and sat at her computer and wrote recommendations to all parties involved.

Suggestions to Airlines:

Create a syllabus that includes hand flying and stall training at altitude, and make this part of ongoing recurrent training.

Require pilots to fly the airplane and perform their takeoffs and landings without automation during all simulator events.

On initial line training require pilots to demonstrate their ability to hand fly the plane without autothrust prior to being released to the flight line.

Enable pilots to maintain proficiency beyond legality by allowing them to visit the simulator if they have not been flying, or assign a trip to allow them to fly. Automation is wonderful, but it can destroy a pilot's skills.

Suggestion to Airplane Manufacturers:

Develop the EICAS to display the first step of flying as a priority— Display pitch and power settings when instruments are lost.

Suggestion to FAA:

Enable pilots to use glider hours toward their 1500-hour requirement to build aerodynamic skills.

Suggestion to Pilots:

Kick off the autopilot, autothrust and flight directors—and fly your plane! You never know when your life will depend upon it.

Plus...it is fun!
Fly safe ~ DB

CHAPTER 41
SEATTLE, ARRIVAL

JULY 3, 2012

KEITH SAT IN the jumpseat an hour out of Seattle. He was at the end of his eight day trip, jumping from plane to plane giving line checks. These were not random checks as they touted. Armstrong selected the 'problems' and gave Keith the list. The problems were pilots who would not keep their mouths shut.

His job was to sit quietly and exert pressure, conveying their career was on the line if they spoke out about anything. He sucked at this. He hated line-checking more than he hated Burt Armstrong. However, during the process Keith got an ear full of what was really happening on the line.

When he found his home in management he would change things. This was bullshit and not the way to conduct business. Darby was right, a chain of command that imbued fear contradicted safety and was no way to run an airline. He just needed to play the game to sneak in the backdoor, then he could create an airline where safety came first.

Darby was on their list. A different list, and one all her own. He suspected it had everything to do with her being the only woman speaking out. That was a slap in Armstrong's face. But more than that, someone had a burr up his butt. He was not sure who held the whip—Armstrong or someone in flight operations, but he *would* find out.

He had no proof, but somebody was definitely playing with her. What was he supposed to do? He had to keep his mouth shut, but he also had to protect her. He was stuck in an impossible position.

The ACARS dinged and he read the message.

"What's that?" the captain asked.

Keith sighed. "Crisis at headquarters. Looks like they can't live without me." He ripped the sheet of paper off the printer that said—*Keith Stone. Call Burt Armstrong ASAP upon landing.*

Keith walked off the plane, found a quiet corner, and dialed Armstrong's number.

"Do you know what Bradshaw did yesterday?" Armstrong yelled.

Keith closed his eyes. "No." He could only imagine.

"She wrote a fucking post about Flight 574 saying the pilots didn't know how to fly."

Keith opened his eyes and grinned. He read the report on the findings the day prior and knew Darby would jump on the story.

"I'm sorry, I was doing line checks and—"

"Those fucking pilots didn't know how to fly," Armstrong said, "Bradshaw told the world! You were supposed to get her to shut that blog down."

Keith cringed. "I'm sure everyone will be writing about it. Her blog will get lost in the mix."

"How quickly can you get to the office?"

"I just got off the plane. I could go home and—"

"I'll see you in fifteen minutes," Armstrong said.

Keith's phone went dead. *God damn that asshole.*

He had been up all night and seeing Armstrong was the last thing he needed. Times like this made the facade all the more challenging.

Whatever was going on with Darby, Keith would figure it out. He glanced at his watch. If he could clear customs quickly, he would have time to stop by his locker before he headed down the street.

Twenty minutes later Keith walked into the training center and headed toward Armstrong's office. He would get evidence that Armstrong was harassing Darby and use it to his benefit, in more ways than one.

He raised his hand to knock, but hesitated when he heard voices. Irritated, Keith knocked harder than he should have.

The door opened.

"Glad you could make it," Armstrong said, stepping aside.

As Keith entered his office, Armstrong poked his head out the door and glanced down the hall and then closed it.

Keith did a double take at the faces in the room. Maybe this was not about Darby...or was it? He pulled the pen out of his pocket and sat with a notebook in his lap.

Armstrong smiled. "You won't need that for what we're going to discuss."

A chill wormed up Keith's spine and the stares pointing his direction felt like daggers. He set the pad of paper and pen on the desk.

"I'm all ears."

CHAPTER 42
SEATTLE, WASHINGTON

JULY 3, 2012

THE POUNDING ON the flight deck door beat on Darby's brain. She wanted to open it, but she could not get up from her seat. She was strapped in, frozen and afraid to move or she would lose the plane. It was falling. Falling like a maple leaf into the sea with its nose held high.

She pushed forward on the control stick, but it would not budge. Someone pounded on the other side of the cockpit door. The first officer to her right was laughing.

"Noooo!" Darby yelled. Trying to force the stick forward, she pressed her body into it to break it free. It snapped and the plane lunged forward into the black water below.

The pounding continued. Darby gasped for a breath. She let go of the stick and unbuckled her seatbelt as the plane sank deeper into the bowels of the ocean. She rolled out of her seat hitting her head on the thrust levers as she fell.

Darby opened her eyes and blinked a couple times. She squinted as the morning sun streamed through her window. Sitting upright on the floor, she pushed the coffee table away and felt the back of her head, then looked at her fingers.

Looking up, she startled. Keith was sitting in a chair staring her way with angst etched into his face.

"That was quite a dream," he said. "Why are you sleeping on the couch?"

"I woke up early. I was going to hide and jump out and scare you when you got home. I must have fallen asleep."

A smile flashed through his eyes, but did not last.

"Are you okay?" she asked. "You look like I felt on my last flight into Seattle."

He raised a hand to his face and rubbed his temple, then stood. Placing his hands on his hips he said, "What the hell are you doing?"

"Excuse me?" Darby said, confusion fogging her brain.

"Why are you writing about the Pacific Airlines crash? They don't even have the final report out!"

Darby's mouth fell open and she stood, yanking the belt on her robe tight. "What the hell are *you* talking about?" Anger trumping confusion.

"Me?" Keith said, pulling a hand through his hair. "You tell the world that the Pacific Airlines crash was the pilot's fault! You've got to stop this fucking blog! What are you thinking?"

"Fuck you, Stone," Darby spat.

She stormed past him and into the kitchen. He was yelling something as she poured herself a cup of coffee. Her heart rate increased with each word he shouted. Anger rushing through her brain made anything he had to say difficult to understand. She dumped in a splash of cream, but did not bother with the sweetness.

"Don't walk away from me when I'm talking to you," he said, entering the kitchen.

"Who the hell do you think you are?" Darby said, sitting on a barstool. She set her cup on the counter and folded her arms. If he wanted a fight she was ready to pull on the gloves.

Keith sucked a deep breath as if he was not sure what to say. He turned and poured himself a cup of coffee and leaned against the counter. His eyes bore into hers. The storm smoldered between them.

Darby took a sip without removing her eyes from his and said, "What's up your butt, anyway?"

"My butt? Oh, that's nice. Where do I begin? Oh yeah, your blog trashing the pilots."

"Did you read it?"

"Not yet, but that's not the point."

"Then what is the point? You can't bitch me out for something you haven't read." Darby glared at him, her heartbeat far from normal.

"Tell me you didn't write that the pilots had no clue how to fly."

She glared. "It's better than telling the world how I'd flown with a captain who had no clue what to do when he had the exact same problem, and that he was an instructor!"

Keith's face turned red and she saw something in his eyes that she had never seen before.

"I didn't say anything." Darby's glare turned into a plea, as tears filled her eyes. "But this is exactly what happened to us and you and I both know why that plane stalled."

Keith walked around the counter and sat on the barstool beside her and stared at the granite. "I'm finally getting where I need to be, and then this. I can't be on Armstrong's shit list because of your blog," he said looking up. "You have to stop writing it. Please."

"Let me get this straight." Darby counted on her fingers. "One, you're yelling at me for something you have not read. Two, you think my blog will put you on the fleet training captain's shit list. Three, you think my writing about a safety issue will hurt your career. Do you hear what you're saying?"

"I'm in the training department, a management pilot. We're dating. What the hell do you think?"

Darby covered her eyes with both hands and shook her head. She wanted to scream. Silence ticked between them like a bomb ready to explode.

"If you love me, you'll shutdown your blog."

She dropped her hands, eyes wide. "*Seriously?*"

"You think you're doing any good? You're not. You're wasting your time. Blogs are a pathetic way to disseminate information."

"This conversation is pathetic," Darby said flatly. "Maybe you should get a woman that Armstrong will approve of."

"Give me a break," Keith said. He turned toward the window and breathed deep. When he looked her way, anguish was etched into his face. He opened his mouth to say something, but Darby would not give him the opportunity.

"Give *you* a break?" Darby said. "The only thing I'm going to give you is a fucking cold shoulder. You can sleep on the couch tonight."

She was so angry at him. Who gave him the right to talk to her that way, and order her around?

"Sweetheart, please—"

She held up her hand and said, "No. I don't want to hear *anything* else you have to say right now. I've heard enough."

With her heart pounding wildly and her body shaking she left the kitchen and stormed up the stairs toward her bedroom.

Fuck him and his little training department, too.

CHAPTER 43
SeaTac Airport

OVER A MONTH PASSED since Darby and Keith's first argument. They had talked and the make up sex was awesome. Yet she stood in the terminal below the flight operations mezzanine alone. He had been sent out to do line checks again.

Glancing up to the flight operations door, she waited for her union representative, Walt Dodd, to come and take her to the gallows.

Shortly after Keith slammed out of her house, Roy, the assistant chief pilot, called and told her to pull the post about the A330 crash. He said, "We are a code share airline with Pacific Airlines and it's a sensitive issue."

Darby pulled the post as they spoke, but a month later she was called in for a social media violation.

It took management in Oklahoma City a month to come up with something to nail her on. Apparently a sensitive issue with a code share partner was not enough.

There were thousands of pilots writing posts about the A330 crash—the topic of the century, yet the company came after her. There was no doubt Dick Foster was still on his hunt, but something she could not prove.

"Darby, we're ready for you," Dodd said as he approached. "Captain Odell didn't want to put a letter in your file, but they're making him. He wasn't sure if they would until about 5 minutes ago, when they faxed it—"

"They're putting a letter in my file? Are you serious?" Darby's eyes opened wide and her hands moved to her hips.

"Calm down. Let's just hear what they have to say."

Darby followed him to the elevator. How the hell did she get behind the power curve with these guys? It all started with her violating the chain of command for a stupid Christmas party. What was done was done—now they were just pissing her off.

They entered the room, and Darby's heart increased a few beats.

"Thank's for coming," Odell said.

"Sure, no problem." *Like I had a choice.*

"We understand you have something for us," Dodd said.

Chief Pilot Odell slid a letter across the table to Darby, and another to Dodd. "We'll need you to sign it."

She took the letter and began to read. Her eyes narrowing with each word. *What the hell?*

Darby finished reading the letter and set it down. There were so many things wrong with it, she did not know where to begin.

"If it were up to me I wouldn't be putting this in your file," Odell said. "Your willingness to pull the post was good enough for me, but Oklahoma said we had to go this route."

Nothing about the letter was true, other than she wrote a post. She certainly did not give permission for a newspaper to publish it and was never called in about her blog once, let alone twice before.

"Don't worry about the letter," Odell said with a wave of his hand. "Global likes to put letters in pilot's files. It's not a big deal."

"My biggest concern," Roy said, "is what if Global wants to place new orders with Airbus? Your blog could have damaged our relationship and ruin negotiations."

Darby's brows knit. "What are you talking about? Since I wrote that post, the head of Airbus Americas is following my blog and we email. I don't think I've offended them. They liked it because I supported the plane. I told the truth…the plane is safe, it was the pilots that didn't know how to fly."

Roy lowered his eyes, and then she asked, "Did you read it?"

"The problem is," Odell said, "you violated the social media policy. You say on your blog that you're a Global pilot, and our policy clearly says that you are not allowed to give information to anyone for print."

"I didn't give anything to anyone, and my blog states that nobody is allowed to take anything unless they have permission. Have you looked through the Internet to see how many Global pilots have blogs and are talking about training and flying, and all their other activities with the airline? Not to mention this accident. Hundreds, if not thousands!" She folded her arms, trying to control her temper. "So why me?"

"Just because people are speeding and don't get caught doesn't mean you get off your ticket," Odell said. "You divulged training secrets."

"What training secrets? I thought this was concerning the post about the Pacific Airlines crash." She glanced around the table. "I didn't share *anything* about my training session."

"You wrote that airlines should give high altitude training," Odell said.

"I didn't get high altitude training."

"Yes you did," Odell snapped. "It was on this year's recurrent scenario."

"No. I'm telling you I didn't get that training. Hell, I didn't even know I was supposed to get it!"

"You have access to the company computer. You can see what's required," Odell said.

"That's the instructor's responsibility," Darby countered.

Red moved up Odell's neck and Dodd squeezed her elbow—a warning to shut her mouth, which was becoming more daunting with each moment she sat in the room.

"Are you guys still spanking pilots with line checks?" Dodd asked, cutting the tension. Apparently the only contribution he had at these meetings.

"I won't get line-checked because I never fly," Darby said glancing at Roy, the little prick who denied her request for a trip buy. She folded her arms again, glaring at the letter before her.

"Social media with this contract is turning into a nightmare," Dodd said. "What are we going to do about it?"

"I don't know," Odell said. "But we can't monitor everyone."

Flabbergasted at this conversation, Darby could not hold her tongue. "Do you see it?" she yelled and the room silenced. All eyes turned her way.

"See what? Dodd asked.

"It's there. Sitting in the middle of the table," she said pointing.

"What the hell are you talking about?" Odell said.

"I'm talking about the elephant sitting in the middle of this table. A plane crashed killing 228 passengers because the pilots didn't know how to fly after losing their automation. They were just as inexperienced on the A330 as I am, and they were not trained at altitude. I wasn't either!"

She pushed her chair back from the table and stood, placing

her hands on her hips.

"I just told you that I did not receive the exact training that could have prevented the Pacific Airlines flight from crashing, and you guys have your panties in a bunch over a friggin social media policy?" She folded her arms. "There is something seriously wrong here."

"The only thing wrong is your behavior," Odell snapped. "Calm down and take your seat."

Darby's heart raced as she looked at her chair, and then to the door. Sense prevailed and she sat heavily.

"I need you to sign this letter," Odell said. "It will be in your file for three years."

Against her better judgment Darby signed and slid it across the table. "May I have a copy of that?"

"Of course," Odell said. "I hate this, but it's really not a big deal."

CHAPTER 44

DARBY WAS FURIOUS by the time she reached the parking lot. After their two-hour meeting Walt Dodd recommended that she forget about the letter. He said, "If you fight it, your head will pop up on the radar." At the time she agreed with him, but the further she got from the office, she was not so sure.

Her chief pilot's assurance that a letter was no big deal and Walt Dodd's encouragement to allow sleeping dogs to lie angered her.

They were missing the big picture. An airplane's system failed, but that failure was no reason for the plane to crash. Pilots should be trained to fly broken planes.

Dodd said that the master counsel was angry at her because she blamed the pilots. The company was angry at her for blaming the plane. The reality was, she blamed lack of training.

She climbed into her car and slammed the door. Taking a deep breath she turned the ignition to start and Wilson Phillips, *Hold On* blared over the radio.

Hold on for one more day—that was exactly what she would do. There was something amiss. She was not sure what, but she sure as hell would find out.

Darby shifted her car into gear, backed out of her spot, drove down the ramp, and headed for the exit.

She would fight them all, and get that letter out of her file, despite the risk of her head popping up on the radar. Hell it was so far up as it was, what did it matter? Then she would do whatever it took to make sure another accident like Pacific Airlines 574 never happened again.

Merging into the line of cars, she waited her turn to exit. Within minutes she stuck her ticket in the slot and the gate opened. As the bar dropped behind her car, her phone rang—scheduling.

"First Officer Bradshaw, we have a trip for you tomorrow."

Darby pulled into her driveway, her resolve strong. She opened her phone and called Dodd.

"I want to fight this," she said when he answered.

"Are you sure?"

"Yes. This is bullshit. Everything they wrote in that letter is a lie except for the fact that I wrote a post about the crash."

Darby ate a light dinner then packed her bags. She called Kathryn and filled her in on the gist of her meeting, then took a bath and prepared for bed. Keith trickled into her brain and she tried to force him back out.

He finally agreed that her post was something that needed to be said, and they should share this type of information with other pilots. He said Darby was doing a good thing and he understood why she needed to write the blog. But he still wanted her to stop writing.

The previous month their relationship was challenged. His mother died and he was dealing with estate issues on his days off. They played email tag and talked on the phone, but Keith was not himself. She loved him more than he knew and wished she could do something to help him work through whatever was bothering him.

Darby climbed into bed and closed her eyes. She tried to sleep, but the thought of her trip and the plane tugged at her eyelids. She had not flown for eight months. Would she remember how?

She glanced at the clock—2108. Her mind running faster than the time.

Rolling to her side she flopped her feet to the floor and reached for her flight operations manual. It weighed a ton, but she dragged it onto the bed and began to read.

When her mind shifted to the meeting and then to Keith, she glanced at the clock—2315. She dialed his number, but it went directly to voicemail. She hung up without leaving a message and focused on her airplane. The next time she looked up, the clock said 0158 and she closed her eyes—just for a minute.

Darby's eyes popped open at 0700 with a manual on her chest and a warning light flashing in her brain. *Shit. Am I legal to fly?*

She did not receive the high altitude portion of her recurrent training or the required oral. They all knew it too.

Jumping out of bed she headed to the bathroom and stared at herself in the mirror. *What the hell should I do? Fly? Deny the trip? Are they setting me up?*

That damned chain. She wished she could wrap it around someone's neck so they could feel how friggin restricting it was. There was only one thing to do at a time like this—coffee.

She dropped her phone into her robe pocket and headed downstairs. With a caffeinated brain she would think more clearly.

After pouring grounds and water in the coffee maker, she pressed the start button. She thought about calling Kathryn, but that would only put her in a position of taking action. This was something Kathryn could not overlook.

She opened her phone and dialed her union rep.

"Walt, it's me Darby, am I legal to fly? The world knows I didn't get my training."

"Hell, I don't know," he said, "call the training department."

"But I'm supposed to follow the chain of command."

"Email Odell. He'll pick it up on his phone even if he's not in his office. Then you could call training records."

"Training records will only know what's in the computer," she said, heading back upstairs. "They'll see me as legal." She sat at her desk and began typing a message to her chief pilot. "I suspect he pencil whipped the high altitude stuff, like he did the oral."

"The question is, do I take the trip when I know I'm not legal?"

"Call the ALPO safety training rep and ask him."

Dodd gave her the number and she said goodbye. She dialed the training rep's number and brought him up to speed.

"Are you signed off?" He asked.

"Yes."

"Then you're fine."

"You're telling me that if I know that I didn't get the training, and they pencil whipped the records that—"

"Don't put words in my mouth!" he snapped. "I didn't say pencil whip."

"Whoa cowboy. Sorry. Let's rephrase…I guess this is a question of ethics. If they signed me off when I know I didn't get my training, you're saying it's okay to fly. That I'm legal."

"I don't know that you didn't get your training."

"I'm telling you that I did *not* get it." She glanced at her watch. "I've got to report in a few hours. Am I legal to fly?"

"I don't know. Why are you calling me with this anyway?" His voice, a few octaves higher than when they had started this conversation, pushed all her buttons.

"Listen," Darby said with a hand on her hip. "I'm calling you because Dodd gave me your number and told me to. So don't go off on me. You're the safety rep. If you don't know, then who does?" She closed her eyes and counted to three. "Just forget I even called."

Darby pressed end and threw her phone on the bed.

Half of her wanted to call in sick, but the other half wanted to fly her plane. She had been begging for a trip for far too many months to give up this opportunity. But without flying for eight months, was she setting herself up for failure? More accurately, were they setting her up?

She checked her email. Odell had not responded. She had no idea what to do.

CHAPTER 45
LOS ANGELES, CALIFORNIA

AUGUST 20, 2012

DARBY PULLED her suitcase down the hall of the Los Angeles Hilton toward her room. It was just past 0600 and she yawned, counting the minutes before she could go horizontal.

The night was long and she stayed up for all of it. She also received a line check. Surprise. Surprise. Like she did not see that one coming.

Someone could put her on a plane and find a check airman to match her schedule, yet they could not find it in their power to buy her a trip for proficiency. Thank God the check airman turned out to be the same guy who gave her the initial line training on the A330.

After she told him what happened in the simulator and that she never received high altitude training or an oral, he told her that they needed to make a self-disclosure.

This was nothing more than notifying the FAA that a violation occurred. The company would make a plan for corrective action and make sure the said activity never happened again. Not a big deal. This was a 'no harm, no foul, people made mistakes and this is how they made sure it never happened again' statement. A get out of jail free card.

If it was unintentional, they would not be fined. This situation would end differently, but still...

She pressed the magnetic strip to the card reader. She dragged her bags into the room and closed and locked the door, then slid the dead bolt into place. She set her computer bag on the floor, dropped her purse, and threw her hat on the bed.

After plugging her computer into the wall, she punched in the access code for the Internet and logged on.

Walt Dodd discovered that the letter of discipline would remain in her file for three years no matter what they wrote. There was no removing it.

The more she thought about that letter, the angrier she grew. She wished her chief pilot had balls to stand up for what was right instead of selling his ethics to the highest bidder. But then, he was just taking care of himself. Something the old chief pilot would never have done—he would have told them to shove it.

Darby hoped that her ethical compass would always point true north, despite the money someone threw her way.

She glanced at the clock. Forty-five minutes until her conference call. There was still time to wash the plane off her body.

Tilting her face toward the water, she closed her eyes embracing the warmth. She missed Keith more than she imagined she would. They talked the night before and he did not agree with getting the union involved. He'd said, "What's the point?"

He was right, but she did not want the company to think they could write letters with false accusations and step on people. Global was an airline of honesty and integrity. Her efforts would be nothing but a rebuttal in her file. At least it was something.

Maybe her chief pilot was just doing what he had to do, to hold onto the job for the greater good. If he stood up for her and lost his position he would lose the war, so he threw her under the bus.

She poured a handful of shampoo into her hand and rubbed it into her hair and rinsed. Keith needed to get over his need to think management was his ticket to success. It might be, but at what price?

She shut off the water and wrapped her hair in a towel, then grabbed another and pulled it around her body.

Back in her room she climbed on the bed with her cell phone, a pad of paper, and a pen. She yawned as she dialed the main office union counsel, in Oklahoma City.

Pete, the ALPO representative from the Oklahoma City base, invited her to call him to discuss the issue.

"Thanks for calling," he said, far too chipper for her mood. "Tell me what we can do for you."

"I'm calling about the letter in my file," she said rolling her eyes. His playing dumb was not appreciated with her level of fatigue.

"I'm looking at it now. What seems to be the problem?"

"The problem is…the only accurate thing in that letter is that I wrote a post about Pacific Airlines. Nothing else is true."

"Weren't you called into the chief pilot's office about your blog in December and January?"

"No. I was called in for the tone of an email in January and for violating the chain of command in December."

"If you violated a policy there's nothing we can do."

"I didn't violate any policy. There is no written policy for the chain of command and the tone of an email is subjective. If they'd written the letter because I'd blogged about Pacific Airlines and that was it, I'd let it go. But I can't allow the other lies in this letter to stay without a fight. Beginning with this being the third time I've been called in for my blog. It's just not true."

"It appears that they've had numerous meetings with you."

"Yeah, because the boys are pissed that I wrote Mr. Patrick. They're playing with me." Darby's voice shook. "I try to do the right thing at all times. I may not always be successful, but I make an effort. I'm also the first person to admit when I do something wrong, but this letter is bullshit."

Darby pulled a hand through her hair, "My blog about Pacific Airlines was accurate, concise, and something that pilots should read. Brock Townsend, the check airman who wrote the systems manual and put the plane into service, said we had a good discussion going, because we did. And it was accurate."

"Excuse me Miss Bradshaw. I'm Mario, an ALPO attorney. I've been listening to the conversation and understand how you feel. I want to help. If you write a letter of rebuttal and send it to me, I'll take a look at it and edit it for legalese. Then I recommend that you contact Brock Townsend and ask him if he'll write you a letter of support. See if you can get the newspaper who published your article to tell you what the public's response was. Do you see where I'm going?"

Darby understood exactly where he was headed. She would gain support to minimize the said damage of her post and attest to the accuracy.

They said their goodbyes and she moved to the desk. She was exhausted and emotionally spent over this situation. Despite the need to sleep, she opened her Gmail account and began to type.

Brock, my blog situation has escalated. The company put a letter in my file. I just got off the phone with the ALPO attorney who suggested I get letters of support for the accuracy. I don't want to put you in a spot, but if you wouldn't mind writing something…your opinion about what I'd written, I'd really appreciate it.

Within minutes Brock responded and said that he was happy to send her something but was on his way to work. He would send it as soon as he returned. She then she typed *New York Tribune* into Google and found a phone number.

Darby dialed the *Tribune* and introduced herself then said, "I wrote a blog that your paper posted. I'm trying to find out what the comments were."

"I'm sorry, I'm not at liberty to discuss this."

"Who can I talk to? I want to know what your readers thought."

"You'll have to speak to a staff attorney."

"Can you connect me?" Darby waited. Two attorneys in one day, she hoped she did not need to go for number three.

"Jacobi. How may I help you?"

"I'm Darby Bradshaw, a pilot for Global Air Lines. My company is after me because your paper printed a post that I wrote about the Pacific Airlines crash. It would help me out if you could tell me what kind of response you received."

Before he could say no, Darby added, "My blog says nothing can be taken without my permission, but I don't care. What's done is done. I'm just trying to find out what the comments were."

"Would you be willing to put that in writing?"

"Absolutely," Darby said.

Darby wrote an email to Jacobi waving her rights to take any recourse in hope of learning what the readers thought. Her intent was to eliminate Airbus fear, not to create it. She pressed send.

Then another email from Townsend came through. Darby's mouth fell open as she read. Her eyes widened. She could not believe what he had written, and so soon.

Darby, This is a letter of support for your blog "Flight For Safety," and specifically the discussion focused on the tragedy of Pacific Airlines 574.

There is a lot of ignorance out there, with no shortage of people making unwarranted disparaging remarks about Airbus aircraft in general and the A-330 in specific. Uninformed claims of bad design, egregious software errors, and composite material failure, among others are easy to find on various discussion boards.

Even those that took the time and effort to read the available accident report do not have enough information (or any basis in fact) to make many of the statements and conclusions they do.

Proper interpretation also requires a knowledge of the airplane's operation to understand such critical areas as the various flight control laws (especially Alternate Law), pitch trim operation, side-stick operation, thrust lever operation, air data computer configuration and more. I thought your explanations helped to inform the ignorant and reduce the fear of the unknown.

No airplane is accident proof. No pilot is immune to error. This is why we study accidents; to promote understanding and enhance safety, while avoiding misunderstanding, misinterpretation, and hysteria. This type of openness is a big reason that aviation and especially commercial aviation is most likely the safest mode of transportation ever devised by man.

I thought your blog in general, and this discussion in specific, did a good job in quelling ignorance and promoting truth, understanding and insight; all the while not reflecting badly on the aircraft, the manufacturer, or Global Air Lines. I was sorry to see that you were forced to remove this excellent vehicle for positive understanding.

Sincerely,

Brock Townsend

Not only did Brock take the time to write before he went to

work, but he wrote more than she hoped he would.

Her phone rang and she jumped. "Hello," she said, as she typed, "Thank You," to Brock for the letter and support.

"Miss Bradshaw, this is Attorney Jacobi from the *Tribune*. It appears that the *Tribune* never printed your blog."

"Would you email me something that states that?"

"My pleasure."

Darby set her phone aside and finished the email to Brock. Then she had one more email to write.

The head of Airbus Industries of Americas communicated with her on several occasions after she wrote the Pacific Airlines post.

Anytime she needed clarification on something Airbus related, Darby wrote him a request to validate the accuracy of her post. After pressing send, she saw another email from Brock—this time from his iPhone.

In response to her 'Thank You' email, Brock wrote, "*No problem. BTW, I just arrived to the schoolhouse and was warned to distance myself from you.*"

CHAPTER 46
SEATTLE, WASHINGTON

AUGUST 25, 2013

EXHAUSTED FROM HER nine-day trip, Darby forced a smile on her face as she climbed aboard the employee bus. She fought to keep her eyes open, but they closed the moment she took her seat. She would rest them for just a few minutes.

What felt like seconds later her head bounced off the window as the bus jerked into the employee parking lot. Stepping into the parking lot, she yawned and scanned the area for her car. Minutes later she was on autopilot for the drive home. Before she knew it, she was pulling into her driveway.

One thing the airlines never addressed were crewmembers in cars and on the freeway after being up all night. Darby arrived safely, but living close to the airport had something to do with that.

Feeling under her seat she found her garage door opener and pressed the button and her eyes narrowed as the door raised.

"What's he doing here?" Darby whispered. "God dammit."

She needed a good night sleep. Tomorrow was the day she would pour herself into the simulator to get special tracked. Dealing with drama of the male persuasion was the last thing she needed, especially after a trip. Besides, he had no right to show up in her home uninvited.

They had a lot to discuss, but now was not the time.

She repositioned her car so not to block his. The least he could do was help her with her bags. She climbed out of the car and slammed the door.

The way the trip worked out, she only received one takeoff and one landing. She was far from legal. But there was something to be said for being part of the crew—something that the assistant chief pilot did not understand.

She pulled her suitcase and flight bag through the garage and closed the door with the button on the wall. She entered through her laundry room.

Normally she would dump all her clothes into the washer, including the uniform she was wearing, but she was too pissed and stormed into the kitchen—empty. The living room was dark, so she headed up the stairs toward her bedroom. *The nerve.*

She had not heard from Keith for five days, not since she talked to the union. He had all but gone missing, not returning her calls or responding to her emails. She had been up all night, was tired, and to say she was in a bad mood would be an understatement.

God damn him. Halfway up the stairs, she heard something below. She hesitated, and then ran back down the stairs, hit the landing and turned the lights on in the living room.

"Hey Sweetie," Neil said, looking up from the comfort of her couch. "When did you get home?"

"Who gave you the right to come into my house uninvited?" She said pissed. "Wrong place at the wrong time, Buddy."

"Babe, don't go off on me now. I've got something you need to know."

She crossed her arms. "You have no idea how capable I am going off on you."

He rubbed his eyes and then squinted at her. "Actually, I think I do," he said, standing.

Darby fought a grin remembering the last time she kicked his ass out the door. "Okay, so you do. But seriously Neil, this isn't right for you to come in here like this. We are not a couple. What if Keith were with me?"

"That's what I wanted to talk to you about."

"You're going to be my dating coach?"

"No, but Stone is up to no good. I overheard he and Armstrong talking about you yesterday."

Darby moved to the couch and sat. "Can't this wait?"

Neil laughed. "That would be a first," he said sitting beside her.

He was right, there was no way her sleep-and-study plan would work with Neil's drama bouncing in her brain. "So tell me what's up," she said glancing his way. "Then leave."

"Armstrong was talking about Stone screwing up and that he'd better get you back."

"What the hell. Is this the first grade or what?"

He leaned on his leg and tilted his head toward her. "I hadn't heard you two broke up. Not that I'm unhappy about that, but the guy's an ass and they're up to something."

"We didn't break up, and you're full of shit."

Darby closed her eyes and dropped back against the cushions. Neil had to be wrong. All the same, a tear leaked from her eye and dribbled down the side of her face. She wiped it away. Maybe that was why she had not heard from him.

"It's the truth," Neil said.

"Then I'm an idiot."

"No you're not. You trust too much."

"Never again."

"We can talk about this later," Neil said standing.

Darby stared at the ceiling. Then pulling a pillow to her chest, she rolled to her side and tucked her legs up and closed her eyes.

Would the boys at Global stop at nothing to get rid of her? *But Keith?*

"Sweetie, it's going to be okay." He touched her hair and she hit his hand away.

"It's not going to be okay," she spat. "Will you just leave? Leave me alone!"

Neil covered her with a blanket, but she never heard him leave.

When she awoke four hours later, the pillow she hugged was mascara stained. She sat upright and shook her head. "This is just great."

She went upstairs, climbed out of her monkey suit, pulled on a pair of shorts and a t-shirt, and returned downstairs and opened the fridge. There was a note on top of a sandwich. *"I may be in the asshole category, but I make one hell of a sandwich. Make sure you eat. Always, N."*

She pulled the plate with Neil's 'Dagwood' from the shelf and grabbed a Diet Pepsi.

When she finished her sandwich, she set the plate in the sink. Neil misunderstood them, but why were they talking about her in the first place?

She and Keith did not break up. They were just having a bit of a rough patch compliments of life.

Darby returned to her computer and clicked the link to her incoming mail, and there was a letter from Keith.

When he went into silent mode on the last five days of her trip she did her best to not catastrophize something that was nothing.

Darby, I've missed you. There is so much happening. I've been dealing with estate issues. Lots going on at work that we need to talk about. Sorry I have not written sooner and hope you had a good trip.

I don't like the way the previous month has been between us. You're right—tense. I'm sorry. To say I feel bad is an understatement. Please forgive me. I've got to go out of town for a few days. I will call the first chance I get.

I love and miss you, Keith

Then Neil's words crept into her brain. The timing of Keith's letter was a little to coincidental. "You bastard," she said, and pressed reply.

Keith, If you think for one second you and the director can play games with me you have something else coming. You're an asshole! No...you're not an asshole...you're a bellybutton! There is a purpose for an asshole and quite honestly I see zero purpose for you. Keith Stone—Fuck Off!

Love always, Darby

She stood and paced, calming with each step. *Do not email when you are tired and emotional.* There was more to what Neil said. She loved and trusted Keith.

A huge sigh escaped. He loved her too. Neil was the proven liar. Darby sat at her computer and pressed delete.

CHAPTER 47
SEATTLE FAA OFFICE

AUGUST 25, 2012

KATHRYN WAS absorbed in paperwork when she looked at her watch, the same moment the phone rang. She was waiting for her boss, Tom Santos, to free up for their morning meeting. The only problem was, it was afternoon.

"Tom has a few minutes now," his secretary said. "You can meet him in the conference room."

"Thanks, I'll be right there." Kathryn hung up and logged off her computer. She opened her briefcase and confirmed both sets of documents were inside. Standing, she took a deep breath then looked in the mirror and adjusted her collar.

"Here goes nothing." She had been waiting a week since the Pacific Airlines preliminary report came through their office to get a meeting with him. Nothing in the FAA moved quickly, but her moment of truth arrived.

A brisk walk down the hall was followed by multiple presses of the up button. She stood tapping her foot with her arms folded. Glancing at her watch again, she thought about the girls and tried to remember if they had soccer practice, or if it had been canceled. Then she thought about the children who died on Pacific Airlines flight 574.

The lives lost were far too many. The devastation of never seeing those you loved again crushed her. Greg's death stung her heart daily. It was hard enough to lose someone in an accident, but to lose them to something so criminal as pilots not knowing how to fly their plane was unimaginable.

Kathryn squeezed the handle of her briefcase a little tighter and tapped the up button a couple more times.

The door finally opened and she selected the seventh floor. She never felt more nervous talking to Tom about anything before this.

The FAA was a different world than the NTSB. Back then she had been confident with her abilities and skills. She knew she was good and that gave her added strength. In this world she was continually slapped down. More for who she was, than her performance.

Sucking a deep breath, she searched for strength with each passing floor.

When the president of the United States intervened allowing her to step into a position with twenty years seniority she upset a lot of people. The assistant inspector general was a surprise. Unfortunately, Tom was included in the disgruntled group of Federal employees.

He grew more patronizing with each day. But if they could work together, he could help to convince the boys at the top of the necessity of this program.

The doors opened and she stepped out of the elevator, turned left and headed down the hallway. The conference room floor was empty. She knocked gently and then opened the door.

Tom sat at the head of the table, leaning back, laughing as he talked on the phone. "Okay, we'll carry this on another time. I've got an appointment waiting," he said waving Kathryn in.

She entered and turned the lights to bright.

Tom set his phone on the table and said, "Thanks for meeting me up here. Just finished a great think-tank session and thought whatever you had to show me might be more fun doing it here." He leaned back in his chair and folded his arms. "Coffee?"

"No thank you," Kathryn set her briefcase on the table and pulled out a chair.

"Before you get too comfortable, could you grab me a cup? Black."

Kathryn sighed. She made her way to the coffee pot and poured him a cup, then placed it in front of him.

"Thank you, Sweetheart," he said.

She cringed at the obnoxious term he only used when they were alone.

"Tom, I'm not your sweetheart," she said. "But I've got one hell of a sweetheart deal." She removed two documents from her briefcase and handed him one. Thirty pages. She retained the other and sat to his right.

"What's this?"

"The future."

"Hmm." He lifted the packet and began to read. His brows knit into one as he flipped through pages, scanning the document. "This looks like a training program."

"That's exactly what it is," Kathryn said, clasping her hands over her copy. "Bottom line is we need to increase training on the automated planes. Pilots need to know how to fly without flight directors, autothrust, and the autopilot. We need to teach them how to fly without the computer. After they've mastered flying with malfunctions and practiced numerous hand flown approaches, we'll teach them how to program the computer and utilize the automation."

"This is anything but the future," he said closing the document. He set it on the table and slid it toward her.

"Please hear me out."

He looked at his watch and said, "The floor is yours. You have ten minutes."

"The training footprints at the airlines have been reduced because of the reliability of the automated aircraft and the ease of flying," Kathryn said. "Not to mention simulator sophistication."

"You have a problem with this?" he asked.

"I do. Airlines see training as a money leak and lobby for us to approve shortened footprints. Manufacturers are pushing for reduced training to make their airplanes sell better. Just because we're recommending pilots to hand fly their planes," Kathryn said exasperated, "there's no verification they are. We're under pressure to approve training programs with minimal amount of time required and it's all backward."

"What's so backward about an industry working toward an economical solution for safe travel?" he asked.

"That's the problem—it's not safe," Kathryn said.

"Excuse me?" Tom slid his chair back and leaned forward pointing a finger at her. "Sweetheart, you had better be a really good shot if you start slinging shit around this office."

"Read my proposal. It's solid."

"I've seen enough. Sixteen days in the simulator for an A330 checkout, who are you kidding? Those planes fly with computers. How long do you think it takes to learn how to program them?"

"That's the point. The pilots are learning how to program computers in abbreviated courses and not learning how to fly. Thank God we have some stick and rudder pilots who knew how to fly a plane before they were hired. What happens when they all retire? Then what? You saw what happened in San Francisco."

"That was a cultural issue."

"That crash was a cultural issue alright. It was the culture of our current industry and pilots who lack ability. If we don't do something, more people will die just like they did on Pacific Airlines."

Kathryn stood and walked to the credenza and poured herself a glass of water and sipped. She needed to cool down before she said something that she would regret. When the glass was half empty, she turned and said, "Had this program been in place two years ago, 228 people would still be alive."

"The final analysis isn't in yet," Tom spat. "Besides, we've got procedures in place demanding higher hours for commercial pilots."

"Yes, but they're learning how to fly and building their flight hours in automated planes with the autopilot. Hell, they would be better off flying gliders. As it is now, when their automation disconnects they won't know how to fly."

"We can't plan for every contingency," Santos said.

"So we plan for none?"

Kathryn walked toward the table. "I joined the FAA because I was tired of cleaning up accidents. I wanted to stop them from happening. This is what I'm trying to do." She sat in her chair and sighed. "Apparently, I'm the only one."

"Don't give me your high and mighty attitude. You have no idea what you're talking about. This goes so much higher than you and I." He slapped his hand on the table and she jumped.

With face red and voice strong he continued. "You think that the government couldn't reregulate the airlines if they wanted to? Fuck yes. But they don't. Do you know why? It's all a fucking game of monopoly. Hell, everyone is in bed with someone. They know what's going on, but they don't care. One planeload of people that insurance covers does not equate to increasing training expenses by millions industry wide."

Kathryn held his stare and neither spoke. Her mind whirled with a thousand pieces of data trying to formulate a response that would help her get him to see the light. His outburst indicated one thing—Tom was frustrated too.

Doing nothing was not the answer.

"Tom," she said lowering her voice. "We both want the same thing. There has to be a way to improve the system. It's training, I know it. This *is* the answer," she said stabbing the document.

"The training programs we've approved are good enough. One accident due to pilot error does not demand an entire industry to change overnight causing millions of dollars in unnecessary training expense."

"One accident, but 228 lives. 574 was more than pilot error. Those pilots did not know how to fly. They also didn't know how to get out of that stall." She left his document on the table and picked up her copy and placed it in her briefcase. "I hope you never have to experience the needless loss of a family member to an airplane crash."

"People die all the time. Do you know how many accidents occur on the freeway daily?"

"We're not responsible for the freeway or the drivers. We're responsible for assuring that our pilots are trained properly in all scenarios. We owe the public that much."

"You can teach a monkey how to fly these planes. They're fool proof."

This meeting was a complete waste of time. Kathryn pushed back her chair. She stood, picked up her briefcase, and walked to the door. Stopping she turned.

He looked at her with eyes wide. "What?"

"Imagine you were taught how to play a piano. You learned your notes well enough to get through a song, but ninety percent of your training was learning how to program a player piano. Then you went on tour and all you had to do for years was know how to program that piano. Then one day your player piano broke, but you still had to play the concert. Could you do it?"

She pulled the door open, hesitated, and then looked back. "I forgot to mention, if you don't play that concert to perfection, you and the 300 people in the audience will die."

CHAPTER 48
GLOBAL TRAINING CENTER
SEATTLE, WASHINGTON

AUGUST 26, 2012

DARBY WALKED INTO the briefing room, pushing Keith from her mind. She needed to focus on flying. Brock was standing when she entered.

"Hey Brock," she said, glad he was the instructor conducting her ride. His reputation was one of being tough, but he was nothing but thorough and a professional. His passion for teaching was trumped only with his knowledge of the plane.

Brock had been her initial instructor and Darby could not have asked for a better opportunity to learn the plane. His lessons were the foundation that saved her ass on the plane she rarely flew.

His checking events were hard, but that was a good thing. Most importantly he always made sure learning took place. Today he could go outside the box and teach her anything and fine-tune her skills. Put the pieces back together.

Brock shook Darby's hand. "I was just upstairs and Armstrong told me we're giving you an oral and a full check ride."

"No. That's not what he told me."

"What's he doing in town?" a man asked, as he walked into the room. "Rob," he said, extending his hand to Darby.

"Apparently he's in town handing out LOEs," Townsend said.

LOE was the acronym for Line Operational Evaluation. She was getting a full checkride. Not that she worried about taking a ride from Brock. He would be fair, but this was wrong on so many levels.

She pulled out a chair and sat with a sigh. "He said that he'd let me do anything I wanted on this visit. That this was a 'customer service' business. He also didn't seem to care that I didn't get an oral or the walk-around the last time we talked."

Darby told Brock and Rob about what happened during her check. They both listened with more than their fair share of facial expressions. Brock finally said, "Well, you're getting an oral today, so we'd better get started.

He asked her a dozen questions and then said, "Good enough for me. Here's the paperwork." He handed Darby a flight plan. "You'll be the pilot flying. Rob will be your captain."

Darby breathed deep as she looked through the paperwork. "Let's go do it," she said, standing.

Brock held out his hand, "Licenses and medical first."

"How soon I forget." She smiled and pulled her licenses out of her purse and waited while he filled out the paperwork. Her nerves tickled below her skin.

After the formalities were complete they headed down to the simulator. Darby climbed into the right seat and looked at the overhead panel. Her mouth fell open.

"What the hell?" she said, not hiding her dismay. The trickle of nerves turned to a chill that ran up her spine.

"I certainly don't need to give you any Easter eggs," Brock said, looking over the panel.

An Easter egg was something hidden in the simulator for the

student to find. A switch moved out of place, low oil quantity... something that needed to be corrected or fixed before flight.

"This is bullshit," she said looking at the overhead panel. "Every button is out of place. This is sabotage!"

Brock laughed, "I'm sure you'll configure the plane just fine."

"Maybe so," Darby said, "But this is a slap in the face. Like someone spraying graffiti on your house while you watch."

"She's right, this is bullshit," Rob said. "Who was in this sim before us?"

"A million bucks says it was Alan Jones," Darby said.

Brock opened his schedule. "That's exactly who it was."

She knew one thing—the fleet training captain talked to Jones, and this was his retaliation.

What bothered her most was that Global had an instructor with this much disregard for safety. He also came from Coastal, which proved one thing—no company was exempt of assholes. She could deal with Jones in the simulator, but on the line she could never be in the flight deck with him. *How far would he go?*

She looked overhead and knew the answer.

When the plane was configured Brock said, "Cockpit, this is the ground. You guys ready to push and start?"

"Standby," Rob said, and then called, "Pre-flight check."

They started engines, completed all checklists, and taxied into position.

When cleared for takeoff Darby moved the thrust levers up assuring power was moving together then placed them in the FLX detent for a reduced power takeoff. After the power was set, she removed her hand from the thrust levers, giving them to the captain for his decision to abort if necessary.

They rotated without incident. As they passed through 1200

feet lights flashed, the autopilot disconnected and bells rang. An electrical abnormal—the exact scenario she experienced months prior. Only this time she was flying with a captain who knew what he was doing and they were each other's support.

"I've got the plane," Rob said.

Darby gave him control. He flew the plane and she handled the ECAM and then the checklist. The ECAM displayed engine parameters, flap position, and messages. The messages told her what steps to accomplish prior to using the Quick Reference Manual—the bible for emergencies.

Other than having an electrical failure with an emergency return, the flight went smoothly and Darby felt confident she could handle anything. She glanced back at Brock and then to Rob. What a difference professionals made.

Once they came to a stop on the runway, Brock said, "Nice job." He turned toward the instructor's console. "I'd like to try something if you guys don't mind."

"Not at all," Darby said thankful they were done. "Thanks for your help, Rob."

"You kidding? Anytime," he said. "Excellent job."

Brock took the plane up to 35,000 feet. While the simulator was catching up to itself he said, "I want to see how this plane reacts at altitude in Alternate Law with a stall. We're going to attempt to relive Pacific Airlines flight 574."

"Rob, when I release the sim, I want you to pull the stick back to the stop and hold it. When you're in a full stall, recover."

"Got it," Rob said. "Ready when you are."

Brock unfroze the simulator and put them in Alternate Law. The nose pitched up as Rob pulled the sidestick aft. Darby selected the flight control page and watched the stabilizer roll toward a full trim up position.

In all the planes she flew prior to the Airbus the pilot was responsible for trimming. The Airbus trimmed itself. Rob pulled back to a 30-degree pitch attitude and the simulator continued cranking in nose up trim to assist in relieving back pressure.

The stall warning cried and the nose dropped. Rob fought to get her flying again. He held the stick forward to fly her out of the stall, but as the jet gained speed in the descent the plane hit a point where the wings wanted to fly. As he came neutral on the stick, the plane pitched up and stalled again. It was as if the plane was a porpoise breaking the crest and diving into the waves. With each dive, it came closer to hitting the ocean floor.

The plane trimmed itself to a nose high pitch attitude to help the pilot when he pulled the stick full aft. Unfortunately, the trim was still aft when Rob wanted to push the nose forward.

Brock said, "I've got it." He froze the simulator in a pitch down moment and looked at the stabilizer trim—the horizontal fin on the tale of the airplane was 27 degrees up.

"Can I try it?" Darby asked.

"Sure," Brock said. He repositioned them to 35,000 feet, put the plane in Alternate Law, and then she pulled the stick full aft.

The nose went up. The plane shook and cried, "Stall. Stall. Stall." When the nose fell, Darby pulled the power to idle—something that Rob had not done.

She pushed the nose forward and held it nose down to gain airspeed. Not until she felt the wings flying again did she smoothly add power, simultaneously raising the nose, and flew out of the stall. She glanced at the altimeter—they lost 7000 feet, but they lived and the plane flew.

Rob's head bobbed. "Interesting."

With cruise power on engines bolted underneath a wing, the plane wanted to lift the wings and fly as the airspeed increased. Pulling the power to idle while pushing the nose over and allowing the trim to undo itself, appeared to be the answer.

"Let's try this again, but with TOGA power," Brock said.

He put them up at altitude and this time the aircraft stalled Rob added full thrust—TOGA. Takeoff and go around power—the most thrust the plane could acquire. He pushed the nose down and the plane rolled over on its back.

At a high altitude with the 50,000 pounds of thrust, with engines hanging under the wing, this created an upward lifting motion and induced an accelerated stall, but Darby noticed TOGA was not much higher than cruise power at their altitude.

Why it rolled, she had no idea, but they were flying outside the parameters the simulator had been tested and certified.

The pilots on Pacific Airlines initially did nothing with their thrust. At one point they increased it to TOGA, but they were not at cruise, they were already falling from the sky with the sidestick held full back. Max power at that point did nothing for them.

All motion stopped as Brock froze the simulator. The screens went blank. Silence. Darby thought about Pacific Airlines' final minutes. They fell flat like a maple leaf drifting to the ocean—at more than 10,000 feet per minute.

If only the crew on Pacific Airlines flight 574 had received high altitude and unreliable airspeed training, something that Jones shortchanged her on. She glanced back and watched Brock punch buttons sending them to altitude again.

If only planes had a reposition button, many lives could be saved.

CHAPTER 49
SEATTLE, WASHINGTON

AUGUST 26, 2012

KEITH PULLED INTO Darby's driveway, not sure what to do with the information he held. He glanced at his watch. In less than an hour she would be out of the simulator. He closed his eyes and rested his head on the steering wheel.

He needed to tell her everything, but if he did he would be putting her in harms way more than she already was. He sucked a deep breath and shut off his car.

Darby jumped into a pad of cement with her unwillingness to give up her fight for safety, and that damn blog. He only hoped he could break her free before they buried her.

The fear of harm coming to the woman he loved took hold, and he could not shake it. Darby always said, "Don't make decisions based on fear." But what the hell was he supposed to do?

Keith climbed out of his car and walked up the path. He stuck his key into the lock, glancing over his shoulder he opened her front door.

He stepped into the entryway and then into the living room. He stopped and looked around the room. He rubbed his chin, then headed down the hall.

Once in the kitchen he pulled open a drawer, then another, and then closed them both. He headed upstairs into her bedroom and sat on the bed. He slid a hand over her pillow and pulled it to his face, breathing deep, inhaling Darby's scent. God he missed her.

Placing the pillow back where it belonged, he looked around the room. His mind spun rapidly with options. When his phone rang, he jumped. He looked at the number and pressed deny. He had but minutes to get the hell out of there and on his way.

He opened Darby's nightstand drawer and grinned at what he saw. He stood with the book and pulled the pen from his pocket and headed downstairs.

Keith returned to the kitchen and set the book and pen on the table. A car drove down the street and he pulled back a sliver of curtain as it slowed. "Shit."

He picked up her mail and sorted through the envelopes until he came to the union bill. Darby always doodled motivations for ALPO on the envelope. She said that they were subliminal messages to help them find their way. This envelope would eventually be looked at—by her eyes only.

His cell phone rang again and flashed the same number as earlier. He pressed deny and picked up a pen from the table and wrote the address on the envelope. He returned the envelope into the mix of mail, then stood and grabbed a knife from the drawer.

CHAPTER 50
GLOBAL TRAINING CENTER
SEATTLE, WASHINGTON

AUGUST 26, 2012

WALKING OUT of the training center Darby took a deep breath. She was glad to have that out of the way. More than that, it felt good to get her confidence back. Global needed more instructors like Brock Townsend.

Darby climbed into her car, but Armstrong hung there like a bad odor. She would not have been upset about his orders if he had not asked her to email him and then responded by confirming she could do anything she wanted in the simulator.

She drummed her fingers on her steering wheel debating whether or not she should go up and talk to him. He set her up. He told her one thing and did another. Not to mention, within the hour after her union call to Oklahoma someone called this office and warned Brock to distance himself from her. There was no question, that warning came from Armstrong.

This was Brock's test to see if he heeded the warning. She hoped his integrity and sense of fairness would not be his demise.

Armstrong anticipated her coming prepared for nothing. Then Keith's warning played through her brain—Never talk bad about one of his instructors. Now she understood why—they get even.

Darby started her car, shifted into reverse, and backed out of her spot. Then she thought about Armstrong talking to Keith about her. She slammed her foot on the brake.

Her name with Keith's out of Armstrong's mouth was wrong on so many levels. Then it hit her. He was putting Keith's instructing job on the line because of her. *That bastard.*

This job meant everything to Keith, and what Armstrong was doing was a bunch of crap no matter how she flushed it.

She wanted it to stop, whatever 'it' was. Putting her car into drive she returned to her parking spot.

Heading toward the training center she ignored the voices that told her 'don't do it Darby'. She scanned her ID into the box and punched in her security code, stabbing the buttons for emphasis.

Darby pushed the door open and headed for the stairs.

One of the rules she lived by was—never let a barking dog chase you. In the plane she set different standards. There was always a time and a place for everything. She was on the ground, just nailed her simulator session, and was ready to kick butt.

Barking back at this dog was the only way she would get him off her ass. There was only one problem—she never dealt with a military trained animal before. But a dog was a dog. They all lifted their legs and licked their balls.

Reaching the top floor she headed down the hall. Surprise covered her face with what she saw. The cubes were empty. The walls were bare. They were actually closing up shop and moving.

Global promised to keep operations in Seattle running and sure enough the wheels were in motion to shut everything down. She never expected it would happen so soon. A graveyard took place where there was once was life and creation.

Sucking a breath, Darby continued her pursuit.

An A330 Fleet Training Captain placard stuck to his door, and a light crept from underneath. Reaching her hand up to knock, she hesitated. Maybe this was not a good idea. As the case would be, sometimes her body had a mind of its own. Before she knew it, her hand was connecting to the wood in a rapid-fire motion.

"Come in," Armstrong called.

Darby opened the door, and confusion flashed through his eyes and then he smiled.

"I'm Darby Bradshaw."

"Nice to meet you Darby," he said leaning back. "What can I do for you?"

She wanted to tell him he'd done quite enough, but instead she said, "I'm done with my special tracking event."

"Good. I trust Captain Townsend took good care of you."

"Better than you could imagine," she said with a grin.

"Glad to hear it." His eyes narrowed.

"How did he know that I wanted an oral and LOE?" Her sarcasm obvious and Armstrong's composure shifted, but their eyes remained locked.

"Glad it was a positive experience for you," he said flatly.

"Oh, it was," Darby said folding her arms. Not sure how far she should press, but she would be damned if she allowed Keith's job to be in jeopardy because of her.

"Anything else?" he asked.

"Just one thing." She hesitated gauging his composure and then sucked a deep breath deciding to punt and let the balls fly where they may. "I know what you're doing, and you're not going to get away with it. Game's over."

CHAPTER 51

KEITH PULLED HIS COAT tight as he closed Darby's front door, then headed toward his car. He hid what was tucked into his waistband. The street was empty, but he felt eyes everywhere.

People died for much less than what he knew.

He did everything possible to get Darby off the radar, but she was just being Darby. She was on the top of the flagpole and pissed the wrong people off. Then her damn blog started them to worry.

Keith climbed into his car and locked the doors.

He did his best to convince her to stop blogging. That just created tension between them. He thought distance would help keep her safe, but they wanted him close to monitor her. As it turned out, that was the only way to protect her.

Darby would never stop trying to make the industry safer. Unfortunately they knew that too, which made her a wild card.

Armstrong knew all about his and Darby's fight. While that worked well for Keith and their believing he was on their team, he was not happy that those bastards bugged her home.

They did everything they could to control her, but they finally realized—there was no controlling Darby Bradshaw. She had a way of walking into the middle of a shit storm and flinging it back instead of ducking.

If he could turn the clock back he would have quit training the day he had learned what they were doing. When he realized why, he was dumbfounded. How the hell they could do any of this was beyond him. Their belief that he would go along with them was their greatest mistake.

Get along and protect her was no longer working. They were in too deep. Telling her what was happening would put her on top of their hit list, but what else could he do?

He sighed. Darby would have an answer. After he took care of business he would tell her everything. They would have a solution by nightfall.

Despite what they thought, he was no fool. He would nail their asses one way or another.

Keith dialed Darby's number and left her a message.

"Sweetheart, I've got to go to Wenatchee to take care of an estate issue. We need to talk. Call me as soon as you get this. It's important. I love you."

CHAPTER 52

DARBY PULLED INTO Kathryn's driveway, and put her car into park. She contemplated going straight home, not passing go, and dropping into bed. But she knew she would not sleep—despite the fact she was still jet lagging from her trip. Thoughts of Keith, training, and standing up to the fleet training captain would slap her awake all night. She needed to talk to Kathryn.

Her life was off balance. Times like this there was no place like Kathryn's home so she opened the car door and dropped her feet to the pavement. She just sat there, having a mental adjustment before she became a Darby Downer.

The boys at Global were definitely playing dirty, but how far would they go? She only hoped Keith was not playing a game of duplicity with her. No. She knew better.

Keith Stone was the most down to earth man she knew. He was always blatantly honest with her. He had no problem telling her about his failures, but he also was not afraid to jump in her shit when she needed it. He was on her team.

But still, something was up.

Darby tilted her head to the sky and spread her arms wide and yelled, "Why can't I just find a normal guy?"

"Hey you," Kathryn called from the doorway. "How'd it go?"

Darby startled and opened her eyes. "Fantastic." She grinned at the sight of her friend's huge smile. Closing the car door she headed toward the house, stuffing the confrontation with Armstrong away for another time.

Kathryn jumped down off the porch saying, "I knew it'd be fine." She wrapped her arm through Darby's and pulled her toward the house. "Can I offer you a glass of wine?"

"You're sure happy tonight. Good day at work?"

"Nope. Just the opposite." Kathryn said stepping through the doorway. "But nothing that alcohol can't fix."

A half empty bottle of cab sat on the coffee table. An empty glass sat next to an open book on the endtable.

"Where are the girls tonight?" Darby asked removing her jacket.

"Overnight at a friend's house."

"And you're not working?" When Kathryn had an empty house and was not trying to fix the industry or the FAA, something was wrong.

"Not tonight. They don't give a shit so why should I?"

"I'm feeling the same way my friend." Darby walked over to the couch and sank in. She picked up the book—*Flight For Control*, and smiled. "What do you think?"

"I feel like I've lived this story. The scary thing is, it's what's going on in the airline industry with the flight crews. It hits way too close to home. If Tom Clancy wrote about airliners, this would be it. You have to read it."

"I did," Darby said, setting the book down, "a couple times." She poured herself a glass of wine, and topped off Kathryn's. "So what's up? Why aren't you working? Are you sick? Do you have a fever?" Darby placed a hand to her forehead.

Kathryn laughed and brushed it away. "Oh I'm burning up alright, but nothing that a thermometer could identify." She lifted her glass and swirled the wine, staring into the red liquid. "My boss is an asshole."

"I've been telling you that for a year," Darby said.

"He doesn't give a damn about fixing anything. I thought he cared and was as frustrated as I was. But if he is, he's a gutless wimp. His ego struts around that building all day, but he won't do a damn thing. The prick is playing with me, and I've had enough."

Darby laughed. *Prick?* This was another side that she did not often see. Her friend—mature and professional—obviously had a boiling point too, or she had been hanging around with Darby too long.

"What'd he say about your proposal?"

"Our proposal," Kathryn said, tipping her glass toward Darby. "He glanced at it. Shoved it across the table toward me, and said they'd never go for it. Blah, blah, blah."

"Did you tell him how you came up with the scenario?"

"He didn't give me a chance."

"A chance for what?" Jackie asked from the doorway. You guys having a party without me?" She wandered into the room and sat beside Darby. "How'd training go?"

"Good, but right now we need to babysit that one," Darby said pointing to Kathryn.

"What happened to her?" Jackie asked.

"Her boss is playing with her."

"Can you blame him? Look at her—she's one hot little mamma."

"Ladies. I'm right here," Kathryn said, laughing.

"What happened?" Jackie asked.

"Proposal." Darby sighed. "And not the marrying kind."

"I wanted to increase the training footprint on the electronic planes. We're going to have problems with pilots not knowing how to fly in the future. Pacific Airlines and San Fran were just the tip of the iceberg. Tom blew me off."

"We'd thought the Pacific Airlines crash would be catalyst to make this a go," Darby said. "Guess we were wrong."

"The guys at work said the crash was the plane's fault," Jackie said, removing her jacket. "They said the computers failed and there was nothing they could do to save it, and that it doesn't fly like a real plane."

"Not true," Darby said. "We just flew the scenario in the simulator. Granted we knew what was happening and were able to anticipate and prepare for what we were going to do. Turbulence and noise from the storm were also not factors."

She sipped her wine and added, "The pilots screwed up from the get go. After they stalled the plane they could have flown out of it if they knew how to do a stall recovery. Besides—"

"So they're going to blame the pilots despite the broken plane?" Jackie snapped. "Airbus needs to take responsibility for building an airplane that pilots can't fly when they lose their computers!"

Kathryn and Darby exchanged a glance and Darby's eyebrow rose with a mind of its own.

"Sweetie, I don't think that's what Darby means." Kathryn placed a hand on her arm.

Jackie's look was one of fear she had not seen in a couple years. Who's to blame haunted Jackie ever since her husband's death, despite the fact they all knew he was just a victim.

"I'm sorry. I don't think the pilots are to blame," Darby said.

"But you just said—"

"I think the airline is to blame for not training them. I blame the FAA for not mandating better training." Darby tipped back her glass and reached for the bottle.

"Not until the public gets mad enough will anything change," Darby said. "Look what happened with the pilots that crashed that triple seven in San Francisco. Nothing."

She topped off her glass and handed it to Jackie. "As long as it's cheaper to pay off insurance claims than it is to train pilots properly, the system will remain broken and people will die."

"I'm afraid you're right. Tom said the same thing," Kathryn said. "I don't know what to do. I've exhausted all options at work."

"If your boss agrees with you, then why isn't he doing anything?" Jackie asked.

"He's a gutless wimp," Darby said winking at Kathryn.

Kathryn smiled. "He says they all know and they don't care. It's all about money."

"Now I'm totally depressed." Darby leaned back into the couch. She knew all too well about political suicide. She took her glass from Jackie and sipped. "You two ready for the laugh of the century?"

"Yes. Please liven up this party," Kathryn said. "We haven't had a good Darbyism in a long time."

"So, I get back from my trip yesterday and Neil's in my house."

"How'd he get in?" Jackie asked.

"Key. Duh," Darby said. "But that's not the point." She handed her glass to Jackie. "So, I find him sleeping on my couch."

"Kind of like Goldilocks and the three bears," Jackie said.

"He has no right to enter without invitation." Kathryn stood and pulled a wine glass from the bar.

"Will you two just let me tell you what happened," Darby said with a laugh.

"Sorry," Jackie said. Kathryn pretended to lock her mouth with an invisible key and toss it aside. She poured a glass of wine and set it in front of Darby since Jackie claimed ownership of the floater.

"So Neil's sleeping on my couch. I wake him up and tell him off for being there. Then he tells me that he'd overheard the fleet training captain and Keith talking about our breaking up."

"I didn't know you broke up," Jackie said.

"We didn't, but Armstrong supposedly told Keith that he needed to make up with me."

"Neil's lying. He just wants you back," Jackie said.

"I know you're right," Darby said, pulling a hand through her hair. "Then Keith sent me an email saying that we needed to talk." She kicked off her shoes. "I trust him, but something's going on."

"This is serious." Kathryn set her glass on the table and leaned forward. "Their calling you in for violating the chain of command, the blog, and being 'reined in'. Now the fleet training captain and Keith? It's all adding up to one stinky mess."

"Don't forget my line check and they sabotaged my simulator tonight." Darby pulled her feet under herself on the couch.

"They sabotaged your sim?" Kathryn said.

Darby nodded, and then over the second bottle of wine she told her friends about what happened in the simulator, followed by her visit to Armstrong's office and that she learned her post on 547 had never been printed in the newspaper.

"You need to go to H.R." Jackie said.

"I think it's time for an attorney," Kathryn added. "They're messing with your career. I'm afraid you've kicked a hornet's nest with that visit to Armstrong. We've been saying this is a coincidence for far too long. It's more than that. I'll shut them down before—"

"Thought you were giving up?" Darby grinned.

"Hell no. Not with this going on. I'm fighting mad," Kathryn said with wine-induced confidence. "We'll beat them all!"

"I don't think Keith's part of whatever their up to," Darby said. "I think their hanging his job in training over his head, trying to get at me. I'm not sure if I'm upset or sad that he didn't have the confidence to tell me." She sighed.

"What are you going to do?" Jackie asked.

"Talk to him," Darby said.

Kathryn laughed. "That's always a good plan."

"Make-up sex is going to be great." Darby raised her glass in an air toast, then dug through her purse and found her phone.

She missed two calls, both from Keith. Just as she was about to press listen, her phone rang.

"Hi, Sweetie," she said. "I forgot to unsilence my phone after the sim."

"I was worried when you didn't answer," he said.

"You don't need to worry about me. Training went great. I kicked butt." Her talk with Armstrong would be saved for a later date when they were sitting together.

He breathed deep and asked, "Can you meet me? We need to talk, and not on the phone. I'm in the mountains at *our* place."

A smile spread across her face, and she glanced at her watch. It was 1845. "I can leave now and be there by seven-forty-five, give or take a few minutes."

Being in Keith's arms was the best thing she could think of. "You're going to have to do some major sucking up when I get there." She winked at her friends.

"I know," he said, "for so much."

"Better yet, I'll see you in the casino at eight. If I'm hauling my ass to the mountains for a guy, I want to get a little gambling in."

"Call me when you're fifteen minutes out," Keith said. "And Darby…be careful."

Darby clicked the phone off, thought about the be careful comment for less than a second, and stood. "Okay ladies, I'm ditching this party. Keith's at Snoqualmie Pass. He has a room and he needs me."

She stuffed her phone into her purse. "Make up sex is mere hours away," she said doing a happy dance.

"You're not going anywhere," Kathryn said. "You're not driving that far after you've been drinking."

Darby stopped mid motion and stared. She opened her mouth and then closed it. Kathryn was right. "But—"

"No buts. The only way you're going to the mountains this time of night is in a cab."

"They won't be here for an hour and that's going to be like over a hundred bucks," Darby said.

"I'll drive you," Jackie said. "I haven't drank that much."

"No. Neither of you are driving anywhere," Kathryn snapped. "Keith can stew for the night. He'll be fine. You can drive up tomorrow morning with a venti coffee in hand."

Darby glanced at the door, then back to Kathryn. She was probably right. Besides, discussions with alcohol involved were never a good idea. Emotions always got involved and distorted issues.

"Okay," she sighed. "Then how about we order pizza. I'll call Keith and tell him I'll see him in the morning."

Chapter 53

Salish Lodge, Washington

KEITH BREATHED DEEP, Darby was on her way. He sat at the desk and stared at Snoqualmi Falls. Arriving at Salish lodge twenty minutes earlier he checked in, thankful room 408 was available. Being on the Spa level it had everything Darby loved—sauna and hot tub down the hall, their own butler, afternoon wine and cheese, couples massages—and him.

He hoped her love would survive what he had to tell her. If it was the last thing he did, he would make it up to her. He stepped into something serious and now it might be too late, but he would tell her everything. He pushed away from the desk and stood.

Keith stopped in Wenatchee before he came to the hotel. He contemplated having her meet him at the cabin, but if she were followed that would be just a little too isolated. They needed to talk in a public place. He turned down the heat, and walked to the window.

He would have gone directly to the authorities, but he was not sure how high this went. If he jumped too soon, he might allow the ring leader to escape and play again. He reached his hand to the window, the glass cold beneath his touch, and gazed out.

Water fell over the Falls with enough power to light a city. He stared for a moment, then grabbed his jacket and turned from the window.

Keith wandered downstairs and out the front of the hotel. He walked across the overpass and unlocked his car door. He turned the key, and then drove out of the parking lot and headed for the casino. He was on autopilot. His mind consumed with what to do about everything. For once he would listen to Darby.

The Salish Casino was over the hill. Five minutes on I-90 and two exits down the street. Within minutes he arrived.

He gave his keys to the valet, and squeezed his way into the casino. The place was packed. He wandered right, glancing at the players as he went. He passed by *Lit*. A quaint little smoke shop bar. Keith loved a good cigar now and again and Darby always said, "I'll try anything once."

The room was filled with smoke. He smiled at the memory of her holding a cigar and mouthing it, saying, "Are you sure you want to light this perfectly good phallic symbol? I have something better in mind." Then she winked.

His heart sank knowing how badly he hurt their relationship by not confiding in her. He left the bar and continued his walk through the casino glancing at his watch as he did. Then he saw *12 Moons Piano Bar,* and pushed through the crowd.

Darby loved piano music. He poked his head inside. The room was small and the pianist was setting up. Keith stepped up to the bar and ordered a Wild Turkey on the rocks.

He was shocked when he learned the truth about what was happening. Did they really think he would go along? Darby was right—they assumed he could be bought and everyone had a price, but his price stopped at the cost of death.

The right place at the wrong time was the story of his life. When they invited him to be part of their game, he played along to buy time. He may have been gullible, but there were some things he would not do.

He gave the bartender a ten-dollar bill, and walked across the room and snagged a stool at the piano.

"Hey asshole," someone said, slamming into him. Keith grabbed the piano before he fell off the stool.

"What the fuck?" Keith said turning. "What the hell are you doing here?"

"Following you," Neil said.

"Get the hell out. I don't have the patience for a drunk."

"I don't have patience for anyone who's screwing with Darby," Neil spat as he steadied himself on the piano.

"We're on the same page, buddy." Keith turned away and took a long drink, trying to figure out how to get rid of the putz before Darby arrived.

"I'm not on any page with you." Neil smacked Keith's arm and half his drink flew out of his glass. "You'd better tell me what the hell you're doing with my girl!"

"Your girl?" Keith wiped his jeans. He set the glass on the piano and placed a five-dollar bill into the tip jar and said, "Sorry."

He pushed past Neil. "Go sleep it off asshole."

"Fuck you," Neil shouted, following close behind. "I heard you and Armstrong talking." Neil grabbed Keith's arm and pulled him back. "I know what you're doing."

Keith yanked his arm free. "You don't know shit. Stay out of it." He turned and headed out of the bar. His goal was to create distance so he wouldn't take his anger out on Neil's face.

Neil yelled, "You're fucking her because Armstrong told you to."

Keith stopped and turned. Neil closed the distance and stood in front of him.

"You have no idea what you *think* you heard," Keith said. "I'm meeting her tonight." He stared at Neil. "I love her. I'm going to marry that woman."

"Over my dead body," Neil yelled and slammed into Keith who fell backward into someone. "She doesn't want to have anything to do with you. I told her what you Dickwads said."

"You did *what*?" Keith's heart free fell to the pit of his stomach as he scrambled to gain his balance. "You fucking don't know what you did."

"Boys, I think it's time you both leave."

Keith looked toward the man touching the gun in his holster and back to Neil. Could this night get any more out of control? "I'm sorry, sir," Keith said to the security guard he'd fallen into. "Just a little misunderstanding."

"I told Darby what an asshole you are," Neil said. "She'll never have anything to do with you." The security guard stepped between them and placed a hand on Neil's chest, holding him back.

Keith closed his eyes and shook his head. She had to be crushed. Yet she was still coming to see him. That was what she meant by he had a lot to make up to her. She listened to Neil's lies and still had faith in him.

Never before had a woman turned his world upside down like Darby did.

He looked from Neil to the security guard. "Officer, I'm sorry," he said. "It won't happen again." He turned, and headed toward the door.

Neil yelled, "Did you hear me? Stay away from her, or else!"

Raising a middle finger over his shoulder, Keith walked out of the casino.

CHAPTER 54

KEITH RETURNED to the lodge and parked his car across the street in the guest parking lot. He pulled his phone out to call Darby and saw that he missed her call.

When he listened to the words that she was not coming until morning, his heart sank. Maybe it was just as well with Neil nearby.

He tucked his keys into his pocket and walked over the bridge to the main entrance of the hotel. His heart still raced from his confrontation with Neil, and more so with the frustration that he could not talk to Darby. She said she would give him a wake up call, 'up close and personal' in the morning. They could talk then.

Walking into the hotel, he climbed the stairs to his room. He lay down on his bed and stared at the ceiling. Little hairs stood up on the back of his neck. He closed his eyes. His time was limited, that he was sure of.

Keith rolled off the bed and sat at the desk overlooking the falls. He pulled stationary out of the drawer and a pen from his pocket and began to write. "Dearest Darby…"

When he was done he placed the letter in an envelope, sealed it, and set it on the desk. He walked to the bathroom and splashed water on his face.

He thought about going to the bar for a nightcap, but did not want to see anyone. Especially Neil, afraid what he might do to him the next time their paths crossed. But then, he too loved Darby. He couldn't blame him for that.

Returning to his room, he pulled on his raincoat and stepped toward the door. He glanced back, returning to the desk he picked up Darby's letter. He stuffed it into the inside pocket of his jacket and zipped it closed.

Keith left the hotel and walked down the path toward the lookout point, the stairs were slick and he stepped with caution.

The roar of the Falls did not block out the hell that became his life. He slipped and steadied himself. He was trapped in a bag of political bullshit. Thoughts of the Pacific crash hung in his mind.

He knew what was going through those pilots' minds when they lost everything and did not know what to do. Fear like that should never be experienced by anyone. Darby saved him. Who saved Pacific Airlines and their passengers? Nobody.

Once the Pacific reports came out he told Armstrong what happened on his flight. His greatest concern was if Keith told anyone. That should have been his first clue. It was not too long after that, until he learned why Armstrong never asked him about the ASR.

Keith was too embarrassed to say anything to anyone. In light of what was pulled from the bottom of the ocean, he needed to tell someone. They needed to tell the world that pilots did not know how to fly their planes. More than that, they needed to tell them why. Armstrong had other plans.

The reasons were all tied into his fucking plan to make a buck.

Keith approached the lookout point. The lodge glowed to his left. He counted floors and then his eyebrows came together. Someone was in his room. Then he realized it was the butler and looked away. His mind flew circles around all that happened.

The wind picked up and whipped through the trees. Keith pulled his coat closed and zipped it to his chin. He walked to the edge and placed his hands on the railing and looked out.

He smiled at the thought of Darby when they stood in this exact spot. She cautiously slid one foot toward the railing, and then the next, before she moved close enough to look over the edge.

Her fear of heights added to the complexity of the bravest woman he knew. Granted the lookout was about 500 feet high, but the railing was strong and she wasn't tall enough to fall over it even if she wanted to. He loved her with all his heart and touched his hand to his chest.

He glanced at his watch—2230. He could be down the hill in an hour and could wait on her porch until she returned home. Or he could go pick her up at Kathryn's. He should not allow another minute to pass without being by her side. Keith pulled out his phone and dialed her number.

A shadow moved across the sidewalk and he turned with the phone to his ear.

Everything happened at once—Darby's voice said, "If you love me, leave a message at the beep." Keith stared, digesting what was happening and then said, "What the hell are you doing?"

The look in his eyes and forward motion answered Keith's question. He slammed into Keith's chest and Keith fell backward against the railing.

The second charge rammed Keith's shoulder and he dropped his phone. The third assault found Keith's upper body bent over the railing and his feet being lifted. He kicked wildly.

"What the fuck?" He yelled.

Keith kicked with all his strength, but that added to his tilting farther off balance. He was over the edge.

Gripping bars, with feet planted on 12 inches of earth outside the railing, he screamed as he held on with all his strength. This could not be happening. He yelled again, but the roar of the Falls muted his voice, and rain kept visitors away.

"You won't get away with this," he cried, his eyes darting left and right for a plan of escape. He glanced down and then looked up, just as a foot smashed into his face.

His arms let loose and his body flew backward as he fell over the ledge. Closing his eyes he said a prayer for Darby.

CHAPTER 55
SEATTLE, WASHINGTON

AUGUST 27, 2012

ROLLING ONTO HER SIDE Darby tried to ignore the pounding. She closed her eyes tight to catch a few more winks and hoped the noise was the continuation of her nightmare so she could remain in bed.

But reality was a bitch and then you became one. She breathed deep, opened her eyes, and swung her feet off the edge of the bed. She put her face in the palm of her hands willing her headache to disappear. When the pounding continued, she yelled, "Coming! Keep your panties on."

Darby stood, looked around the room and her face turned to a scowl. "What the hell?"

The drawers in her room all hung open a smidge—one of her pet peeves. She peered inside one and her stuff was askew. Her closet was cracked open too. She opened the door wide and everything was off.

Lesson of life—do not search for anything drunk. She pressed her drawers closed, but for the life of her could not remember what the heck she had been looking for. The pounding continued.

Taking a deep breath she was halfway down the stairs when she stopped and looked at her attire. She contemplated going back upstairs for a robe, but pressed on. When she reached the bottom of the stairs, she looked around. Her living room was in the same condition—nothing in place. She shook her head and turned toward the pounding.

She pulled the end of her t-shirt down to cover her red panties and opened the door.

"Cute outfit," Kathryn said from her porch. "You ready for our run?"

"Hardly. What time is it anyway?"

"Time to run off our headaches with a sprint to Starbucks. I'm buying. I left my car there, so it's a one way run for you."

"How about you dash off to get coffee, and I'll go back to bed."

"Okay," Kathryn said. "Here's your paper." She handed Darby the *Seattle Times*. "Call me when you're human."

Darby nodded and closed the door. She wandered into the kitchen, tossed the paper on the table, and filled her coffee pot with water and added coffee. She poured herself a half glass of orange juice, opened a bottle of ibuprofen and swallowed three pills.

She was not going back to bed. She needed a shower and then was off to the mountains where she and Keith would go back to bed together.

Darby headed for her bathroom to shower while her coffee brewed. With one foot on the first stair the pounding at the door began again. She smiled, closed her eyes and shook her head. *Friends, you gotta love 'em.*

"The answer is still no," she said opening the door. Kathryn was not standing there. Instead, two police officers stood on her front porch.

"Are you Darby Bradshaw?" the young one asked.

"Yeah," Darby said, trying to connect the dots as to why cops were at her door. *Oh shit. How did I get home?*

"Miss Bradshaw, we'd like to come in and talk to you."

Darby hesitated and then said, "Sure...Wait...Can I see your ID?" She heard too many stories of fake cops entering homes. She glanced at the driveway and realized they would have to be driving a fake police car too. "Never mind, come in," she said. Holding the door open wide she stepped back and both men entered.

"Thank you," the older guy said, tipping his hat. "Would you mind putting some pants on?"

Darby pulled the edges of her shirt down and said, "I thought you were my girlfriend. Make yourself at home, I'll be right back."

They entered the living room and she ran up the stairs.

"Stumbling as she pulled on her sweat pants, she tripped and fell. She righted herself and looked in the mirror. "Double shit." Pulling a brush through her hair she tied it back into a ponytail and rubbed a finger under each eye removing the remainder of mascara.

Walking softly down the stairs, she peeked over the railing and scrunched her brows as the young officer lifted a magazine, while the other officer opened her purse with his flashlight.

Apparently 'make yourself at home' had it's own meaning when you were a cop.

"Excuse me?" she said, startling them both. "You guys have a search warrant?"

"Do we need one?" the old cop asked.

"How the hell should I know? I have no idea why you're here," she snapped as she rounded the landing. Standing in the entry of her living room, with hands on hips, her eyes narrowed. "But I do know you're not supposed to be looking in my purse."

"Where were you last night?" the older cop asked.

"My girlfriend's house," she said stepping into the living room.

"When did you return home?" he asked.

Darby stared with a major blank. She ran the night's events through her mind in fast motion. They finished three or four bottles of wine. Kathryn took her keys around bottle three...and then she sent her home in a taxi, clueless of the time.

"I don't know."

"Do you know Keith Stone?"

"He's my boyfriend. We work together. Why? What'd he do?" Darby's mind flashed to him being in jail for drunk driving. God she hoped not. That was all they needed.

The officers glanced at each other and then the young one said, "He's dead."

"No he's not," Darby said, with a shake of her head. "I just talked to him last night. He's at Salish waiting for me."

"I'm sorry," the old cop offered.

Without warning Darbys ears began ringing and her vision narrowed. The recurring nightmare of her life flashed before. She was instantly transported to another place and time when she heard those exact words, 'he's dead' followed by her screams.

She dropped to the couch and said, "No. He's not dead." They had to be mistaken. Keith was in the mountains, in bed, waiting for her to join him.

"They found his phone. Yours was the last call he made," the older officer said.

"He was murdered," the older cop said.

"You're wrong," she snapped. Tears filled her eyes as she fought to maintain control. "Who'd want to kill Keith?"

"We don't know," the young cop said.

"Do you have proof of your whereabouts last night?" the older cop asked.

Darby looked up, tears stinging her eyes, and choked out a, "yes." She looked through her purse for her cell phone. When she couldn't find it she picked up her house phone and dialed Kathryn's number.

"Change your mind for the run?" Kathryn asked out of breath.

"Cops are here," Darby sobbed. "They...they said Keith's been murdered. Please come back." She dropped the phone without hearing Kathryn's response.

It was not long until the door burst open and Kathryn entered. "I'm Kathryn Jacobs," she said. "I work with the FAA. What's going on?"

"Keith Stone is dead and Darby Bradshaw is the last person he spoke to. We need confirmation of her whereabouts last night."

"She was with me until shortly after midnight when I put her in a cab and sent her home," she said, handing the officer her identification.

Darby sank into the couch and fell into another world. This could not be happening. She wanted Keith. She needed to tell him that she loved him.

The ringing grew louder, blocking out everything they were saying. Darby pulled her legs close and hugged them. With eyes tight she prayed they were wrong. Keith was not dead.

Kathryn sat on the couch beside Darby and wrapped an arm around her, bringing her back to the present. "It's going to be alright, Sweetie," she said.

But Darby knew it would never be all right.

The old guy's phone rang. "Excuse me." He turned his back to them and walked toward the entryway. He spoke quietly, then ended his call and turned. "Looks like they found a suspect. They're booking him now."

"Who?" Darby asked, between sobs, ready to kill the bastard.

"A pilot. He had a fight in a casino bar over some girl."

Darby's heart slammed into her chest. "Please don't tell me it was Neil."

The older officer raised an eyebrow. "Jordan? You know him?"

"Shit. Shit. Shit." Darby placed her face into her hands. "This cannot be happening," she mumbled.

"What is it?" the young cop asked.

"Neil's her ex-boyfriend," Kathryn said. "He hated Keith."

Darby blew her nose on her t-shirt. "Neil's an ass, but he wouldn't hurt anyone."

"People do strange things for love," the young officer said. "I'm sorry for your loss."

"What is that damn buzzing?" the old cop snapped.

Darby listened for a moment and then said, "My phone."

She followed the noise to a planter beside the couch. She brushed off the dirt and looked a the screen—voicemail.

CHAPTER 56

THE POLICE LEFT and Darby curled up on the couch and bawled for over an hour. As her tears dried, she grew quiet and her sorrow shifted to anger. When she breathed deep Kathryn patted her back and said, "I'm taking you to my house."

Kathryn left her alone. When she returned she told Darby to follow her. Darby blinked a couple times and did as she was told. That was so much easier than thinking.

Keith was calling her when he was attacked. She put him on speaker, and they all heard the fight and his plea for help, as well as his falling over the railing and the roar of the Falls. Eventually... nothing.

It was the nothing that stabbed her heart. The silence of where life once was. The police took her cell phone for evidence. They said they were pulling the recording and would return the phone soon.

Why they needed the phone to get a message that was stored in some database did not go unnoticed. Her phone had no recording. They wanted to track her whereabouts. See whom she called. She didn't care and there was nobody she wanted to talk to anyway.

Someone saw the fight, but their statement was sketchy. The cops found his phone on the ledge. His body was missing, but it would only be a matter of time until they found him.

Darby sat in silence all the way to Kathryn's house, running a picture of what happened through her mind. When they arrived, she followed Kathryn inside, moving on autopilot.

Once she was tucked in on the couch, Kathryn handed her a cup of hot chocolate.

"You heard what he said. Keith knew who pushed him," Darby said taking the cup with both hands. "Something more is going on than boyfriends arguing. As much of a dipshit Neil is, I don't think he would do this. Besides, Keith had twice his strength. How could he push him?"

Darby stared into her cup. The wheels inside her head cogged along and then a thought occurred to her and she scowled.

"What are you thinking?" Kathryn asked, sitting beside her.

"What if all this has something to do with me going into Armstrong's office and telling him I knew what he was up to." She held eye contact with Kathryn. "What if something *was* going on? What if he thought Keith was going to tell me, or had."

"Then you could be in danger and we need to tell the police."

"If we do that and they question him, he'll know that I don't know anything, and—"

"You'd be safe," Kathryn said. "If you're right about this and we don't do anything, then you're a target."

"We don't have anything on him." Darby set her cup on the table. "This is stupid. I'm grasping at straws. What if someone was mugging him?"

"At ten-oclock at night, in the rain, at the edge of the Falls? Highly doubtful," Kathryn said. "Your first thought was right, and my vote is to keep you alive."

Alive had such less meaning without Keith by her side, but Kathryn was right...this was not a mugging.

Kathryn sipped her cocoa, then said, "Keith knew who it was, but the fleet training captain?"

Darby shrugged. Blaming the fleet training captain was far fetched, but she had to blame someone.

"He knew who it was and Neil doesn't have the balls, or the strength, so who?" Fresh tears sprung to her eyes. "He went up there because he wanted to tell me something. He emailed me and said something was going on at work and we needed to talk. I'm going to find out what it was."

Kathryn touched her shoulder. "It's going to be okay."

Darby grabbed a napkin and blew her nose. "I never believed anything Neil said, but why didn't Keith talk to me? Why didn't he trust me?"

She should have taken the cab to the mountains. She should have been there with him. Maybe she could have done something. Closing her eyes she fought the urge to tell Kathryn it was her fault. If Kathryn would have let her go in the first place, then none of this would have happened.

"He didn't tell you, to protect you," Kathryn said.

"So he is dead because of me."

"No. He's dead because somebody pushed him."

Tears filled her eyes, again. She looked to the ceiling and took a deep breath, then wiped them away.

When she regained her composure she said, "I loved him Kat. I wanted to marry him and have his kids. This wasn't like Neil. This was the first time I thought there was hope since Brian. I wanted a family with Keith, and we were headed that way."

Kathryn opened her mouth to say something, but no words escaped. When she opened it again, still nothing. She was trying to find a way to tell Darby that everything worked out like it should, or this too will pass, or you'll find love again—all the things she always said to make someone feel better. Finally Kathryn took a deep breath and simply said, "I'm sorry."

Darby nodded.

"So what are we going to do?" Kathryn asked.

"I know what we're not going to do. We're not going to let his murderer get away." She pushed her cup aside and sat up a little straighter. "First thing tomorrow I'm going to visit Neil in jail and find out what happened on that mountain."

Chapter 57
Police Station, Seattle Washington

August 28, 2012

D ARBY LEFT HER PURSE locked in her car and carried her keys inside the police station. She made it through the metal detector without her knee setting off alarms, but they still patted her down.

After waiting forty-five minutes a guard came to get her and walked her down a long empty hallway. She lied and told them she was Neil's sister, not knowing if they would let her see him if she was not family.

Halfway down the hall she glanced over her shoulder and caught a glimpse of one of the officers who had been at her house. He nodded. They knew she was there and that she lied about her identity.

They would be listening to their conversation. She was sure of it.

If Neil had anything to do with Keith's death, she would get it out of him and then his ass could rot in jail for the rest of his life.

Deep down she knew he was incapable of murder, but once again, nothing surprised her.

Inside the room a wooden table held center stage. Two chairs, one on each side of the table, were in clear view of a mirrored wall—just like in the movies.

Neil was not there yet, so Darby walked to the mirror and pulled a hand through her hair. She wiped a finger under each eye, as her mascara ran with her emotions on the way to the station. The temptation to share that special finger was as overwhelming as was the urge to wink. But she stifled both urges.

The door opened behind her and she turned. Neil was in an orange jumpsuit with his hands cuffed in front of him. Red and swollen eyes lay flat against his pale skin. His forehead hosted drops of perspiration.

"No touching. You have fifteen minutes." The guard moved Neil to a chair and pushed him into a seated position.

Once the door closed, Darby said, "You look like shit."

"Touché."

"So what the hell happened last night?"

Neil hung his head. "I don't know."

"Start at the beginning," Darby snapped.

Neil looked up from his cuffed hands and said, "I was in the training department finishing up some paperwork that Armstrong asked me to do, and I heard your name again. When I popped up from my cube, nobody was around. So I asked the secretary if she knew where Stone was. She'd said that he took a personal day for family business, and gave me his contact number."

He squirmed in his chair. "I called the number. It was the Salish Lodge."

"Why would the training department have that number?"

"How would I know? Sometimes the guys give their contact info when they're on call."

This made no sense. He was not on call. "Why wouldn't they just use his cell phone?"

"Maybe it didn't work in the mountains?" Neil shrugged.

Darby sucked a deep breath, fighting for patience that she did not have. "So how'd you end up at the casino?"

"I drove to Salish, found his car and waited in the parking lot for him."

"And?"

"And nothing. I was on my fifth beer when he finally came out. I followed him and he drove to the casino." He lifted his hands and rubbed them over his face, then said, "I wanted to see if you were going to show up. I didn't want to be a dick and jump on him in front of you."

"What if I'd been there?" Darby snapped. "What were you going to do then?"

"I don't know." He lifted his hands and scratched his neck.

"What happened after the argument?"

"I don't know that either. That's the thing. I had one drink after he left and then headed to my car. I was coming back to Seattle."

He closed his eyes tight and said, "I don't remember anything but waking up with a headache in the parking lot of the Lodge." When he opened them, he added, "I don't know how the hell I got there."

"You were so trashed you blacked out and were going to drive to Seattle?"

"I didn't think I was that bad."

She leaned on the table. "The bar fight is all over the Internet on YouTube."

Neil raised his brows. "Shit."

"Somebody video taped you." Darby tapped a chipped nail on the table. "It's going to be great evidence at the hearing."

"Fuck you."

"Fuck you back," she snapped. "It's your fault this happened!"

"Why's it my fault?"

"You're the one that told me that shit about Keith and…"

"I told you the truth. I told you what I'd heard." Neil lowered his voice. "This is not my fault. He probably went up there to hide from you. When you get pissed God himself needs to run for cover."

She opened her mouth to respond, and then closed it. She would not fight with Neil. Not now. Not ever again.

"We had a date." She bit her lip, and then added, "Someone is setting you up."

"I didn't do anything but yell at his ass. I swear."

Darby felt sorry for the shell of a man that sat in front of her, but all she cared about was Keith. Their times together flashed through her mind like mini movies, while the reality of 'never again' filled her eyes with tears and her heart with sorrow.

"Don't worry, Sweetie, my name will be cleared," Neil said. "I'll be okay."

She closed her eyes and shook her head. She did not care if his name was ever cleared. She wanted to know what happened to Keith. "Did you and Keith have any problems in training with each other?"

"No."

"What about Keith and anyone else?"

"Nope. Nothing. Stone pretty much did what Armstrong or anyone said to do. He was a puppet."

"Puppet or not, he didn't deserve to die." She shifted in her chair. Tears filled her eyes again. She wanted to pound Neil's face, but she needed answers more. Besides, battery would be a direct pass to an adjoining cell with the cops watching.

"Ah shit," Neil said. "You were in love with the douche-bag."

She glared. Her and Keith's relationship was none of his business. If he had not opened his big mouth she would not have gone to Armstrong's office in the first place. Keith would still be alive, that she was sure of.

"You'd better help me figure this out," she said, "or your sorry ass will fry." She raised a finger and said, "One...You and Keith both worked for the same airline. Two...You both worked in training. Three...You both had me as a connection." She held up three fingers. "What else connected you?"

"Nothing."

"Was there anything in training that Keith was upset about?"

"No." He rubbed his wrist and said, "Well, maybe."

"Maybe?"

"He was pissed they were firing Townsend, and that they'd made that first officer who was on the New York flight an instructor.

"I worked with Brock in the simulator two days ago. He didn't say anything."

"Maybe they haven't told him yet. When all the simulators move to Oklahoma City, they're not taking any of the seniority-list check airmen."

"Keith knew this?" *What the hell is going on?* Why hadn't he told her? Her mind flew Mach one and then landed on New York. "What New York flight?"

"The guys that didn't activate their approach. They went around twice and then slammed it on the runway. Damn near went off the end. I thought you knew because you wrote about it on your blog."

"No, I didn't." Darby scrunched her brows trying to figure out what he was talking about.

"Your post about what happens if you forget to activate the

approach."

"I seriously hadn't heard." Darby covered her face with both hands and shook her head, then looked up. "This actually happened and Keith knew about it?"

"Stone was pretty upset about their hiring that instructor." Neil squirmed in his seat. "If you ask me, I bet that instructor wanted Stone gone, especially if Stone was going to make problems for him."

Darby dropped her hands to the table and stared at Neil, shaking her head. "You seriously think someone would push him over a cliff for a training position?"

"Hell if I know, but who was Stone to talk," Neil said. "He had no experience when he was hired."

Darby glared. "You don't know shit about the plane either."

Neil shrugged. "It doesn't matter much now anyway, does it?"

CHAPTER 58

AFTER VISITING NEIL in jail, Darby retrieved her phone and went home for a futile attempt at a nap. Tossing and turning, she tried to sort out the reality of Keith being pushed and who did it. Finally giving up on sleep she grabbed her purse, snuck out the back to avoid the media, and headed back to Kathryn's house.

Something told Darby there was no way that Keith was dead. They should have found his body. She had visions of him surviving and crawling to safety. Or better yet, he walked away and was in hiding while he created a plan to nail whomever pushed him.

Darby arrived a little after five. She hugged both Kathryn and Jackie and settled onto the couch.

Jackie set up the scrabble game on the coffee table and Kathryn carried in a tray filled with fruit and cheese. The twins were having an overnight with some friends, and Chris was visiting his grandmother.

They decided to distract themselves with a girl's night of game playing. Rules were they would not talk about Keith being pushed, but Keith was all Darby could think about.

Kathryn filled their wine glasses and set the bottle on the bar. "You ladies ready to start?"

"Draw a letter," Jackie said.

Darby reached into the bag and pulled out the letter T, and Kathryn a pulled the letter C.

"Guess I'm first," Jackie said. "I got an A."

Kathryn and Jackie were making a huge effort to cheer her up by pretending everything was normal. As hard as she tried to focus, her mind drifted to Keith and tears filled her eyes. Kathryn handed her a box of tissue.

"What did Neil say," Kathryn asked.

Darby sighed. "Pretending nothing happened sucks. I don't know how much longer I could fake it."

They filled the scrabble board, each taking their respective turns, while Darby told them everything that Neil said about the flight to New York, the instructor changes, and that Keith was upset with all of it.

"How'd they bury that New York flight?" Kathryn asked.

Shrugging she drew her letters. "Nobody wanted to believe the Pacific Airlines crash was due to pilots not knowing how to fly. The New York incident would have been in the same category, right up there with the San Francisco flight, and mine into Seattle."

Darby played with her letters. "The New York pilots forgot how to manage the computer and were afraid to disconnect the autothrust, but then they could have been the SFO crash all over again if they didn't know what they were doing."

She leaned back and sighed. "Keith didn't tell me about the incident because he knew I'd write about it. Apparently I did anyway."

"That damn blog," Kathryn said elbowing her. "What's the union doing about that letter in your file concerning the Pacific post?"

"Nothing. It was like pulling teeth. But...Oh shit!" Darby said, "Brock wrote me a letter of support. He was warned to distance himself from me, which he didn't do. I told Armstrong he gave me a fair checkride. Do you think I have anything to do with his getting kicked out of training?"

"I doubt it," Jackie said. "Brock knows too much about the Airbus. I think he intimidated Armstrong."

"Maybe so, but the coincidence shouldn't be ignored."

Kathryn lifted a branch of grapes. "Do you think Keith fell out of their good graces too?"

"That's what I'm afraid of," Darby said. "Keith's disappearance has to do with something going on in the training department. Something he saw and was about to tell me."

The more she thought about it, the stronger her resolve that Armstrong was at the heart of Keith's being pushed.

"Kat, will you do me a favor?" Darby asked. "Tomorrow, check and see how many other ASR reports have gone through with Global besides mine and that go-around fiasco in New York."

"That's a good idea," Kathryn said playing with her letters, and then she looked up. "Am I thinking what you are?"

Darby nodded. "And ladies...I don't think Keith is dead."

CHAPTER 59

Kathryn entered her office and set her venti sized latte on her desk. Tossing her purse underneath, she slid into her chair. She pressed the power on button and reached for her coffee. Sipping the warmth she wondered what the hell was going on at Global Air Lines as she waited for her computer to come to life.

The boys over there were giving Darby one hell of a time. But there had to be more than their just being arrogant jerks.

To be called in for violating the chain of command for a Christmas party was childish and a meeting for a tone of an email asinine. Putting a letter in her file and manufacturing data for violating social media, along with forcing her to remove her blog about the Pacific Airlines accident...there was more to this story.

Keith, a Global pilot instructor, was dead. Despite what Darby thought, there was no way he could have fallen off that cliff and survived. She did not have the heart to tell Darby that.

Kathryn stepped to the window with her coffee. She gazed over the top of her cup at the parking lot below, then glanced at her watch. The cubicles would start filling up in another forty-five minutes. Turning, she leaned against the windowsill.

This was quite a hornet's nest that Darby stirred up. Was it all connected or coincidence?

Darby made a complaint about an instructor, and that turned

on her. They would not allow her to pick up a trip when she told them that she did not feel proficient. They line checked her. Her union told her they hoped there was a crash so things could change—an interesting comment from an organization who was supposed to assure safety.

Global's training department practices for hiring and firing instructors had a lot to be desired. Then she came back to Keith being murdered.

What the hell is going on over there?

She returned to her desk, but remained standing as she pressed buttons. Clearly somebody was setting up Neil. But why? What did he have to do with anything—other than his being part of the training department and in love with Darby.

Kathryn walked to her doorway and peered out. She closed her door and returned to her desk and sat in front of her computer.

Logging in with her ID number and security code, she accessed the main database for all airlines and scrolled down to Global and then typed an additional series of numbers, enabling her access that very few had, and waited.

An error message flashed. *What the hell?* She typed her password and the airline codes again, and the same response—INVALID LOG IN.

There had to be a malfunction. She had access to all airline ASRs. She checked Alaska Airlines with the same result. Kathryn picked up the phone and dialed the help desk. Tapping her foot with each ring, her heart beat faster. Something was wrong.

"Tech support. What can I do for you?"

"Kathryn Jacobs, employee number 35249200. Attempting to access the main database for the ASR reports for Global Air Lines. I'm getting an error message."

"Standby, please."

Closing her eyes, Kathryn silently counted while she tapped a pen on a pad of paper.

"Miss Jacobs, you've been denied access."

"Why?"

"Inspector Roberts of internal affairs blocked you yesterday afternoon. I suggest you ask him."

Internal affairs? Kathryn set the phone down. "God dammit," she whispered. Why would somebody block her? She needed to see those ASRs.

Lifting her pen she chewed on the end and an idea sparked. Kathryn pushed back from her desk and headed down the hall toward Brent's cube.

His morning ritual was to pour out the old coffee, look at the bottom of his cup, fill it, and then get to work. She smiled the first time she witnessed the ritual and he'd said, "A reminder where I work."

She glanced behind her, and then at her watch. She needed to hurry. Brent's cup was sitting on the desk, half-filled with yesterday's coffee. She dumped it into a plant and looked at the bottom and grinned. FUBAR. She returned it to his desk and lifted a paper to read his employee number and...

"What are you doing?" Santos asked.

She jerked and looked up. "Good morning, sir." Her heart skipped a beat and then pounded hard. *Keep it cool.* "Just leaving Brent a note. We need to go over the report on Alaska Airlines," she said lifting a pen.

"See me when you're done. We need to talk."

"I'll be right there," Kathryn said. He walked down the hall toward his office. She quickly copied Brent's ID number and wrote the word FUBAR—Fucked Up Beyond All Reality—on a scrap of paper. She slid a hand over the coffee dribble and wiped it on her black pants, then turned the opposite direction of Tom's office toward her own.

Back at her desk, she logged into her computer with Brent's ID. Within minutes she accessed Global Air Lines data. Her eyes narrowed. *This can't be right.* There had to be a mistake.

She typed another code, and paged forward. She logged out and logged into Alaska's database, then plunged back into Global's with the same result. Her foot tapped quickly.

"What the fuck?" She said, shaking her head.

"That's exactly what I was going to say," Santos said. His breath hot on her neck. "What the hell are you doing?"

CHAPTER 60

THREE DAYS PASSED since Keith was pushed, and Darby just returned from her first run. She could not outrun the pain or the vision of him falling off the ledge. She would never be able to outrun the ache in her heart if he were dead, so she pushed that thought from her mind. Believing he was alive.

Pounding the street with music blasting in her ears—songs that she and Keith enjoyed together, brought tears. She tried to outrun them too, but was not fast enough. By the time she reached home an hour passed, and the wolves hunkered down on the street corner thinned to two vans.

To avoid being seen she climbed the fence and ran through the backyard, entering on the side of the house as she did earlier that morning when twice as many vans lurked out front.

Darby held the blender under the faucet as she cooled down. Two thirds full of water, she added a raw egg, then a scoop of chocolate protein powder, and placed the craft on the base. She stabbed the blend button. Lifting the lid she dropped ice cubes in one at time. As each cube crushed between the blades she envisioned they were the head of whomever pushed Keith.

A guest from the lodge had watched the struggle and saw Keith go over. By the time security showed up, the person disappeared. By the time the search and rescue crew made it to the bottom.

Keith's body was gone. Three days later his body was still missing.

Darby flipped on the TV. They were talking about her again and she glared. An 'anonymous source' said, "A female pilot—Captain Stone's ex-lover—and her current boyfriend may have plotted to murder him together."

They said that she lured Keith to the mountains where she and Neil were supposed to have killed him in a crime of passion. It was clear the police did not believe the rumors.

With the flash of Keith's picture, tears welled up again. *Damn I'm such a baby.* She shut the TV off.

"Suck it up, Darby," she whispered, stabbing the stop button on the blender.

She spent the night at Kathryn's house after their scrabble game, but left early before Kathryn and Jackie awoke. Their failed attempt at games, morphed into staying up late talking and crying with memories of their past flooding forward.

Kathryn finally said, "You have a broken heart, but time will heal. Force yourself to go through the normal motions of life. Each day will get easier."

Somehow she was not sure that would be the case if Keith were dead. He had to be alive and she would find him.

Darby's morning run was forced, but well worth the effort. Energized, there was no better time to get the bastard that pushed Keith. *Nothing like today for justice.* She lifted the blender and took a large drink, then poured the remaining liquid into a glass.

She moved to the kitchen nook and sat. Peeking through the curtains she raised an eyebrow as the last van pulled away.

Allowing the curtain to fall back into place, she returned her attention to her drink. She needed a plan of attack.

Goal one—force herself to exercise. Complete.

Goal two—intake nutrition. Complete.

Goal three—find the bastard who pushed Keith and nail his nuts to the floor. In progress.

Darby picked up the stack of mail and sorted through it, glancing at each bill. She opened her mortgage payment and then her phone bill. Tears filled her eyes when she saw Keith's phone number filling two pages. She came to the union bill and cringed.

They did nothing for her alleged violation. Not that it mattered now, anyway. GPA, Global Pilots Association was on the move. They finally reached the number of cards to enact a vote for new union leadership. Time would tell.

She gathered the mail into a stack and tapped it in her hand, then set it on the table. She glanced at her phone—0845. Kathryn would be at her office and already have pulled the ASR reports.

If Darby were right, there would be many. She and Kathryn suspected that Keith got himself into trouble because he was arguing about the non-qualified instructors being hired and the many incidents that occurred on the flight line. The combination of cancelling ground school with non-qualified instructors was a recipe for disaster.

Keith was going to speak the truth about a majorly fucked-up training department and they silenced him because he would not play their game.

But who were 'they'?

Pushing away from the table, Darby walked to the sink. She took one last swallow and poured the remains of her drink down the drain, then rinsed out the blender.

What she could not figure out was why they hired that pilot who nearly crashed in New York to be an instructor. She doubted someone would kill for a job, but then you never knew what people were capable of until they did it. Whomever pushed Keith had one intent in mind.

She shivered and wrapped her arms around herself. The stench caught her by surprise. She was seriously beginning to stink, and in much need of a shower. As she turned to leave the room when something caught her eye. She lifted the envelope with an address written on it—*Wenatchee?*

She slid a finger over the address. Keith. It was his writing. *When did he write this?* More importantly, why? That was were he went before going to the lodge. She held tight to the envelope, grabbed her purse and headed upstairs to her computer.

Pulling herself up the stairs with the help of the railing, she thought about Keith carrying her over his shoulder and smiled.

Once in her room she tossed her purse and envelope onto her desk and flopped onto her bed and closed her eyes. She lay there a moment thinking about covering her head with the covers and hiding, but she bounced up.

Today would not be spent in bed. She kicked off her shoes, then pulled off her socks and tossed them into the hamper. Today was 'take Kathryn's advice' day. Force herself to do the normal things in life and wait for Keith to come back to her.

Darby pulled off her t-shirt and dropped it into the hamper and then climbed out of her sweat pants and sports bra and tossed them in the basket. There was one more thing she needed. Smile therapy.

If a person smiled, even if it was forced, their body received health benefits. Clinically depressed patients were actually able to get off their meds just by smiling. She plastered a smile on her face.

If the police stormed her house they would arrest her for looking stupid. Naked with a cheesy grin and red swollen eyes, she put Kenny Loggins on her CD player and pressed shuffle. The first song that came up was *Danger Zone* from *Top Gun*. And her smile became real.

Stepping into the shower she was back with Keith and his attempt at romance on their first Valentine's Day. He bought a bottle of champagne and set a bowl of M&Ms in the middle of the floor. He even built a fire. Quite the feat, despite his never having been a boy scout. That was their first night at the Salish Lodge.

He planned the perfect romantic movie night with *Top Gun*.

The M&Ms were because she told him there was a chemical in chocolate that a woman's body produced when she had an orgasm. He mistook that as giving one. He figured if one piece of chocolate was good for one orgasm—an entire bag would bring great pleasure.

He planned for her to get horny with champagne, aroused with the chocolate, and then after the volleyball scene he would move in for her final pleasure.

The plan from the male perspective was top notch, but he forgot whom he was dealing with. The champagne did its magic. The M&Ms tasted great—Keith pulled out all the green ones just for her. The fire crackled and she lay snuggled in his arms, enveloped in warmth.

Sliding into to a seated position, Darby tilted her head back and allowed the warmth of the water to take her. Almost three years passed since a psychopath tried to kill her in this very spot. Had he, she never would have known Keith.

She wrapped her arms around her legs and imagined they were Keith's arms holding her tight.

The fire crackled and she felt the warmth of his love, even now. He planned the entire evening to go like a lesson plan—everything had its time. But when the fighters began taking off the aircraft carrier and *Danger Zone* began to play, Darby was so turned on that she attacked him.

He said, "Wait. It's not time. I heard the ladies really liked the volleyball game." The confused look on his face was priceless.

Her smile broadened and she began to laugh, but her laughter turned to tears and then to sobs.

"I will get whomever pushed you, Keith. I promise." Holding her legs tight, she rocked until the water turned cold.

She climbed out of the shower and wrapped a towel around her body. Darby forced the smile back on her face, but it would take a long time for it to return to her eyes. She would remember the good times until he was with her again, and then they would make more.

Darby carried her phone to the bedroom and tossed it on the bed at the same time it rang. Startled, she jumped for it and said, "Hold on, I've got to turn the music down."

She rushed across the room while Kathryn was talking, but Darby could only make out a couple words.

"What'd you say?" Darby asked, as she silenced the music.

"I'll be there in twenty-minutes," Kathryn said before the phone went dead.

CHAPTER 61

DARBY DRIED her hair, pulled on her only clean pair of jeans, then slipped into a t-shirt that Keith bought her on their trip to New Orleans. The front was a body of a reptile without a head. Her head made the picture complete. Underneath the picture, Swamp Monster was written in bold letters.

"Time to let this monster out," she whispered.

When a car pulled up out front, Darby rushed to the window and peeked out the curtain. She ran down the stairs and opened the door before Kathryn could knock.

"Get in here before anyone sees you," Darby said, looking for remnants of camera crews. She grabbed Kathryn's arm and pulled her inside in one movement.

"Where'd the vultures go?" Kathryn asked heading toward the kitchen. She tossed her purse on the counter then opened the fridge and pulled out a can of Verve, Darby's answer to the healthiest energy drink.

"What happened?"

Kathryn shook the can three times and popped the top. "I was locked out of our computers at work. My association with you has led to the question of whether or not I deserve to work at the FAA."

"That's bullshit," Darby said. "The police don't think I have anything to do with this."

"Apparently the FAA has another version." Kathryn leaned toward the window and peered through the curtains, then pulled out a chair and sat at the table with a sigh. "When I realized I was blocked, I borrowed a coworker's ID number and password." She sipped her drink glancing over the top of the can.

"My hero," Darby said. It wasn't often that Kathryn broke the rules, but when she did she made it count. "What'd you find?"

"Global Air Lines has no air safety reports."

"As in *zero*? But...I..."

"Exactly. Let's pretend that everyone else did everything perfect, there should be yours and that New York flight. What happened to those?" Kathryn's foot tapped. "It took me a minute to realize Tom was leaning over my shoulder."

"Oh shit," Darby said. "Maybe we can get a cell together."

Kathryn held her gaze. "Somebody at Global has figured out how to bypass all reports from being logged into the system."

"What about other airlines?" Darby asked.

"They all have events. Global is the only 'perfect' airline."

"How could the Feds not see that?"

"The only thing that triggers a serious look is with too many incidents. Nobody looks for something that's not there. We're understaffed and all too busy. There's no reason to look."

"Shit," Darby said running a hand through her hair. "What'd your boss say?"

"He was upset that I accessed the data illegally. But he came in early to warn me of what was coming down the path."

"I thought he hated you."

"Well, apparently he hates the fact that someone is playing with the data more." Kathryn sipped her drink. "He's an ass with a major character flaw, but frustrated with the bureaucracy too. It wears on you after awhile."

Darby sat heavily, unsure of what to think.

"Tom recommended that I take a leave of absence until this is over. He said he would grant it with full pay before internal affairs got there to pull me."

"What could they have possibly done to you?" Darby asked.

Kathryn shrugged. "I didn't wait to find out. I got the hell out. I actually think they were going to detain me." Tears filled her eyes. "What would've happened to the girls?"

"Nothing would ever happen to those girls. They have me and Jackie." Darby slid her chair back and stood, then began to pace. "So what does Keith being pushed over the Falls have to do with ASR reports? Could he have known what was happening and was going to rat them out?" *What if he were involved?*

What was going on at Globlal? Too many things bounced through her brain—too many paths leading to nowhere. She leaned against the counter, folded her arms, and closed her eyes to think.

"Obviously training is involved. I think he found out and was going to tell you," Kathryn said. "Now you and Neil are being set up for his mur...disappearance."

Darby gave her a sideways glance. "I suspected as much." Moving her pinky to her mouth she chewed on a frayed nail while her mind whirled. Then she turned and opened her junk drawer, removed two permanent markers and set them on the table.

Kneeling she opened the cupboard beneath her sink and pulled out a brown paper bag. She ripped it apart and spread it on the table between them. "What do we know?"

Kathryn lifted a pen and wrote zero ASR events for Global, at the top of the bag. "Here's where we start."

"Then we have Keith being pushed," Darby said, drawing a

mountain on the right side of the paper and wrote Keith inside it. Below the mountain she wrote Neil.

"They think you're an accomplice," Kathryn said, adding her name.

They stared at the bag in silence. "This is stupid." Darby pushed away from the table. "We have nothing," she said in exasperation.

"No. It's not nothing. Look here," Kathryn said. "There's a connection between Keith and Neil."

She drew a line from each of their names into the center of the page and wrote training department. "There's also a connection to you," she added, drawing a line from their names to Darby.

Darby returned to her seat. "Let's also look at everything that's happened to me since I came to Global."

She wrote the list on the left side of the page. 1—Requesting to fly. 2—Not getting proper training. 3—Called in for tone of emails. 4—Called in for violation of social media for the Airbus blog. 5—Called in for violating the chain of command.

"What do numbers one through five have in common?" Kathryn asked.

"Idiot pilot managers," Darby said.

"Well, besides that." Kathryn drew lines from the list to Darby's name, and then to the training department. "You're tied to the training department too. You're standing up for quality training and complaining about lack of proficiency."

"I never complain. I'm being proactive." Darby grinned.

"That you are, and someone doesn't like it." Kathryn tapped the pen on the paper. "Then we have your writing an ASR, that we now know was wiped out of the system—"

"What if the POI pulled them. He had motive and allowed them to cut back our training program and cancel ground school."

"The POI is a good place to start," Kathryn said. "But maybe a bit too obvious. Why would he pull the reports?"

"He's being paid to look the other way so Global can shorten their programs more than they should."

Global Air Lines had been approved to use a shortened course on the A330 that was originally designed only for those who had flown the A320. Pilots who did not make it through the program were provide extra training—using AQP and 'train to proficiency' to their benefit.

More than half her class needed extra simulator sessions to pass. For those who stayed on footprint, they suffered in their own way. This firehose training provided too much information too fast for the student to absorb, and did not last long term—the primary reason why so many pilots did not remember how their planes worked.

"If the program's too easy the POI could be fired, but only if a plane crashed would there be an inquiry," Kathryn said. "On the other side of that coin, he could be fired if he makes the training too long. Political pressure that training is unreasonable would start at the top of Global Air Lines and come down on the POI's head."

"So the CEO complains to the top of the food chain at the FAA and shit falls downhill burying the POI?" Darby asked.

"More or less," Kathryn said nodding. "But Global's training program could also be looked at if there were too many ASRs."

"If he could be fired for mandating a program that's too long what if he cut it short, but went too far? Then he had to pull the reports to cover his ass."

Darby chewed on the end of her pen. "But why remove them? Why not just beef up the program if they were having problems?"

"Someone doesn't want the program beefed up," Kathryn

said. "They're paying him to pull the reports."

"But how much could they pay the him to try and kill someone? And who would pay it?" Darby asked.

"I'm wondering that too. POIs make a good living, but there have been cases where airline execs provided extravagant gifts for them to look the other way."

Darby tilted her head back and closed her eyes, running the POI scenario through her mind. Allowing training programs that put less than proficient pilots into planes was one thing, but pushing someone over a ledge was a different story.

"I'm not sold on the POI angle," she said.

"I'm also not seeing anyone trusting him enough to keep his mouth shut," Kathryn mused. "The guy's a worm."

"Besides, worms are harmless," Darby said. "Maybe we need to look at how badly someone in my company wanted to shut me down after writing that Pacific Airlines blog."

Darby played with the tab on the top of her can. "I didn't violate social media. That letter in my file was to scare me. They didn't want the public to know that pilots were not being trained properly. Hell, I wasn't trained properly." She drained her can and crumpled it. "Those two crashes could have been my plane."

"You're right, but we can't rule him out," Kathryn said pulling the cap off the marker and adding 'POI' to the paper.

"I think someone is in bed with someone," Darby said when her phone rang. Jackie's name flashed across the screen.

"Quick, turn on the television," Jackie said.

CHAPTER 62

DARBY AND KATHRYN sat on the couch with eyes unblinking. All channels played the same drama—Lawrence Patrick, the CEO of Global Air Lines, being pulled out of the Oklahoma City corporate headquarters with his hands cuffed behind his back. FBI agents carried out boxes of files in mass. Yellow tape blocked sidewalks and roads were closed to through traffic.

Darby never saw anything like the show that played out before them.

"Ladies and gentleman, we're standing out front of Global Air Lines corporate office, Oklahoma City, with shocking, but sketchy news at best." The reporter spoke breathlessly. She wiped a hair from her face. "As you can see behind me, FBI agents are removing documents in this dramatic raid.

"What we know is that the CEO, Lawrence Patrick, is at the heart of a serious breach of ethics. We have reports from reliable sources that Global Air Lines has been falsifying training records and short-changing pilots' training.

"In light of this news, and the murder of one of their pilots, we have to ask ourselves— did CEO Patrick have something to do with that pilot's death?"

"Holy shit," Kathryn said. "Mr. Patrick killed Keith?"

Darby glared her way, and pulled a pillow close and squeezed.

"Keith went to the corporate golf game and bragged about playing with him. They were on a first name basis. Maybe he'd heard or saw something he shouldn't have."

She pulled her legs onto the couch and tucked them under her. "That's why he was on edge and yelled at me about my blog. He knew what was happening and wanted me to shut up."

The news switched to their local affiliate station, KOMO, and reporters stood outside the Seattle corporate office.

"Look," Kathryn said, elbowing Darby. "McDermott's in Seattle."

The Vice President of the airline stepped in front of a handful of microphones. Camera's flashed. He ran a handkerchief over his face, and then stuffed it into his shirt pocket.

"Sir, can you tell us what's happening here?"

McDermott's silver hair was uncombed and an evening-shadow put him on the edge of sexy. Clearly his night had been long. Behind him the Seattle Global Training Center was roped off and boxes were being removed from that building too. His look was one of angst as he glanced over his shoulder and then to the reporter.

"There's not much I can tell you. All I know is that Lawrence Patrick is a good man. The best CEO this company could have. Whatever they've accused him of, they're wrong. We run a top-notch airline. We pride ourselves on honesty and integrity, with safety our highest focus."

Kathryn wrapped her arm into Darby's and squeezed. "It's over," she whispered as McDermott continued to speak.

"I wish I could tell you more," he said, sticking his hands deep into his pockets. Looking over his shoulder at the training center, he shook his head then turned back to the reporter and said, "This will be sorted out quickly and we'll be moving forward in no time."

"What about the murdered pilot?" The reporter asked. "Does that have anything to do with what's happening here today?"

"I'm sure we'll find that had nothing to do with any of this," McDermott extended his arm toward the activity behind him.

"But he was an instructor who worked in this building, as was the pilot sitting in jail who's being accused of his murder," the reporter said.

"There have been no convictions, and I'm not at liberty to discuss anything about that at this time," Mc Dermott said flatly.

"What about the female pilot—Darby," a reporter yelled from the crowd. "We understand that she identified numerous transgressions in training and was harassed because of it."

Darby's eyes widened. "Who the hell was that? How did she know what was going on?"

"I'm not sure," Kathryn said. "Look at McDermott's reaction. See the red around his neck and the way he hesitated? You can be damned sure he wasn't expecting that question either."

"We are grateful for all our pilots stepping forward. Especially Miss Bradshaw," he said. "If it wasn't for she and her blog, I doubt any of this would have come to light."

"Thanks to me and my blog?" Darby said. "What the hell."

CHAPTER 63

KATHRYN SAT IN FRONT of her computer inspecting Alaska Airlines Air Safety reports. After the CEO was taken into custody, Tom called and apologized for the trouble. He gave her the remainder of the week off and told her to have a great holiday weekend. He said he needed her help and to be at work 'bright and early' Tuesday morning.

As it turned out, he needed her like a hole in the head. Each member on the Seattle team was assigned to a different airline to review ASRs. She had been given Seattle's sweetheart—Alaska Airlines.

She was also assigned with Jake Bryant, like she was not good enough to have her own airline. Pushing her attitude aside, she continued to search for something that was not there.

Kathryn glanced at her watch—fifteen minutes until she could escape for lunch with Jackie and Darby. There was a time when she worked through lunch, but today she could not get into the flow. Forcing her attention back to the computer, she sighed.

From what she could determine, there was a normal pattern of events with Alaska Airlines. Nothing out of the ordinary.

"Excuse me," Tom said, standing in her doorway. "Do you have a moment?"

"Certainly." Kathryn gladly stopped and pushed away from her computer, then glanced at her watch. "My friends will be here any moment. We might be interrupted."

"This will take just a minute." Tom stepped in and closed the door. He pulled a chair to her desk and sat. Despite his being a condescending ass, he came to her defense when she needed it.

She had such mixed feelings for Tom Santos. He was one of the most respected agents at the bureau, but he lacked all social skills.

She gave him her full attention.

He spoke in low voice, "I think we have a mole."

Kathryn leaned forward. "What do you mean?"

He glanced over his shoulder at the closed door, then back to her. "I think someone was working with the CEO at Global. I don't think something like this could've been pulled off without someone inside the FAA helping."

This was nothing that she and Darby had not discussed, she had just not wanted to believe it.

He took a deep breath and leaned back, running a hand through his hair he said, "This is a Coastal Air Lines scandal, all over again."

She stiffened with the comment.

"I'm sorry," Tom said. "I didn't mean anything by that. It's just that there always seems to be fucked-up people who don't give a shit about anything but themselves."

"Who in our department would have motive, let alone the skills to pull something like this off? More importantly, why?" Malcolm Anderson, Global's POI, flashed before her eyes.

"Money, sabotage, making a name for themselves, I don't know." He leaned forward and said, "I think the reports came into the system and then they were removed."

"There has to be someone inside Global to cover the tracks that they were not receiving the reports on their end."

"Perhaps." He locked eyes with hers. "I need a favor."

"Anything."

"I gave you Alaska Airlines with Bryant for one reason only—I know what we're dealing with, with them. He can handle it alone. I needed you free. I want you to operate under the ruse that you're helping him, but instead I want you to search our database and see if it was possible that reports came in and they were stopped or removed. More importantly—who stopped them."

"But how? I don't have that kind of access."

"I'm giving you access to everyone's data, including mine." He pushed back from the desk. "You are the only person I can trust. If you find anything, we'll hang the bastard."

"Is it possible that the IT department at Global would have the ability to fix something before it came our way?"

"Nothing is impossible. We'll hit that path once we determine we're clean. The FAA does not need one more scandal."

Tom pulled an envelope out of the inside of his shirt pocket. "Here are the security codes. If they figured a loophole, they could have used anyone's access instead of their own. Yours, mine, who knows." He hesitated and then said, "I'm counting on you."

There was a knock at the door and Kathryn said, "Anything else?"

"That's all for now." Tom opened the door.

Darby stepped back and looked from Kathryn to Tom. "Is Kathryn here? Can she come out to play?"

Kathryn rolled her eyes behind Tom's back.

Tom laughed. "She's all yours, but make sure she's back in an hour. There's work to be done." Tom extended his hand. "You must be Darby. I'm Tom Santos."

She shook his hand and said, "Darby Bradshaw and president of the Kathryn Jacob's fan club."

Tom laughed, "You two have fun. Nice to meet you." He turned to Kathryn and said, "Thank you."

Kathryn nodded and Tom left.

Darby entered the office and shut the door. "The ogre you always told me about is not quite the man I envisioned. He's charming. Nice laugh. Not too bad to look at." She wiggled her eyebrows.

"Don't even go there," Kathryn said, her mind on the envelope he left with her. "You ready to go? We can meet Jackie in the lobby."

"We're rescheduling. Jackie's having lunch with John, and I'm going to the mountains to find Keith," Darby said as Kathryn's cell phone rang.

Kathryn held up a finger and answered.

"Have you seen Darby?" Neil asked.

Kathryn looked at Darby and mouthed, 'Neil.' Darby shook her head.

"No, I haven't. Why?"

"They let me out and I have to find her."

"They dropped the charges?"

"No."

"Then why did they let you out?" Kathryn asked.

"Someone posted bail. The only person who would've done it is Darby."

"Neil, let her be. When she wants to contact you, she will." Darby gave Kathryn a thumbs-up.

"But I want her to know I'm out."

"If she posted bail, don't you think she already knows?"

"I guess," Neil said.

"If you love her, I think you should give her some space until this is over." Darby gave her two thumbs up.

"I just wanted to—"

"Go home Neil. I'll tell her you called." Kathryn ended the call and switched her phone to vibrate.

She turned her attention to Darby. "Did you bail Neil out?"

"Hell no! The slammer is the best place for him."

Pushing Neil from her mind, Kathryn looked at the envelope, then sighed. "I wish I could go to the mountains with you, but Tom just gave me a project."

"I'm good. I'll be back before dinner." Darby walked to the door and opened it, then turned and mouthed, "hottie alert."

Kathryn shook her head with a grin and Darby closed the door.

She opened the envelope and read the list of names. Having everyone's passwords and full access made her feel like a criminal. She turned the page and knit her brows at the codes Tom Santos gave her. This was deeper access than she'd had at the NTSB.

If someone was playing on the dark side, she would damn well find them and shut them down. She started at the first name. The biggest jerk in their office—Malcolm Andrews, Global's POI. She would love to put him away, but life was never that perfect or easy.

Malcolm would be the most challenging because he had reason to be near Global, their ASRs, and anything they were involved with concerning training. She was not sure what she was looking for, but when it appeared she would know.

Then something occurred to her. Did Darby say she was going to 'find' Keith?

CHAPTER 64

NOT READY TO face the reality of life, Darby pulled off the freeway and exited toward the casino. Going to the lodge to look for Keith sounded like a great idea, but she was having a hard time controlling her emotions the closer she got. What if she was wrong and Keith was dead? *Don't go there Darby.*

She pushed those thoughts aside as she pulled in front of the casino. Leaving her car with the valet she headed inside.

The place was like a morgue. The fact it was 1300 on a Tuesday might have something to do with that. An odd feeling came over her as if she were being watched. She looked over her shoulder, and the doorman nodded. She smiled and then headed across the casino passing by the slot machines.

Bells rang and someone screamed to her right. Darby jumped. Gambling was more about the win and had less to do with the money. Well…maybe a little to do with the money. But winning was the real thrill and would be her revenge. She would find the bastard who pushed Keith and make him pay. If she and Keith could do it together, all the sweeter.

Darby wandered through the casino toward the *12 Moons Piano Bar*. She held her breath as she poked her head in the door.

Praying that he would be sitting there and this was a nightmare, was short lived. The room was empty, other than the bartender.

Darby sat at the piano and a chill crept through her body. This was the place where Neil confronted Keith. She glanced around at the bar then slid her hand over the piano. This was the last place Keith was seen.

He had been there to see her—to explain something. Tears filled her eyes. *Goddamn you, Stone. Where are you?*

If only she would have called a taxi they could have talked. What was a hundred-dollar cab ride? Nothing. She glanced toward the bar, took a deep breath and walked toward the counter.

"What can I get you, Sweetheart?" The bartender asked.

"Were you working when this guy was in here the other night?" Darby asked, showing him a picture of Keith.

"He's that pilot they pushed off the ledge," he said glancing at the photo. "Yeah, I was here."

"Do you know what he was drinking?"

"Sorry, I don't. A friend of yours?"

Fresh tears stung her eyes, and she looked away.

"Let me get you something," he said. "On the house."

"A Diet Pepsi, would be nice."

Raising an eyebrow he said, "How about something with a punch to it. Looks like you could use it."

"What the hell," she said wiping tears off her cheek. "How about a Wild Turkey on the rocks."

"That a girl."

He filled her glass, added a lime, and set it in front of her.

"Thanks." She took her drink to a table in a dark corner and sipped, hoping to find the courage to drive five minutes east on the freeway. Courage did not take a DUI and she was stupid to have accepted it. Somehow common sense was lost in the moment.

The liquid gold trickled warmth where the chill had been. The drink took her back to when they sat in this exact spot and killed a couple turkeys together. She wanted to do that again.

It was stupid to be sitting here. What good would this do? Her eyes dropped to her drink. The answers in a bottom of a glass were always wrong. The truth was, she was afraid to go to the lodge.

"Hey Darlin, what's a cute little thing like you doin all alone?"

Darby startled, looking up she adjusted her eyes to the unfamiliar figure standing in front of her. "Leaving," she said.

She slid off the seat, ducked out the bar, and flew nonstop to the front door.

Darby gave the guy in the valet booth her ticket and a five-dollar bill. Within minutes her car was sitting in front of the casino. She climbed in and headed for the lodge.

When she pulled into the parking lot it was nearly empty, mirroring the feeling in her soul. A huge hole filled the space where Keith once lived, a vacuum that sucked the life from her.

Keith, you cannot be dead. She put her car into park.

Kathryn told her there were always clues. The answers could be right in front of her if she looked in the right place. If a clue were here, she would find it.

She headed over the ramp toward the hotel. Once inside she glanced around the lobby. They remodeled since she and Keith were there, but the cozy lodge feeling still held.

She walked to the front desk. The young woman tossed back her hair and said, "May I help you?"

"They said my boyfriend was..." Her eyes filled with tears.

The young lady placed a hand to her mouth. "You're that pilot?" Placing a hand on Darby's she said, "I'm so sorry. This totally sucks."

"Could I see the room he was in?"

"We're not allowed to go in it," she said and then whispered,

"Someone saw him pushed and he put up a pretty good fight."

Darby fought her emotions and said, "I just wanted to see if—"

"Oh my God. You think his ghost is here. That would be totally awesome if he haunted the lodge, but wouldn't he be out on the ledge?"

Seriously? If the situation were not so grave Darby would have found humor in their conversation.

"I won't tell anyone you let me in. Please."

The girl glanced to her right, and then whispered, "Here's the deal. It's room 408. I'll code the key, and then I'm going to the ladies' room. I didn't give it to you. Don't touch anything. Just look. Then come back and tell me what you find. Okay?"

Darby nodded.

"I'm sorry miss, I can't help you," she said loudly. "Now, if you'll excuse me I have to go to the bathroom." She winked at Darby and walked down the hall.

Rolling her eyes Darby picked up the plastic card and headed toward the elevator. She pushed number four.

Her hand shook as she stuck the key into the slot. The lock gave way and she pushed open the heavy wooden door. The room was beautiful. They remodeled the rooms too, but the fireplace was exactly as she remembered. Darby slid her hand on the wood and then walked to the window and looked out to spot where Keith went over the railing.

Wrapping her arms around herself she hugged tight as a chill slithered into her soul. She looked out to the evergreens and then closed her eyes, fighting nausea that grew greater with each passing minute. When the thought of vomiting passed she opened them.

She stood frozen in place. Waiting. For what, she was not sure. She looked around the room, slid her hand over the mirror and then dropped to her hands and knees. She looked under the desk and chair. She crawled to the bed, and lifted the skirt. She opened the drawers, pulled them out and looked behind and beneath. Nothing.

By the time she was finished searching, she faced the stark reality that there was no clue left behind. She sat on the bed and ran her hand over the bedspread.

When the phone rang, she startled but did not answer it. She wandered to the bathroom and grabbed a handful of tissue and blew her nose.

"Keith, someone will pay," she whispered.

Closing the door behind her she headed for the front desk.

"No ghost. Sorry," she said.

"That's okay, I guess it's just as well. I work the night shift and I really don't have time for ghosts."

Darby smiled. This chick was seriously demented. "You've got a lot of work at night?" she asked sliding the plastic card across the counter, not anxious to go outside and look over the railing.

"A ton. They do everything the old fashioned way here. You'd think they would catch up with the times and get this stuff on computers."

"Thanks for letting me see the room."

"No problem," she said. "I really am sorry."

Darby nodded, and then walked outside. She turned left and walked around the building, heading down the path toward the lookout point. Her body shook with more force the closer she got.

The rain started again. Walking carefully, her mind drifted to Barbie at the front desk. Then she stopped. "Holy shit." How could they have been so stupid? She turned and ran back up the path.

The rain shifted from falling to pouring as she ran across the bridge to the parking lot. Raindrops chilled her bones as they slapped her across the face. She ran to her car and yanked the door open.

Sliding into the driver's seat she pulled her shoulder harness on and buckled her lap belt, then started her car. She put it into gear and backed out of the lot. She drove too fast through the small town as she headed toward the freeway. Ten minutes later she was flying down I-90 toward Seattle.

Her speed was approaching 60 miles per hour, but the poor visibility made driving any faster a challenge. The rain pelted the windshield and the wipers could not keep up.

Darby reached a hand into her purse and found her phone. She glanced at her cell and selected favorites, pressed Kat, and shifted her eyes back to the freeway.

Kathryn said, "Speak of the devil, I was just thinking of—"

"The records. The boxes..." Darby said as she stepped on her brakes, but they were nothing but mush. "Shit!" she yelled and dropped her phone and put both hands back on the wheel.

CHAPTER 65

TEN MINUTES PASSED since Darby called. Kathryn dialed her right back, and then multiple times since, but no answer. She feared the worst and hoped to hell that Neil did not follow her to the mountains. That was the last thing Darby needed.

Kathryn was not convinced that Neil was innocent in whatever was happening at Global. He should never have been hired as an instructor with his limited experience. It was he who spent too much time in that office, but then so did Keith.

Records and boxes? What was Darby talking about? When Darby yelled 'shit' followed by silence, Kathryn's worry turned to panic.

If she was not answering her phone that meant only one thing— she couldn't. All Kathryn could do was wait.

Focusing on her work gave her little reprieve. Lightning flashed and she went to the window and looked toward the sky. Kathryn glanced at her computer shaking her head at the tedium in front of her. Thunder boomed loud and she jumped as the wrath of Seattle prepared for attack.

She glanced at her watch. The kids movie would be done in thirty minutes. She lifted her cell and called Jackie.

"Can you pick up the kids?" she asked when Jackie answered.

"Sure. Everything okay?"

"Darby went to the mountains and—"

"I know. She called before she left," Jackie said. "Isn't it great they let Neil out? I told him Darby went to the lodge. I thought it would be a good idea if she wasn't alone."

"Tell me you didn't," Kathryn said.

"It's okay I told him, isn't it?"

"I hope so." There was no undoing it now. "She's not answering her phone. I think something's happened."

"Oh my God," Jackie said. "What can I do?"

"Get the kids, I'll start making calls. We'll find her. I'm sure she's fine. I'll meet you at my house."

Too much time had passed without word, so Kathryn dialed 911.

"Is this an emergency?" the operator asked.

"Have there been any accident reports on Snoqualmie Pass within the last hour?"

Kathryn closed her eyes. She tilted her head back listening to thunder slam against the sky as she waited for what she feared would be bad news.

"Are you okay?" Santos asked.

Kathryn jumped. She placed a hand to her heart. How long had he been standing there? She covered the phone and said, "I think Darby might be in trouble."

"Anything I can do?" he asked.

"Ma'am," the operator said, and Kathryn held up a finger to Tom. "We've had a report of an accident. They've dispatched a medic response team. I suggest you call the local hospitals."

Tears stung Kathryn's eyes as she told Tom, "I think Darby was in an accident."

"Go. Get out of here. This can wait," he said. "Take all the time you need and let me know what happens."

CHAPTER 66

D ARBY PRESSED HER FOOT on the brake pedal and pumped. "*Shit. Shit. Shit.*" There was nothing there. She glanced at the speedometer—her speed was increasing.

She pulled the emergency brake—nothing. Her heart raced faster than her car. Traffic was light, but it would only be a matter of time until she hit the town of Issaquah.

If she did not get this machine stopped before then, she would be a missile and take out everyone at the bottom of the hill. She had maybe 15 minutes.

She pulled on her emergency flashers and glanced right.

Plowing into the guardrail might be an option. She glanced at the speed again. It was going faster with each second. She had to do something and quick.

A horn blew and she jumped as a huge rig pulled up beside her. Adrenaline shot through her veins. She glanced at him, then right at the railing and prayed for courage.

Her eyes darted to the speedometer. Her speed had increased and there was a steeper grade ahead.

She inched toward the railing. "One. Two. Three. Ready or not," she whispered.

The screeching was as startling as were the sparks. She yanked away and fought to keep the car on the road.

The semi paralleled her car. With his window down he yelled and waved, but she couldn't hear him over the noise.

The semi pulled forward, inching into her lane, just enough to block her from passing.

What the hell's he doing? Doesn't he see my flashers?

She pressed her horn multiple times.

They flew down the freeway, him a good three feet in front of her. Their speed close to even, but hers was increasing.

His rig blocked her from passing, and she was closing in on him. She glanced to the railing again. Then the light bulb came on.

She pulled her car toward the middle of the road directly behind the truck. The distance between vehicles narrowed.

Inches away, her car closed in on his truck. Their autos were about to become very good friends. Bumper buddies.

The thud was hard and metal crunching stabbed her senses. The airbag exploded, hitting her windshield and smacking her in the chest and face, knocking the wind out of her. Her head flew back with a jolt and the airbag pinned her to the seat.

Closing her eyes was a reflex, but there was no way to shut off the noise of glass shattering, and metal bending, or the screeching of the semi's brakes.

With a mouthful of airbag, breaking of glass and squealing brakes, she became a passenger. For a moment she thought Keith was with her. She trusted his voice and went for the ride, then everything went black.

CHAPTER 67

DARBY AWOKE to the sound of thunder, sitting in the cab of a large truck. She touched her forehead and felt for glass, then looked for a smear of blood on her fingers that was not there.

Glancing in the side mirror revealed the traffic jam she created. Lights flashed from behind and the trail of cars extended as far as she could see. A tow-truck was in the far right lane, inching forward as cars shifted to make room.

"You okay, little lady?"

Darby startled and looked left. A large man wearing a U.W. Husky sweatshirt was sitting beside her. "Yeah, I think so." Glancing into her side mirror she added, "I guess I know how to stop traffic."

"Yup," he said, chewing on a toothpick. "You need new brakes."

"You think?" Darby smiled and closed her eyes. She was soaked and a chill gripped her body something fierce. She opened her eyes and asked, "How long have we been sitting here?"

"Ten, maybe fifteen minutes." He glanced into her side mirror and Darby's eyes followed just as the tow-truck broke free from the jam. Her car was half the size as when her day started. "Someone played with 'em."

"Seriously?"

"Watch your back," he said as their eyes met. Darby nodded.

A siren blared causing her to jump. Her nerves were on the

other side of stable. She pulled the blanket tight and worked to calm her breath.

The ambulance driver looked into her car and shook his head. He then spoke with a police officer who pointed her way.

"Please don't tell them I blacked out."

Mr. Husky raised an eyebrow, then opened his door and jumped out of his truck. He walked around the front and spoke to the officer and paramedic and then gestured toward her. All eyes turned her way. She smiled and gave a little wave.

Darby opened the door but did not climb down. Whoever tried to wipe her off the mountain was still out there. Besides, her body ached and she had no intention of seeing if everything worked just yet. She liked exactly where she was seated.

"Can you step down, Miss?" the officer asked. Before she could say no, Mr. Husky stepped forward, slipped his hands inside the blanket and lifted her down in one gentle motion. He adjusted the blanket over her shoulders and she pulled it tight.

"Are you okay?" the paramedic asked.

"Oh, yeah," Darby said. Her ribs ached and her heart raced. As long as she did not have to take a flight physical anytime soon she would be fine.

"What happened," the officer asked.

"My brakes went out." He stared for a moment as if she was supposed to say more, so she complied. "This guy saw me flying down the freeway and gave me a hand to stop."

"A buddy radioed me from back yonder," Husky said, nodding up the pass.

The tow-truck guy wandered up with hands in pockets. "Where do you want me to take this beast?" he asked to nobody in particular.

"Can you take it to Carlos Auto Repair and Detail in Burien?"

Darby said. Not that there was a chance of bringing her car back to life.

"I know them well," he said. "Need a ride?" he asked eyeing her.

She pulled the blanket tighter shivering, and turned toward Mr. Husky. "Can I hitch a ride with you?"

"My pleasure, ma'am."

The officer's radio came to life and he said, "Standby." He walked five feet in front of the semi and stared into the cabin while he spoke.

Mr. Husky lifted Darby into the cab and joined her.

"Thanks for not telling them I blacked out."

"No problem." He reached behind the seat and pulled out a can of Diet Pepsi. "Cold. Want one?"

"I'd die for one."

"Yup, almost did that."

Darby laughed. She opened the can and drank half before she said, "Thank you."

"So why didn't you want them to know you blacked out?"

"I'd lose my medical, and it would be hell to get it back."

"What do you do when you're not flying down the freeway?"

"I'm a bus driver," she said and he nodded.

The officer stepped to the left side of the truck and waved them on. Darby allowed a breath to escape that she did not realized she was holding.

Mr. Husky started the engine and put the big rig into gear and slowly inched forward. With a head nod to her mirror he asked, "A friend of yours?"

Darby did a double take at the figure running after the truck. *What the hell?*

"Can I borrow your phone?" she asked, shaking her head.

CHAPTER 68

Kathryn made it home before Jackie and the kids. She had called all the hospitals—nothing. She waited. There was nowhere to go and nothing to do. She stopped pacing and peeled apples. Baking always calmed her nerves.

Just as she stuck the pie into the oven, the front door slammed against the wall.

"Did you find Darby?" Jackie whispered, after rushing in.

"No. I called the hospitals and—"

"Hospitals?" Jackie said, covering her mouth. "Oh my God."

"I'm sure everything is fine," Kathryn said.

"Apple pie. Yummy," Jenny said, entering the kitchen.

"Do you have anything to eat Mrs. Jacobs?" Chris asked opening the fridge.

"Chris," Jackie snapped. "Watch your manners!"

Kathryn took a deep breath and wiped her hands on a dishtowel and said, "Where's Jessica?" handing Chris an apple.

"She went to Sarah's house," Jenny said.

"I hope that's alright. The girls told me they'd cleared it with you," Jackie said.

"They did, I just forgot. What time's the dance?"

"Six. But I'm not going," Jenny said.

"Why not?" Kathryn asked.

Jenny shrugged. Kathryn and Jackie exchanged a glance.

"I've got a great idea," Jackie said. "Why don't you come home with Chris and I, then I'll take you both to the dance, and you can spend the night."

"Can I, Mom?"

"Of course. You have to do something fun to celebrate the last day of summer." Kathryn hugged Jackie and whispered, "Thank you."

Their Memorial Day weekend had been killed with the events, and she did not want the girls home if something had happened to Darby. That was one conversation she would never be prepared to have.

"Hey kiddo, why don't you go get your stuff," Kathryn said.

Chris and Jennifer left the room at the same time Kathryn's phone rang. The number was unknown. She held her breath and answered.

"I'm alive," Darby said.

"Where the heck are you?" Kathryn dropped into a chair fighting the urge to cry. "You had me scared to death. I'd heard there was an accident. I thought that you—"

"Whoa. Slow down," Darby said. "I'll tell you when I get there. I'm getting dropped off at your house in about thirty minutes." Darby's voice cracked as she asked, "Can I spend the night?"

"Of course," Kathryn said. "What's going on?"

"You mean besides being set up for pushing Keith, and an E-ticket ride down the mountain?"

"Stay where you're at. I'm coming to get you."

"Not necessary. I'm safe now. But Kat, keep your doors locked until I get there."

CHAPTER 69

DARBY'S HEAD WAS CLEAR by the time she arrived in front of Kathryn's house. Mr. Husky, real name Joshua, was her sounding board on the drive down the mountain.

She told Josh that the bus she drove had wings, as well as everything that happened to her since the merger with Global, about Keith being pushed over the ledge, her ex-boyfriend was in jail for the alleged murder, but he had been the guy chasing the truck.

He listened and nodded as she rambled. Then after he pulled in front of Kathryn's house he turned toward her and said, "When you find out who's causing you grief, you just tell em that all 250 pounds of Joshy is going to have fun making them squeal like a pig."

Darby laughed, "There are a few I'd like to hear squeal." She placed her hand on his. "Thank you."

He smiled, lifted her hand to his mouth and kissed it gently. Then he jumped out of his truck and jogged to her side of the cab and opened the door.

"Are you sure I can't hire you as a bodyguard?" she asked as he lifted her down from her perch.

"No job I'd like better, but if I don't get this load to Portland before dark, I'll have my ass in a ringer."

Darby threw her arms around his waist and hugged tight.

"Thanks Josh. I owe you my life."

He grinned and said, "Take care of yourself. Call if you need anything." He jogged around the front of his truck and climbed in. Honking twice he headed down the road.

She stood for a moment then turned toward the house. Kathryn was off the porch and running toward her.

"Who was that?" Kathryn asked hugging her.

Darby pulled back, grabbed her friend's arm and pulled her toward the house. "We've got a problem Houston."

Kathryn poured two glasses of merlot and Darby took a healthy drink, working hard not to spill through her shakes.

When she set her glass on the coffee table, she took a deep breath and said, "Someone messed with my brakes. If it hadn't been for Josh, I'd be a pancake on the bottom of the hill."

"The same person who pushed Keith. But who?"

"It couldn't be Neil. I saw him on the pass, but...if he wanted me out of the picture he wouldn't have hung around to get caught in the act, let alone chase after me."

"He's never been that bright," Kathryn said. "But none-the-less, I think you're right."

They both slipped into thought.

"Do you have our plotting paper?" Darby asked.

Kathryn left the room and returned with the paper bag. She unfolded it on the coffee table. She had brought it home to add to it, but clearly no progress had been made.

Darby slid to the floor and knelt. With palms on her thighs, she stared. "Here's the deal. All the players on this sheet have either been in jail, are in jail, or were involved in an attempted murder... except for one." She picked up a pen and circled the fleet training captain's name. "Burt Armstrong."

Kathryn laughed. "That doesn't mean he's guilty."

"Why not?" Darby asked. "When they said, 'when pigs fly' I think they were talking about him."

Kathryn smiled and tapped the pen on the paper. "Tom thinks it might be someone working for the FAA. He's got me going through everyone's computers. I hope to hell he's wrong."

Darby took the marker from Kathryn and wrote FAA on the page beside the POI, then reached for her glass. She stared at the paper trying to figure out the motive for anyone in the FAA, other than the POI, to falsify documents.

It was one thing to look the other way to cover your butt. But to openly destroy evidence—that was another issue all unto itself.

"What about the files?" Kathryn asked.

"Files?" Darby said, looking up confused. "What files?"

"Your call. You said—"

"Oh shit! That's what I wanted to tell you. Everything in this world has gone electronic. So why were they pulling boxes of files out of the CEO's office?"

"Huh?"

"Missing ASR reports. This is an electronic issue. What was in those boxes?"

"Oh my God." Kathryn leaned back, with eyes wide. "Training records...that were planted."

"Exactly," Darby said.

"But why try to kill you?"

"Everything I've been blogging about has ruffled feathers. All of it had to do with training...or lack of. My first problem was emailing Mr. Patrick. I think it flagged me as a problem."

Darby stood and stretched, bringing life back to her legs.

"They've wasted a great deal of time and resources for a chain of command violation. What corporation would be so insecure to react that way in today's world? Especially where the CEO touts an open door policy."

Darby reached for her wine. "I think flight operations is hiding behind this 'military' thing because they *want* us to think that's the reason they don't want us going over their heads."

Kathryn furrowed her brow. "I'm not following."

"Just like Vegas," Darby said. "They don't want us exercising the open door policy because they want everything that happens in flight ops to stay in flight ops. To stay hidden from Mr. Patrick… who is one hell of a CEO. His only problem is enabling assholes to run flight operations.

"He's responsible for the company," Kathryn said. "If they're to blame, so is he."

"True, but keeping your hand in every pot with a company this size is not an easy thing. He has to allow people to run their departments and make decisions. I'm not giving him an excuse, but it's a valid reason he's lost track of what the kids are doing with their airplanes."

"Playing devil's advocate," Kathryn said, "if flight operations pilots are involved—"

"I don't think it's the flight ops guys," Darby said. "Maybe they were involved in policing the pilots. Hiding ASR reports, what's their motivation? I think they're just being insecure assholes."

"Then who?"

"Training. The fleet training captain…maybe the director of training." Darby held up her hand before Kathryn could speak. "This goes beyond Armstrong being an ass. I really believe there is something going down in that department. It fits."

"Okay. So why?" Kathryn asked.

"Money, in the form of millions," Darby said. "Their salaries and bonuses are tied to MBOs—the more they save in their department, the more they make at the end of the year. They could be using training funds to fill their own pockets."

"Management by objectives or not, I can't believe pilots would sell their souls by allowing training to be shortchanged. They're supposed to be the safety net for the rest of you. If they're not, why have them in those positions anyway?"

Darby raised an eyebrow. "Seriously? Who do you work for?"

Kathryn grinned. "I know it's an FAA mandate to have pilots in those positions, but only because non-pilot managers don't understand what you go through and the logistics of line flying. But they're still pilots."

"Yeah, pilots selling their souls." Darby sighed. "Were there ASRs on any Global planes, or just missing on the A330?"

"Nothing for *any* fleet at Global," Kathryn said.

"Then that says the director of training more than Armstrong."

"We need more than assumptions. If we do this wrong, the rat will burrow deep and we'll never get him."

"Without ASR events, could training be cut without question?" Darby asked. "They've been cutting all training programs. My plane is just the highest profile because pilots are having problems with the new technology."

"They could. So, let's say the director of training is involved." Kathryn took the pen and wrote Frank Dawson on the paper. "Could he get away with this by himself?"

Darby shook her head, "I doubt it. I doubt any of these pilots in this management regime could do anything by themselves. They probably go to the bathroom together." She sipped her wine and thought for a moment. "Maybe he and Mr. Patrick are in this together. Whomever it is, I know one thing—we need to pull them out of hiding so I can skin their balls."

Kathryn chuckled. "You shouldn't joke. This is bigger than we think, and you're in danger. "

"I don't think so. None of them have big balls. Skinning will be easy," Darby said, then winked. She laid her head on Kathryn's shoulder and sighed. "How are we going to catch them?"

Kathryn laughed and pushed her upright. "We're calling the police. Telling them what we suspect."

"No, we're not," Darby snapped. "What are we telling them exactly? There is no proof of anything other than my brake line was cut, and idiot Neil will be the first suspected of that. Who got him out of jail anyway?"

Kathryn shrugged. "I don't know, but we need help."

"Can we call John?"

"I'm not sure what he could do," Kathryn said. "Besides, since he moved his office out here he's been pretty busy."

"Not too busy to spoil Jackie," Darby said.

"That man is seriously trying to impress someone." Kathryn and Darby exchanged a glance and smiled.

"If I could get Dawson or Armstrong to incriminate themselves on a recording we'd have someone's ass by the weekend," Darby said snapping her fingers.

"That would be nice, but we need it legal to hold up in court."

Darby chewed on her lip. "Then we need John's help."

She knelt in front of the coffee table and stared at the paper. She touched Keith's name then looked up at Kathryn. "We're missing something. Why did they push him?"

"He knew what they were doing," Kathryn said. "He was going

to tell you or the authorities. It's that simple."

"More than knowing something. I think he had something," Darby said, "and they're looking for it. Someone went through my house the night he was pushed."

"What?" Kathryn snapped. "Why didn't you say anything?"

Darby shrugged. "At first I thought it was me. Hell, for all I know, they could have been there when I came home that night. We'd drank so much that I flopped into bed after I stumbled in. When I awoke, my drawers were definitely compromised."

Kathryn raised an eyebrow and Darby rolled her eyes and said, "My dresser drawers."

"I didn't say anything." Kathryn stood and peeked out the curtains and then turned toward Darby. "Sooner or later they'll figure out you don't have anything."

"Then we better make them think I do. Besides, they tried to kill me so they must think I know something."

"Or you know where it is," Kathryn said.

"Exactly." Darby nodded and her stomach grumbled. "All this brain work has made me hungry. Do you have anything to eat?"

Darby followed Kathryn to the kitchen.

"Maybe we should order out," Kathryn said, opening the fridge. "I haven't done much shopping lately. I have pie."

Darby sat on a barstool and folded her arms on the counter. Then something caught her eye—Kathryn's pile of mail.

"Holy shit! I'm such an idiot. I know where it is," Darby shouted as she jumped off the stool.

She ran to the living room and grabbed her purse, then flew nonstop to Kathryn's office.

CHAPTER 70
FAA OFFICE
SEATTLE, WASHINGTON

SEPTEMBER 6, 2012

KATHRYN PULLED INTO the FAA parking lot and sighed. She pulled her keys out of the ignition and held them tight in both hands. Closing her eyes she said a quick prayer that they were on the right track.

She dropped her keys into her purse, climbed out of the car, and pressed the master lock before closing the door. Looking up to the building she took a deep breath.

A million concerns filled her head about the stupidity of Darby's plan. But as hard as she tried, there was only one reason that they could fail—if her worst nightmare came true. She had to trust and believe there were good people in the world who could not be bought, no matter what the price.

Kathryn headed into the building. Just before reaching Tom's office, her phone rang and she stopped to answered it.

"Hey," Kathryn said, "are you ready to go?"

"Yep. I'm sitting at Starbucks and operation 'squeal like a pig' is ready to go," Darby said.

Kathryn laughed. She placed her phone back into her purse and poked her head through Tom's open door. "Can I talk to you for a minute?"

"Come in, please."

She entered his office and closed the door. "I know we have a closed case. They have Mr. Patrick and so far our search has turned up nothing in our office, but…"

Tom sat against the edge of his desk. "But what?"

"I don't believe Mr. Patrick acted alone on this. I think the A330 fleet training captain and the director of training are involved."

"You've got my attention," Tom said.

"They've been harassing Darby for the most ridiculous things over at Global. But when they made her pull that Pacific Airlines post and fabricated a letter, they changed the game. Someone was worried she would bring attention to the lack of training, leading us to noticing those missing ASRs."

"What do you have to back this up?" Tom asked.

"Nothing, yet. But I don't think Keith's being pushed was at the hand of the CEO. I also don't think he cut Darby's brake lines. Someone else is involved. We think Keith had something on them. It makes sense. He worked in that department. He was connected to Darby. He tried to get her to stop writing that blog and then he ends up missing."

Tom folded his arms. "A lot of speculation."

"For now," Kathryn said. "It won't be long until we have something solid."

Tom's eyebrows raised.

"Keith left Darby an address written on the back of an envelope. She had stuffed it into her purse, but with all that was happening she forgot about it. We Googled the address and discovered Keith's mother left him a cabin in Wenatchee."

"You think something's there?" Tom asked.

"Absolutely. Whatever he has on the training department is

hidden in that cabin. He was pushed for something important." Kathryn sighed. "Darby's headed there today, and I'd like to go. Unofficially, of course. I need the day off."

"If these guys are willing to kill, I don't think it's safe for either of you to do this." He pushed back from his chair and walked to the window with his hands on hips. Turning toward her he said, "We need to take a team and search the place, make it clean and official."

"I couldn't agree more," Kathryn said. "But this is a closed case. They think Neil killed Keith over a lover's quarrel and the CEO screwed with the airline."

"It may take a few days, but I can set something up," Tom said. "Let's let the sleeping cabin lay for one more day."

"I couldn't agree more, but I can't stop Darby from going."

Tom sat on the edge of his desk and folded his arms. "Does she have the right to go into his cabin?"

"Actually, she does." Kathryn said. "The records indicated that Keith transferred ownership to her two weeks ago. "

Tom nodded slowly then said, "Then you go with her. Call me if you find anything."

"Thank you, sir," Kathryn said.

"If you find something, don't touch it. This has to be a legal search to hold up in court. Despite having the CEO in a tight little bundle, we're still responsible for tracking those records. I want to personally nail whomever is involved."

"You got it," Kathryn said, walking toward the door.

"Kathryn," Tom said. She hesitated and turned. "Be careful. I don't want to lose you."

CHAPTER 71

KATHRYN MET DARBY at Starbucks and within minutes they were on their way to Lake Wenatchee.

The directions were easy to follow. With a little over an hour and a half on the freeway, they were minutes away from the cabin. Their venti-sized coffees were long gone and Darby sat in silence. Every time they passed a car Darby startled, but she had not moved for the previous fifteen minutes.

Kathryn glanced right to see if she was asleep, as neither of them had much the night before. Darby's forehead rested on the glass as she stared out the window, lost in another world.

Glancing at the photo of her twins pinned to the visor, Kathryn prayed she was doing the right thing. With any luck they would be done with this mess and home by dinner.

Kathryn clicked the blinker and pulled off the freeway. With a quick glance at the directions and back to the road, she turned right and continued down a hill. The car hit a pothole and bounced Darby's head against the window and she sat upright as Kathryn pulled onto the property.

"Are we here?" Darby asked, coming back from wherever she had been.

"Yep," Kathryn said, putting the car into park. She looked up at the cabin. "Welcome to the moment of truth."

The cabin was a nine hundred square-foot A-frame with fresh paint and a new roof.

They climbed out of the car and Kathryn locked the doors. They walked up the path to the front door and Darby placed her hands on the window and peered in.

"Wow," Darby said. "This is amazing." She stepped back and Kathryn took her place.

"Not your typical cabin in the woods," Kathryn said.

"Close your eyes." Darby stepped forward holding a large rock.

Kathryn turned her back and Darby smashed the rock into the window. She broke the lower right pane in the door and then smashed the glass a second time breaking away the sharp pieces around the edges. She reached inside and unlocked the door.

"Looks like you're a master of breaking and entering."

Darby shrugged, "Some things you never forget." She winked and opened the door.

Kathryn wished she knew how to pull Darby out of the funk she fell into on the drive. Instead, she reached for the light switch and lifted it. "Power. Nice." Then her eyes swept the room—one large open space with stairs off to one side heading up to a loft.

A stone fireplace filled one wall and large window panes filled another facing the lake. Kathryn's eyes landed on Darby who was sliding her hand over the back of the leather couch.

"This came from his house in Arizona," Darby said. "My favorite. He fixed this place up for us." Her eyes glassed over. "This was why he was out of touch last month." She walked to the island and sat on a barstool.

"Maybe this wasn't a good idea," Kathryn said, sitting beside her. The pain in Darby's eyes was unbearable.

Darby brushed away a tear. "No. This was the best idea, but…"

She hesitated and said, "I was hoping he was hiding here, but the closer we got I realized we would have received a call."

"Oh, Sweetie—"

Darby waved a hand. "Stupid I know. But without a body, I just hoped…" She sucked a deep breath, wiping a tear, and said, "Whoever pushed Keith did it for a reason. They're looking for something." She glanced around. "This is the one place they've yet to be. Let's find whatever it is."

Darby climbed the stairs to the loft. She stood at the top and stared into the darkness, then turned and looked toward the view of the lake and returned downstairs.

She and Kathryn exchanged a glance. Kathryn reached out and touched Darby's arm. Then they began searching.

They searched through drawers, on the bookshelf behind books, the desk, through the DVDs under cushions, in the freezer. Anywhere they could think of and found nothing.

"Nothing's here," Darby finally said flopping onto the couch. "Why leave me that address?"

"He gave you the cabin. He wanted you to know it was here. Let's not give up hope and keep looking."

"How long should we stay?" Darby asked.

Kathryn glanced at her watch. "Maybe a couple more hours."

"We need a snack," Darby said. She opened the pantry and pulled out a box of popcorn and unwrapped a package. She placed it in the microwave and pressed start. She turned and leaned against the counter with arms folded.

Kathryn did not know what to say. The best she could do was just be by her side and wait it out.

They listened to the pop, pop, pop of the kernels. The time between each pop decreased, and then simultaneously with the microwave beeping, the lights went out.

They exchanged a glance in the shadows.

"Blow a breaker?" Darby asked.

"Let me check," Kathryn whispered.

Kathryn opened the drawer beside the sink and pulled out a flashlight. She had found the electrical panel during her search and headed toward the back of the cabin.

While daylight streamed through the windows in the main room, the back hall was dark. She turned on the flashlight and found her way to the closet that housed the panel. She opened the door and flipped the breaker off, then on.

Lights illuminated the hallway and Kathryn relaxed. "It was a breaker," she said walking down the hall. "Looks like we're up and..."

Darby stood in the middle of the room with a man behind her holding a knife to her throat.

CHAPTER 72

IF A KNIFE WERE NOT pressing into her neck, Darby would have laughed at Kathryn's expression. They both hoped to catch a scumbag, but a knife to her throat was not part of the plan.

Darby had stopped by the training department and told the fleet training captain she was sorry for all that happened, and that she was putting the past to bed. She also mentioned Keith's cabin in passing.

She finally convinced Kathryn that Armstrong and Dawson were responsible. Keith was in training and ASRs were missing. This was nothing short of a training department game.

They hoped for a confrontation with a confession, not a knife to her throat. Holding her breath, she waited for a moment to escape before things got messy.

There were a million things she wanted to say to the asshole, but she was afraid to open her mouth. Even if he did not plan on cutting her, the alcohol seeping from his pours made an accidental slashing more probable than not.

"What do you want?" Kathryn asked, "We don't have any money."

Good job Kat. Playing dumb always worked well in situations like this.

"I want the tape," he said.

"What tape," Kathryn asked.

"Don't play dumb," Armstrong spat. He pushed Darby to the floor. "I've been sitting outside for the last hour and you two bitches are making popcorn? Enough is enough, hand it over."

"What? You want popcorn?" Darby asked pushing to her feet.

He stomped a foot toward her and she scrambled backwards.

"You'd better run."

"Kat, meet Burt Armstrong. Global Air Lines A330 fleet training captain and proverbial piece of shit," Darby said, nodding his direction. She knew Armstrong was involved, now they just needed him to incriminate Dawson and they would have them.

Giving a little wave Kat said, "Kathryn Jacobs."

"I know who you are. Give me the tape and I'm out of here."

"Yeah, right," Darby said. "You killed Keith trying to get it, and if we give it to you, you'll kill us too."

"Grow up little girl," he said. "You have no idea what you're talking about."

"If it was an argument and you struggled," Kathryn said inching closer, but remaining in the kitchen with the island between them, "they'll go easier on you."

Darby slowly worked her way toward the stairs. Armstrong looked her way and then to Kathryn and back to Darby.

"How'd you pull the ASR reports anyway?" Kathryn asked.

"Shut up," he said. "Where's the tape?"

"We couldn't find it," Darby said. What they found instead was the flying pig.

"Then you're both useless to us."

"Hardly," Darby said keying on the word 'us'.

He looked her way and glared. He was about to say something, but hesitated and grabbed his phone instead. He fumbled pushing buttons with his left hand while he held the knife with his right.

"They didn't find anything...Yeah...I'm not stupid," he said, and then ended the call.

"If you kill us this will be premeditated," Kathryn said. "You'll get life. You won't get away with it."

"The hell I won't," he sighed. "Stone had one task—control that bitch. He could have been rich. What does he do?" Armstrong glared lustfully at Darby. "You must be some piece of ass."

"You'll have to kill me first to find out," Darby said with both hands planted firmly on her hips.

"That can be arranged," he said with a laugh.

They had nothing on him, and their minutes were numbered.

"Why'd you and Dawson pull the reports?" she asked, inching toward the stairs. "Was it because you don't have a clue how to manage, and you were having difficulty hiding your incompetence that you can't fly a plane or a desk?"

"You fucking little bitch," he said, gripping the knife so tight his knuckles turned white and his face reddened. He raised his arm.

"Armstrong!" Kathryn yelled.

When he turned his head toward her, she threw a bowl at him. He swatted it away with his hand, but that was all the time Darby needed.

She bolted up the stairs. Armstrong flew after her. She was half way up when she stumbled and he dove for her legs. He grabbed a foot and she kicked wildly. Pulling free, she left a shoe behind and sprang to the top and into the darkness.

Armstrong chased her with the knife held high.

CHAPTER 73

WHEN DARBY SCREAMED from above, Kathryn ran toward the base of the stairs. The next thing she heard was a thud followed by silence.

"Darby? John?" Kathryn called.

"We got him," John yelled.

"I'm good," Darby said, leaning over the railing. Kathryn placed a hand to her heart.

She had asked John, her old boss from the NTSB, to help. His moving to a Seattle office for a mysterious project, led to unanswered questions. The extra funds were a little too suspicious. The rental car he drove was a little too nice. None of this added up to a government salary. Yet he was the only one she could turn to.

She thanked God he was for real.

He drove up to the cabin at zero dark thirty and set up the equipment to tape, and she and Darby broke in for a show.

John appeared at the top of the stairs with Armstrong in handcuffs, slumped on the floor, out cold. John propped him into a sitting position. He glanced at Darby. "You want the honor?"

A smile spread across her face for the first time that day. She knelt behind Armstrong and gave him a push. He toppled down, stopping midway, and she scooted down and pushed again until he reached the bottom.

Darby followed him, picked up his phone and stuck it into her pocket, then grabbed her shoe. John came down the stairs, and they stared at their trapped animal.

"Now what?" Kathryn asked. "Did we get anything?"

"I'm afraid not. Other than an assault with a weapon." John shook his head. "With the right attorney, he won't spend a night in jail."

Darby sat heavily on the bottom stair. Her foot involuntarily extended and met Armstrong's head, and then she pulled on her shoe. "We need that tape."

"At least we know what we're looking for," Kathryn said.

"We'll find it," Darby said. "Keith probably has it with him."

John leaned against the fireplace and folded his arms. "I'm not sure Keith had a tape. I think he said that to threaten them. Our only hope is to cut a deal with this one."

"Then that's what we'll do," Kathryn said. "He won't want jail. He'll talk."

"He's a princess," Darby said. "He won't last a minute in prison."

"He'd also been drinking," Kathryn added. "He might not remember what he said."

"I could help with the brain damage part," Darby said, going to the kitchen. She pulled a pitcher from the cupboard and filled it with water and added ice.

Kathryn laughed. "That would be nice, but I think John needs him in one piece."

She wished Darby could unleash her fury on Armstrong. If it could bring Keith back, she would kick the shit out of him herself. Instead, they needed to negotiate a deal.

"Unfortunately, Kathryn's right," John said.

"Then let's get this party going." Darby lifted the pitcher and threw ice water on Armstrong's face.

Armstrong coughed. "What the hell," he said sputtering.

"Time to go for a ride." John rolled him on his face and took a handful of cuffs. "Stand up asshole," he said as he yanked him to his feet. "Kathryn, are you okay to secure the loft? Still good with procedures to not contaminate the site?"

"Absolutely." It had been years since she worked an investigation site, but she knew exactly what to do. More importantly, what not to do.

"Get Kathryn's keys and we'll drive her car," John said to Darby. "You two up front. I'll sit in back with this piece of shit."

Darby followed John as he pushed Armstrong out the door. Kathryn went up to the loft, and flipped the light switch to on.

After finding his camera, she snapped photos of the knife, pulled on rubber gloves and put the knife inside a plastic bag. She carefully picked up his tools and then secured the recording equipment.

Enough proof for speculation only. *Big deal, he had a knife.* She shook her head and pulled off the gloves.

She was closing the box with the recording equipment, when a loud cra-ack echoed outside. Kathryn dropped everything and ran for the stairs.

CHAPTER 74

DARBY STOOD ON the top step and watched John as he pushed Armstrong down the stairs. When he stumbled John let go, allowing him to face plant. Being anything but gentle John yanked him to his feet.

She would remain optimistic, but somewhere deep within her gut she knew Captain Burt Armstrong would get away with whatever he was up to. If it were the last thing she did, she would make him pay.

She hopped off the steps and led the way to the car. She stopped halfway and turned. "Ooops," she said as her foot accidentally connected with Armstrong's crotch.

Armstrong fell to his knees with a howling moan and glared her way. "Your days are numbered."

"The only days that appear to be numbered are yours," John said, yanking him to his feet. "I'm seeing a long life in the state pen." He pushed him toward the car.

"Can you say, butt toy?" Darby smirked.

"You have nothing," Armstrong said smugly.

John threw him against the hood of the car and placed an arm against his neck and pressed. Armstrong's eyes grew wide.

"I'd kill you right now, but death's too easy for a scumbag like you," John growled. "Every day you rot in prison will be another day I'll smile." John released him and he slid to the ground.

Darby glanced at the lake. Ripples percolated as the wind picked up. The sun cresting above the cabin cast a glow across the mountain on the opposite side of the lake. If only she and Keith could share this together. They needed to find him.

Glancing down at the pathetic example of a human being, she lifted a hand to her throat. The fact he drank first was not the sign of a criminal with a stomach. He was a robot, and someone held the controls. Dawson, she was sure of it.

John bent down and pulled Armstrong to his feet as Darby unlocked the doors. She opened the back door for him to throw in the trash.

He pulled Armstrong around the door, and brain matter and blood splattered everywhere followed by a loud cra-ack. Darby hit the ground and scrambled to the other side of the car.

Her heart pounded as if it were trying to break free from her chest. Her jagged breath echoed in competition with the ringing in her ears. She pulled her shirt up and wiped the brains and blood off her face.

Within minutes the front door to the cabin flew open and Darby yelled, "No!" But not quick enough to keep Kathryn from running out.

CHAPTER 75

KATHRYN HEARD Darby yell, but her momentum was too great to stop. She tripped, hit the ground, and ate a mouthful of dirt, afraid to move.

"Darby?" she called.

"I'm okay," Darby yelled. John said nothing.

Kathryn shifted her eyes toward the car, but all she saw was the top of a head soaked in a pool of blood oozing outward.

"Where are you?" she called to Darby, afraid to lift her head.

"Car. Passenger side."

Silence gave time for anger to replace fear. If she and Darby were going to be killed, they would have been shot by now.

Kathryn raised her head, scanning the area as she shifted to her knees. Kneeling in a sprinters start she dashed toward Darby and dropped to her side. The two friends hugged, but they stayed crouched behind the shield of her car.

"John?" Kathryn whispered.

"I don't know." Darby said. "I've been trying to get a look under the car, but it's too dark to tell."

"What if..." Kathryn's voice cracked. She was the one who convinced John to come along on this escapade.

"He's okay," Darby said. "He has to be."

Kathryn wished she could believe her, but the silence told her otherwise. John was dead and Armstrong escaped, or worse—he was sitting in wait for them to move.

"I dropped your keys on the other side of the car," Darby said. "But the doors are unlocked. I've got my phone so we can call for help."

Oh God. Yes. "Let me have it. I'll call John."

Darby handed her phone to Kathryn, who then dialed John's number. They jumped when a phone rang behind them.

John stood three feet away. With hands on his knees he was breathing hard, scanning the horizon.

"We thought you bit it," Darby said.

John stepped forward extending his hands toward them and they each took one. He pulled them to their feet and said, "Someone nailed him with a rifle. I heard a car up the hill and went through the brush to cut them off. I didn't get there in time."

He continued to scan the area and said, "Go inside, wait for the authorities. I'll check out our boy."

Darby sprinted to the cabin and Kathryn followed.

She rushed Darby to the sink and helped her clean the death off her face and out of her hair.

When they finished, John was already inside. He stood beside the window and glanced out. Darby moved to the couch and pulled a blanket over her shoulders, back in a funk she played with her phone.

"They're here," John said.

Kathryn turned from Darby and walked to the window and peered out. Two police cars pulled down the driveway, lights flashing, with an ambulance in tow.

"He called someone," Kathryn said. "Where's his phone?"

"I've got it," Darby said. "The only number on it is John's."

CHAPTER 76

DARBY SAT IN KATHRYN'S living room watching John and Jackie sit way too close. Jackie held onto his arm, and Darby looked away feeling jealousy that she wished she could lose.

She was happy for her friend, but the emotion of wanting what Jackie had was almost unbearable. Darby experienced it twice, but both times it was stolen. If only she could have a do over. Unfortunately there were no such buttons in life.

Not finding Keith hiding in the cabin gave her reason to believe he might be dead—unless he was injured somewhere. His body had yet to be found, but her hope was waning. She also could not have been more wrong thinking bloodshed in his honor would make anything better.

The television was on, but muted, as they waited for the 11 o'clock news to see what the media would broadcast concerning the day's shooting. John placed a guard at the cabin until authorities arrived to do a proper search.

"Who do you think shot Armstrong?" Darby finally asked.

When Darby saw John's number on Armstrong's phone her heart had skipped a beat. She did not say anything until the police arrived, just in case. As it turned out, Kathryn had used it to call John while they were sitting by the car.

"Your guess is as good as mine," Kathryn said. "Dawson?"

"Maybe." Darby reached for a cookie. She had been thinking about something Armstrong said to them in the cabin.

"They already have Mr. Patrick," Jackie said.

"I'm not so sure he's involved," Darby said. "A little too much for a CEO to be in the woods hunting and playing with brakes. Not only would he ruin his suit, but the guy's out on bail. I think someone would be watching him."

John shifted his eyes from Kathryn to Darby. "Then who?" he asked giving her his full attention.

"Kat's boss," Darby answered. "Tom Santos."

"Why would you think that?" Kathryn asked. "He gave me access to everyone's data, including his. Why would he risk exposing himself if he were involved?"

"He wanted verification that whatever he did, could not be traced back to him," Darby said.

"Why Santos?" John asked. He raised his cup to his lips and eyed her over the rim. "He's got a reputation for being one of the best. "

Darby looked at Kathryn. "Remember when Armstrong said he knew who you were? Why would he? Then I asked myself how the heck your boss knew who I was when I came to your office." Darby dropped the cookie onto the plate without tasting it.

Kathryn's eyes widened."That's right. Both Jackie and Darby were supposed to meet me. I told him as much, but I only said my friends."

"He called me by name without being introduced."

"You were all over the news," John said.

"Name only," Darby replied. "Never my picture."

"I told him about the cabin," Kathryn said. "How could I have been so stupid?"

"I was the one that convinced you it was Armstrong and Dawson," Darby said. "I should've known that neither of those numbnuts were capable of doing anything alone."

"Why kill Armstrong?" Kathryn asked.

"Get rid of an accomplice." Darby hugged a pillow. "Armstrong was there to get rid of us. Santos knew what an incompetent putz he was and needed confirmation of the kill." Kathryn seriously needed to watch more television. "When we came out of the cabin, and he saw we were alive and John was there, his next choice was four bullets or one."

"You think?" Kathryn said.

"Four bullets and one of them a director of the NTSB...he's got a case open that won't go away," Darby said. "No brainer. Besides, he knew Armstrong would talk to save his ass."

"What about motive?" John asked.

"I've been thinking about that. Rumor has it that Santos tried to get hired by both Coastal and Global as a pilot many years ago. He couldn't get hired by either airline." Darby stood and stretched. "He could have a hard-on for Global."

"I'll be right back." Jackie squeezed John's arm and got up to leave when Live News Report flashed across the television screen.

"Turn that up," John said.

Darby was already increasing the volume.

"We're in front of a home on Lake Washington and Global Air Lines is back in the news," the reporter said. "The director of training at Global Air Lines, Frank Dawson, is dead."

The reporter hesitated. "Standby," she said, holding a finger to the wire in her ear.

"They're saying this was a suicide. He died by a self-inflicted gunshot wound. We don't have confirmation that his death has anything to do with a murder that occurred earlier this afternoon in Wenatchee. We can only speculate as the two victims worked for the same Airline."

A body was being wheeled out of the home in the background, and the reporter said, "We're minutes away from the complete story. More to come at eleven. Live on KOMO Four."

All mouths hung open and eyes wide. Darby broke the silence when she said, "If they could only find Keith. We'd have all the answers. I know there's a tape and he's got it on him."

She stood and walked to the window and looked out into the darkness. She sighed and turned toward the room. "He's up there alive somewhere. They're not doing enough. We need to search the mountains."

Kathryn and Jackie exchanged a look, and John scratched his head, then cleared his throat.

"I better get going," he said. "This is going to be a long night."

CHAPTER 77

Kathryn stepped off the elevator. She took a deep breath and adjusted her jacket. John wired her that morning in hope they could get something on Santos, while she hoped they were wrong.

When she arrived at his office, Tom's door was open. She knocked on the frame and he looked up with a broad smile.

"Good morning. I heard you had quite a time in the mountains yesterday," he extended his hand to a chair. "Sit please."

Kathryn turned her attention to the photos on the wall. Photos she never paid much attention to before today. "You're a hunter," she said quietly. When he did not comment, she turned his direction.

Eyes bore into hers and his smile turned her blood cold.

"No better thing than the hunt," he said, "other than a good kill."

Kathryn breathed deep and sat. "Armstrong confirmed we're looking for a tape." If her heart were racing earlier, it was now at the end of a marathon. The fact he would not do anything to her in the office, gave her little comfort.

"You came up empty handed?"

"Not completely," she said. "We know there's a tape, there's been a trail of bodies and someone wants that recording awfully bad. I think it's you."

His smile remained.

"Apparently I gave you a get out of jail free card by searching the computer system."

Santos look shifted to one of confusion. "You did what? You searched computers? Whose?" He wagged a finger at her. "If your computer shows a trail going anywhere it shouldn't, that could mean only one thing."

Kathryn froze. That son of a bitch was setting her up. "What have you done?"

"What have I done?" He leaned back in his chair. "I found my mole. Security is pulling your computer as we speak."

"You bastard." Kathryn watched her life fly out the window. More than that, she allowed this urchin to get the best of her. She felt as if she were falling off that cliff with Keith. "You'll never get away with this."

"Get away with what?" Santos said. "Fire you? You're right. It would take an act of congress. But I can have you transferred. How does the Detroit office sound? Maybe Fargo?"

"There was a reason I didn't tell you that John was joining us at the cabin. We knew you were involved," she lied.

"You mean that NTSB punk out of jurisdiction? They have Patrick for falsifying records. The director of training killed himself after admitting he shot the fleet training captain." He pushed back from his desk and added, "For gods sake lady, he even had the rifle in his possession."

"An unregistered rifle."

"Hell, he left a suicide note."

Santos sauntered to his credenza and poured himself a cup of coffee. "Would you like some?" he asked, over his shoulder. "I'm buying."

"You'll never get away with this."

"I knew they couldn't pull this off without inside help," he said turning. "Just like your husband. Shame on you."

"You bastard."

Santos laughed, and returned to his desk. He sipped his coffee and watched Kathryn over the brim. Her mind shot all over the place searching for something, anything to nail him with.

"It's time for you to leave," he said, shooing her away with the back of his hand. "I'll put your transfer in tomorrow." He leaned on his desk and added, "If those little girls of yours would like to go hunting before you leave, I could teach them a lesson or two."

Kathryn's blood went from cold to boiling in an instant. She jumped to her feet, knocking the chair backwards as she did.

"You fucking little twerp. You can threaten me with jail or a transfer, but don't you *ever* threaten my family," she said stabbing a finger his way.

Every part of her body shook, fear attacked her senses. She just put her daughters in harms way. Her phone rang and she pulled it out of her purse. "Yes?" she snapped.

"They have Stone's body," John said. "Get to the police station, I'll meet you there. And Kat...tell Santos."

"I'm on my way," she said, still shaking, and pressed off. "Looks like they found Stone's body. Your days are numbered."

CHAPTER 78

DARBY SAT IN A POLICE station briefing room beside Kathryn. John stood, as he attempted to rationalize why he lied to her for the previous twelve days. She tried to keep an open mind, but it was getting harder with each ticking minute. They found Keith's body the night he was pushed, but had kept it secret.

"I'm sorry," John said. "We've been watching this for eleven months. After the San Fran crash we looked into our local ASR reports to see if the U.S. was having a problem with our pilots not being able to fly their automated planes."

John pulled a hand over his face. "We learned that Global Air Line's ASR reports were non-existent. After finding Pacific Airlines black box, the situation escalated to top priority."

He pulled out a chair and sat at the table across from her. "They called me because of the people involved. When Stone was murdered we figured we could catch more fish with bait." He reached out and covered Darby's hands with his. "I wish I could have told you the truth earlier. I'm sorry."

Darby jerked her hands away and put them in her lap. Each day that passed gave her reason to believe that he was injured and hiding. Stupid, she knew, but she built up hope.

Hope was denial's best friend and now she had nothing. It was true—Keith was gone. She could not even bring herself to go see his body. She wanted the memories of him alive.

"So there's no tape," Kathryn said.

"No." John shook his head.

"Now what?" Darby asked, without looking at either of them.

"It gets better," Kathryn said. "Santos set me up and threatened the girls. He's behind it alright, but we've got nothing to prove it."

"I'll review the tape this afternoon."

Darby pushed back from the table and stood. "This is a fucking nightmare. Santos is getting away with murder!"

She was so friggin angry at everyone. Glaring at John she said, "But nobody kills three people for a pilot job. Especially how the industry has ended up." Darby held his stare. "There has to be more."

"We're checking his banking transactions to see if there has been a transfer of funds. We'll watch him," John said. "Eventually he'll make a mistake and we will get him."

"So we do nothing? And what about Kat and the girls?"

"We've got a number of positions we can transfer her to." John turned toward Kathryn and said, "Or, we could keep you in that office looking over his shoulder."

"If it weren't for the girls I'd stay and fight," Kathryn said. "But until he is behind bars, I don't want them in the same city with that monster. We have to move."

John nodded.

"I'll go with you," Darby said, sitting beside her.

"Where's Santos now?" Kathryn asked.

"He's down the hall reviewing the evidence."

Kathryn and Darby looked at each other, and then to John, with confusion.

Darby froze. "What evidence?"

"Why does he have access to anything?" Kathryn said.

"Santos had a warrant standing by for first access to Stone. Part of his investigation."

"If there's no tape, then what evidence?" Darby asked again.

"Wallet and contents," John said. Glancing at Darby he added, "And a letter."

"Letter?" Darby's heart began to race.

"Keith wrote you a letter," John said. "It was on his body when they found him."

"What the fuck?" Darby jumped up and knocked her chair over. "Keith wrote me a letter and that scumbag is reading it? What happened to personal property?" She pulled a hand through her hair and placed the other on her hip.

"You knew, and you didn't say anything?" Darby yelled, and then dropped to her knees and began to cry.

She looked up between sobs and said, "How could you John? I trusted you. It's mine...he has no right."

"I'm sorry, Sweetheart. He didn't mail it. It was on his body and part of his effects. Santos will find nothing and then we'll hand it over to you."

"Why are they doing this now?" Kathryn asked, kneeling by Darby. She placed a hand on her back and rubbed.

"The case is officially closed," John said.

"No!" Darby cried. "It can't be over."

CHAPTER 79

September 21, 2012

Two weeks had passed since they closed the case. Darby was curled up on her couch, alone. The TV was on and the news blasted in the background, but it was nothing but noise. She called in sick with no intention of going back on duty anytime soon. How could she return to work?

Kathryn invited her over for dinner with Jackie, John, and the kids. What she once loved, now reminded her of what she would never have. Besides, she was angry. Angry at all of them.

If Kathryn had not kept her from driving to the mountains that night, she would have been with Keith and he would be alive. He would not have been on that ledge. They would have been in bed curled up in each other's arms. Together they could have figured out what to do.

She was so mad at Keith for not trusting her enough to tell her what was going on.

John lied to her too. He knew Keith was dead the entire time. He had a letter that belonged to her. There was something wrong with all this.

Darby unfolded her letter. This was her only connection to Keith and she could not read it often enough. Tears filled her eyes, but it was getting easier each time.

Dearest Darby,

If you are reading this without me by your side, then the worst has probably happened. I won't go into any half-assed explanations, excuses, etc., because if you don't know what's happened, then it's safer that way. I want this letter to find you. To tell you how much I love you.

I hurt you. I'm sorry. Please don't let my stupidity keep you from the love you deserve. I never anticipated things would turn out like they did. I was never part of it. Believe that. I left my cabin to you. It was supposed to be for us. Every hour I spent working on it, was an hour spent envisioning us together. (We had a really good time.) I want you to make memories of your own. The address is on your ALPO bill.

It was going to be a surprise for your birthday. But, don't feel obligated to keep it. You can do anything you want with it. But before you do...

I want you to know one thing—you were the best thing that ever happened to me, and the Best Chapter Of My Life...

Remember that, always..."The Best Chapter!"

I love you. I will love you forever and four days...

Yours, Keith

Darby folded the letter and pulled it close to her heart and closed her eyes fighting pain that shredded her heart and soul.

She envisioned the cabin and all its beauty. She wanted that with Keith. She needed it. She set the letter on the table, and her phone rang. Kathryn, again.

She allowed the message to go to voicemail. Her last five calls were nothing but trying to talk her out of her funk. Darby no longer wanted to talk, and she sure as hell was not ready to get out of her funk. Maybe next week.

The ringing stopped and the message pinged. She set the phone on the table and rolled over, pulling the blanket up to her chin.

That bastard Santos was still floating around the halls of the FAA. His living and her wanting to kill him, trumped everything else she felt. She hated him with every bit of her soul.

Within minutes pounding began on her front door and then it opened.

"Darby, it's me," Kathryn said. "If you won't come to dinner, dinner will come to you."

Darby pulled the blanket over her head.

Jessica and Jennifer were arguing about something when they came crashing in. Chris was laughing. Jackie and John's words were muffled as they entered and then the smell of Chinese Food punched her in the gut. Her stomach grumbled.

Someone ran up the stairs and then Jackie yelled, "She's not up here."

Darby held her breath until the blanket was ripped from her head, and Kathryn stared down at her.

"I don't care if you hate me. I don't care if you hate the world. But you will *never* hate Chinese Food and you need to eat. So get your ass off that couch now."

Darby blinked a couple times. Half of her wanted to prove that they couldn't push her around by barging into her cave. If she wanted to be depressed and hate everyone, she had every right. But the smell of Moo Shu pork smacked those thoughts from her brain.

"Okay," she said with a smile.

"Good girl," Kathryn said. "Besides, John wants to talk to us."

Darby sat up and pulled the blanket over her shoulders, and followed Kathryn toward the kitchen, setting her letter on the bookshelf along the way.

"Did you bring wine?" Darby asked. "Being depressed is getting old. Maybe I could drink myself better." She tossed the blanket in the corner.

Kathryn hugged her. "Welcome back."

Next week she would feel the sweetness of revenge. She would get on her feet and find proof to nail that bastard Tom Santos, if it were the last thing she did.

"Think you brought enough?" Darby asked looking into the box. There was enough food for the entire neighborhood.

Jackie watched the kids fill their plates and John stood close, touching her. She was happy for Jackie. She and Kathryn exchanged a smile. They knew it would not be long until Jackie became Mrs. McAllister.

The kids took their plates to Darby's game room, and a pain stung her heart. She envisioned her kids playing with Keith in there. *Shake it off Darby.* She sucked a deep breath and filled her plate.

"I hope you got chop sticks," Darby said, looking through the box. "It should be against the law to eat Chinese food with a fork."

"Put me in jail," John said, holding up his fork. "I'm starved."

"What's up with Santos?" Darby asked.

"We've got nothing on him, and worse yet he's built a solid case against Kathryn." The room quieted with John's words.

"And I thought I could destroy the mood of a party," Darby said. "It won't stick." But the look on Kathryn's face said she did not believe that.

"This sucks," Jackie said. "Nothing about it is right."

"You and the girls can live with me. If you have to move I'll change bases with the airline," Darby said.

Kathryn leaned over, with tears in her eyes, and hugged Darby. "Thank you."

"That's what I'd like to talk to you about," John said to Darby, and set his fork on the plate.

Darby's eyes went from John's fork to his eyes and a chill wormed through her body. She gripped her chopsticks waiting for a pair of shears to cut them in half.

"McDermott talked to the union and offered to pay you to take early retirement. The union said they would present the offer when you came off sick leave."

"Pay me off?" Darby snapped. "Why?"

"Maybe with all they put you through, they're afraid of a huge lawsuit," Jackie said.

"They said they were making up for the pain they caused you," John said. "They think, with all that's happened with Global, that it would be uncomfortable for you to stay."

"Uncomfortable?" Darby said confused. None of this made sense. She tapped her sticks on her plate as her mind whirled, then it kicked into high gear.

"What if we have it backwards? What if those shits in flight operations were involved in this too? That's why they were harassing me."

"Don't over think this. It's a good payday," John said. "Four million dollars good."

Darby dropped her chopsticks. *"Seriously?"* John nodded, and the table went silent.

She closed her eyes and pressed her face into her palms. *Oh My God.* She could buy a little plane, become a flight instructor and actually fly a plane, again. But retire early?

Darby dropped her hands and eyed the barbequed pork. Lifting a piece with her chopsticks she dipped it into the hot mustard. She would let this offer sit on the table. There was Chinese Food to eat first. One thing she learned a long time ago, never make a decision based on fear, on emotions, or when you were hungry.

"Four million bucks is a lot of money," Jackie said. "You could write a book about all this."

"Well…" John hesitated. "There's a problem with that. The only way they'll pay you is if you sign a disclosure to keep your mouth shut about what happened."

"Interesting," Darby said. "So if I take money, then we're done? A double jeopardy kind of thing."

"That's about the size of it," John said, stuffing rice into his mouth. "They're going to offer this when you come off sick leave. I'm not supposed to be telling you."

Darby nodded. She chewed on the idea for a moment. She always swore she could not be bought, and that was exactly what they were trying to do. Yet, how could she go back to work for that airline after all that has happened?

"Why are they buying me off?" she asked nobody in particular.

"Good question," Kathryn said. "One I'm asking myself."

"There's only one reason that they don't want me working," Darby said. "All the trash has not been taken out at Global Air Lines."

CHAPTER 80

ONCE DARBY FINISHED eating more food than a body had the right to in one sitting, she excused herself from the table and went to the living room. Why in the hell were they trying to buy her off?

What were they doing? On the other side of that coin, how much fun would it be to have four million bucks to play with. She picked up the remote to kill the news, and froze. Her eyes went wide. *Oh Shit.*

Vice President McDermott was back on TV. Global Air Lines had been in the news for two weeks with updates on the murders.

Lawrence Patrick was out on bail awaiting trial and Vice President McDermott was officially running the airline.

"John!" she yelled. "Who made that offer?"

He walked into the living room followed by Kathryn and Jackie. "McDermott. Why?"

"I know who the trash is." Darby rushed to her video cabinet and dropped to her knees. She had taped every news report with Global since this all started. She searched through the labels and found it. *CEO Goes to Jail.*

"What's going on?" Jackie asked.

"Here we go," Darby said and stuck the disk into the player. Darby allowed the scene to play out with Lawrence Patrick being taken to jail and then the video shifted to Seattle. McDermott stood in front of the Seattle office." Darby pressed pause.

"What's this all about?" Kathryn asked.

"McDermott knew my name, too. Just watch."

"What about the murdered pilot?" The reporter asked. "Does that have anything to do with what's happening here today?"

"I'm sure we'll find that had nothing to do with any of this," McDermott said, splaying his hand toward the activity behind him, as he did the first time they watched.

"But he was an instructor who worked in this building, as was the pilot sitting in jail who's being accused of his murder."

"There have been no convictions and I'm not at liberty to discuss anything about that at this time."

"What about the female pilot—Darby. We understand that she identified numerous transgressions in training and was harassed because of it."

"Transgressions, my ass," Darby mumbled.

Kathryn touched her arm.

"Watch McDermott's reaction, here," Darby said. "Remember the red around his neck, his hesitation and that stupid phony smile?" Darby pressed pause. "It's the next part that's the key. Listen to what he says." She pressed play.

"We are grateful for all our pilots stepping forward. Especially Miss Bradshaw. If it wasn't for she and her blog, I doubt any of this would have come to light."

Darby pressed pause again.

"I don't get it," Jackie said.

John scratched his head and sat heavily.

Darby could see Kathryn's wheels turning.

"There are over 15,000 pilots at Global," Darby told Jackie.

"Why would the Vice President of the airline have a clue what my last name is? He wouldn't."

"Yes he would," Kathryn said. "Your name was plastered all over the news."

"I'll give you that, but why would he know about my blog?"

"The guys called you in for it," Kathryn said. "Of course he knew about it."

"McDermott is on the company side," Darby said. "Miles Carter, the chief operating officer, is the conduit between flight operations and the corporation. The corporate side only knows what Wyatt tells Carter, and I know that Wyatt would never tell upper management about my blog."

"Why not?" Jackie asked.

"Because it wasn't their idea and it was having a positive impact."

"This is all circumstantial," John said squeezing the bridge of his nose. "There's no way we can go after the vice president of an airline for knowing your name or that you wrote a blog."

"McDermott is behind this with Santos," Darby said. "I know it and I'll get the proof." She sat heavily. "But who the hell asked that question about me anyway?"

"I'm wondering the same thing," Kathryn said.

CHAPTER 81
GLOBAL CORPORATE HEADQUARTERS
SEATTLE, WASHINGTON

SEPTEMBER 28, 2012

DARBY SAT IN HER NEW SUBARU Forester outside the Seattle office and opened Keith's letter and read it one more time. She was the best chapter of his life, as he was hers.

She folded the letter and put it back inside her purse and picked up the newspaper. She came off sick leave but delayed acting on the buyout for two reasons—she wanted them to think she was considering it, and needed her ID to have access to Global.

John said that it was over. The hell it was.

Darby had spent the week playing detective. She was on reserve and counted on not flying so she could sit outside the office and wait for McDermott to leave so she could follow him. Eventually he would meet up with Santos and she would have them both.

The first night she learned he was staying at the Double Tree at SeaTac. That amounted to a nine-hour sit outside headquarters, and a five-minute follow to the hotel. She had gone home for a quick sleep and was parked back in the hotel lobby at 0500 the following morning.

Five days of the same behavior, her patience was wearing thin, as was her time. One more week and the Seattle training center would history. The Seattle corporate presence gone forever.

Darby drummed her fingers on the steering wheel waiting for him to do something.

She had looked through Keith's stuff for his recording pen, but could not find it so she decided to use her cell phone. This was a better plan than anything anyone else was doing, which amounted to a big fat nothing.

Now all she needed was them together.

All charges were dropped against Neil, and he finally gave her space. He quit training and started flying high time so he was not around. Kathryn was on administrative leave for three weeks until her transfer to Denver. The kids were in crisis mode leaving their friends. Jackie was working overtime trying to schedule pilots after they moved the Seattle simulators to Oklahoma.

John stayed in town with Jackie, continuing to work out of the Seattle office, but said there was nothing he could do with the situation. He suggested they all move on with their lives and wait and see what happened.

Darby took his advice—sort of. He did not tell her exactly where to wait.

The temperature dropped inside Darby's car as quickly as it fell outside. She pulled her wool cap over her ears and then turned on the ignition to warm up her home away from home. She tapped the buttons on the radio and then turned it off and pulled on her gloves. Her mood sank deeper than the day before.

Each day she moved her car to a different location. During her watch she would start it every two hours for warmth, listen to tunes and eat something non-healthy. Most of the time she would sit in silence. Today the silence was replaced by the growl of her stomach as Starbucks crept into her mind.

She sat on her butt for a living, but doing it in a car left a lot to be desired. She looked at her watch and figured she could escape for twenty minutes. What were the odds of his coming out the minute she left? Zero to none.

She put her car into gear at the same time her passenger door opened.

"Going somewhere?"

Darby startled. Her mouth opened, but nothing escaped. She choked on her reply, staring into the barrel of a gun.

CHAPTER 82

DARBY HELD HER breath, unsure of what to do. She glanced at the gun, now firmly in her gut, wondering if he would shoot if she jumped out of the car. Unfortunately her seatbelt was already fastened.

"Drive," Santos said.

She hesitated, then put the car into gear. Looking over her shoulder she pulled out onto the street. "Where are we going?"

"Mountains."

She pressed the gas pedal to the floor and ran a red light at an intersection, then headed up the hill. Her eyes darted left and right. There was never a cop when you needed one.

"Slow down," Santos said. "I've got a concealed weapons license, and I know where the Jacobs brats go to school."

Lifting the pressure off the gas pedal, her car slowed to the speed limit.

"Good girl. You know the way, lover boy's cabin."

She merged onto the freeway and headed north on I-5 then connected to 405. They drove in silence, but the voices in her head chatted wildly as they worked to figure a way out of this situation.

Traffic was thick but moving. She glanced at the clock—they would be there in less than an hour.

"Is that a real gun or did you get it out of a gumball machine?"

"*What?*" he said pulling his attention from the window. His stare burned and she wished she had kept her mouth shut.

"Imagine my irritation when McDermott tells me you were following him. How the hell did you know he was involved?"

"You told me."

"Don't screw with me," he snarled. "How'd you know?"

"The same way I knew you were involved—you're an idiot."

He pressed the gun deep into her side. "You can make this easy, or painful. Your choice."

She allowed the atmosphere to settle. As the gun relaxed in his lap she asked, "What is going on?"

"McDermott wants you to disappear."

"The feeling's mutual."

He grinned raising the gun to her chin. Sliding it down her throat he touched it to her breast. "I'll be sure to tell him your sentiment."

Darby's skin crawled and sweat dripped down the side of her face. She raised her arm to pull off her hat, knocking his hand away in the process.

He fumbled with the gun, but regained control. "Keep one word in mind when you play games—twins."

"Sorry. I was warm."

She pulled her gloves off and threw them in the back seat, then reached into her pocket. His hand flew to her arm and grabbed her wrist. He yanked her hand out of her pocket, and she held a chapstick.

"It's not going to hurt you," she said. "Unless I shove it up your ass. Oh wait...there's no room, your heads in the way."

He released her wrist and said, "Have your fun, but I'll be the last one laughing."

She angled the mirror toward her, glancing his way. Santos was watching so she winked. He grunted and looked out his window just as a police car pulled up beside them.

"Don't try anything," he said, staring straight ahead.

Darby slowed, turned on her blinker and merged right pulling behind the cop. During the distraction of her merging maneuver, she dropped her chapstick into her pocket, removed her iPhone and set it beside her on the seat.

Don't be stupid," he said his eyes not moving from the front window and the officers car.

"If we're behind him, he can't see inside the car." She said, slipping her hand to her side and pressing the record button. "So what are you and McDipshit up to anyway?"

He glanced her way but continued to look straight ahead. They drove in silence for ten minutes before the weasel made a noise.

"I figured out what they were up to, then I made them a deal they couldn't refuse."

"So you pulled the reports for them?"

"Hell no, that was McDermott's game, and what I discovered."

"Were they cutting training to save the airline money so they hid the reports because of all the incidents? Was Patrick involved? What about the guys in flight ops?"

"You're sealing your death sentence," Santos said.

"Oh God," she said rolling her eyes. "You've got a gun to my head. We're going to a remote cabin. Who am I going to tell?"

Santos laughed. "Good point." He picked up her chips. "Do you mind?" He ripped open the bag and stuffed a handful into his mouth before she could tell him hands off.

He extended the bag to her.

She shook her head no. The last thing she wanted to do was eat something his slimy hands had touched.

Darby drove with the irritation of his smacking and crunching killing her brain cells. She wanted to smack him. The thought of driving off the freeway flashed through her brain, but that would give McDermott a free ride.

Time was her friend. She glanced in her rearview mirror hoping she would see someone following her, but the freeway behind was empty. If only she had told John what she was up to.

"Lawrence Patrick's not involved, but he's not as innocent as you think. He puts pilots in management positions, pays them big bucks, strokes their egos and tells them they're gods." Santos shook his head. "Pilot egos. You feed them bullshit and before long, they believe it. Give them enough money, and they'll do anything."

"How did McDickless get involved?"

Santos laughed. "This was all McD's game. Cutting training would cause an inordinate amount of incidents. Eventually an accident or two. He needed a boy in the training department to make the plan work, so he planted Dawson during the merger."

"What plan?" Darby asked confused.

"McD thinks he should be president of the airline."

"Training cutbacks and risking passenger's lives were because he wanted to be president of the stupid airline?"

"People have killed for far less."

"So all you do is look the other way?"

Santos laughed. "That, and take care of problems."

"Was Keith part of this?"

He glanced her way. "No."

"Then why kill him?"

"He had one task, to get you to shut up. We didn't need any attention brought to the Airbus, and sure as hell didn't need you thinking you could email Patrick. Stone lost his life because he chose the wrong side."

"So he knew what was going on?"

"He showed up to a meeting because that idiot Armstrong said he could be trusted. Said we needed him. Armstrong assured me that Stone would go along." Santos stuck a handful of chips into his mouth and crunched while he spoke.

"That bastard played along, but wanted nothing to do with any of it. By then it was too late, he knew too much and had the nerve to blackmail me. Said that he'd taped our meeting and would shut us down if we didn't lay off you."

Keith died trying to protect her. The rain mirrored her emotions, and Darby turned the wipers on, but her feelings of loss could not be wiped away. Her rage grew stronger with each passing mile.

"Neil Jordan was perfect to take the fall," Santos said.

"Who killed Keith?"

"One of my finer moments."

Darby took slow calming breaths and counted silently as she worked to control her emotions. It took everything to not smack his ugly face right there. She hit number thirteen before she was able to speak. "So you're the hatchet man."

"I prefer problem solver."

"Where's the tape," Darby asked.

"That my dear, is the multi-million dollar question. Quite honestly, I don't believe there ever was a tape, but we had to be sure."

Darby glanced his way. Keith did not make idle threats. He had something. The question was, where is it?

"Is this why they're firing all the Coastal instructors? Because they're objecting to your shortened programs?" Darby asked.

"Firing instructors was Captain Wyatt's doing to cut expenses.

Patrick supported him."

He shifted in his seat and adjusted the gun. "There's no reason to pay captains four times the amount they could hire retired pilots to do the same job."

"Seriously?" Darby snapped. "If they retired off the Airbus, yes. I had an instructor who didn't have a clue how the plane worked, how to teach, or how to operate the simulator, and they just fired the check airman who put the plane into service!"

Santos laughed. "And there's the problem with hiring women. Your too damn emotional." He poured potato chip dust into his mouth. "It's just business, Sweetheart. Something you wouldn't know about." He crushed the bag and tossed it out the window.

Darby kept her emotional female brain focused on the street.

"We also got the company a hell of a contract with your ALPO boys. McD was furious when they signed, but now he couldn't be happier." Santos tapped the gun in the palm of his hand.

"The contract was part of this?"

"Smoke and mirrors," Santos said. "Patrick offered your union a teaser contract with an immediate bonus for signing. McD fed them a bunch of bullshit of what would happen if they didn't." Santos laughed. "McD lied to Patrick. Told him they'd sign it out of fear. Patrick wasn't so sure and McD never thought they'd do it."

"They didn't think we'd sign?"

"Hell no. McDermott never thought dangling a little fear would make them bite so hard. He thought there'd be employee unrest and incidents on the flight line would increase due to stress, pilots getting even, or some other bullshit. The stock price would fall and he'd take a couple chinks out of Patrick. Then an accident would knock him out of the ballpark."

Santos shook his head grinning. "Your union surprised us all."

"But why hide the ASRs?" She glanced his way.

"He needed something to pin on Patrick for a conviction."

"So the incidents on the line had nothing to do with your plan?"

"Nope. They're all compliments of the reduced footprint and pilots losing their skills thanks to automation."

"But if Mr. Patrick approved the training cuts, then—"

"A plane goes down and he's to blame," Santos said. "But the investigation would turn up the missing ASRs and he goes to jail for a very long time."

"How the hell are Wyatt and Clark allowing them to cut training? Are they involved too?"

"Hell no." Santos grinned. "I told you...pay a pilot enough and they'll do anything. Hire pilots who don't fly and they don't have a clue what's needed."

"How was this supposed to end?"

"Patrick in jail and Dawson and Armstrong missing."

"And you?"

"I'd learn the truth and become the hero nailing Patrick's coffin closed. McDermott would wire my new life to the Caymans." He sighed. "But you changed the course. Same plan, just a new route."

Santos patted her leg. "You just moved the finish line up without a crash."

She cringed at his touch, but the thought of how many times the previous year a plane should have crashed sent chills up her spine.

"Do you know how many incidents occur daily because of the reduced training?"

"You're preaching to the choir, but shortened footprints are the future. Automated planes are reliable and airlines have the right to train accordingly," he said sarcastically. "They're saving millions and still able to give congressman incentives to maintain status quo. If a plane goes down they've got insurance."

"Kathryn and John know you're involved."

"Perhaps, but they have no proof. With time that suspicion will wane. If it doesn't, the pressure of being a suspect will give me reason to retire early—a multi-millionaire."

Darby's skin crawled. Not because they were approaching her exit, but because of the thousands of lives that were in danger.

"This is just wrong."

"Paying management pilots to look the other way is a brilliant business model. One that I'm sure McD will carry forward in Patrick's honor. What better way to control a pilot than give him a management title, pay him a shitload of money and create an organizational model where shit flows downhill. The only people accountable are at the bottom of that chain. They're expendable."

Darby took their exit and headed toward the cabin.

"I have one last question," she said. "You're up here with me, in my car. I'm assuming whatever you do will be an accident. So how exactly are you getting back down the hill?"

Santos grinned, "McDermott's on his way."

Darby pulled in front of the cabin, and put the car in park and turned toward him. "Are you sure?"

CHAPTER 83

JOHN RETURNED FROM LUNCH and was unlocking his office door when his phone rang. "McAllister," he said.

"Have you heard from Darby?" Kathryn asked.

"No why?"

"She's been following McDermott. I dropped by to take her lunch, but she's not outside his office and doesn't answer her phone."

John rushed to his desk and unlocked the drawer. "Her car's gone?" he asked pulling the tracking device out.

The Department of Transportation suspected McDermott all along, and the government backed John to do whatever it took to get him.

Unfortunately the guy never made a mistake.

John planted the information about Darby in the media to gauge McDermott's reaction. He had been right, but that was still not enough to get him. Then Tom Santos popped up on the radar screen. He was a surprise.

Darby would not back down so he placed a tracking device on her car. After four days of monitoring her, it turned into a huge nothing. He went on with business as normal. His attention grew less on Darby.

"What's going on John?" Kathryn demanded.

"We've been tailing McDermott for almost a year. I've had the funding and approval to stick to him like glue. We added Santos with recent events. His car has a tracking device, too. He never stays at the corporate offices more than twenty minutes. But..."

"But what?"

"He's been there for two hours. McDermott's car hasn't moved all day." John's heart sank. "Ahh... Shit," he said. The green light flashed indicating Darby's car was on the move.

"John!" Kathryn yelled. "What's happening?"

"I've been tracking Darby. She's headed up Snoqualmie Pass as we speak."

"The cabin." Kathryn said. "If you're tracking her, how the hell could you not have followed her?"

"I'm on it," John snapped.

CHAPTER 84

Tom hesitated, fighting the urge to smack Darby Bradshaw in the face. He would not allow her the pleasure to know his deepest fear—that McDermott would sell him down the river too. Santos had him by the short hairs. Still, the fear of betrayal tickled the back of his neck.

There was no better opportunity than for an airline executive to have a Fed in his pocket. As long as McDermott believed that Tom Santos was his, he would be safe. It was only a matter of time until he shutdown the entire fucking airline. To hell with McDermott.

"Get out," Santos said with a wave of the gun. "Don't forget your phone."

Darby opened her door as Santos opened his. He watched her every move not allowing the gun to relax. Once in front of the cabin, he waved it toward the door. "Go."

She walked to the door and fumbled with her keys. He stood back and pulled on leather gloves. She eventually found the key and unlocked the door, and he followed her inside. He slid the deadbolt into place. "Erase that recording."

After they searched the place, he'd had the glass replaced in the door. Success was always about the details.

A pile of firewood sat in the corner, which made step-one easier. Tom looked at his watch. Twenty minutes before he needed to be on the top of the hill. His eyes settled upon the gas can, and he smiled.

"Build us a fire," Santos said swinging the gun toward the fireplace. He grabbed her phone and pressed play—nothing. "Good girl."

Darby knelt in front of the stone structure, big enough to throw her into. She wadded newspapers and tossed them inside. Then made a teepee of sticks and piled them around the paper, then angled two larger logs against each other.

She was quite the girl scout. He walked to the kitchen and opened cupboards. "I need a drink. There any booze in this place?" He laughed, knowing exactly what was in each cupboard.

Santos turned toward Darby as she rolled her eyes. He allowed the disrespect for one reason only—within fifteen minutes she would be dead.

"Grab a chair and pull down your pleasure," he said moving aside.

When she did as instructed, he went to the fireplace and reached up inside the chimney and made sure the flue was closed. He turned and watched her on the chair.

She had a nice ass. Something stirred that he had not felt in a long time. There would be no reason he could not have a little fun. He glanced at his watch, but the minutes were ticking down.

Santos reached for the Wild Turkey and opened the bottle. He took a sip and smiled, wiping the opening with his sleeve.

"Get a glass," he said.

Darby pulled down two.

"One."

She returned the other to the shelf.

"Set it over here," he said pointing to the counter.

She set down the glass, and he filled it and said, "Drink."

Darby picked up the glass and sipped.

"Down it."

"I haven't eaten."

"All the better," Santos said. "Drink."

Darby drank half the glass, never allowing her eyes to leave his. She was smokin' hot. He removed a bottle of Tylenol PM from his pocket and handed it to her. "For your headache."

She picked up the bottle, her eyes not leaving his.

"Open it," he said, "and dump them out on the counter."

She complied. He used his gun and separated a dozen from the pile. "Eat."

Darby scooped them up in her hand and said, "I would rather be drunk and passed out dead, than spend one waking moment looking at your butthole face." She swallowed the pills then set her glass on the counter.

"Take off your jacket."

"It's cold."

"Not for long," He lifted the whiskey, took another swig and winked at her. "I'd love to warm you up."

"Fuck you," Darby said, stepping six inches in front of him. "You are the last thing I would do."

"Your wish is my command." Santos grinned. "But we don't have time." He stepped back creating space.

Darby folded her arms, "Ha. Ten seconds is more than enough time. I'd give you two tops."

His arm had a mind of its own when it swung toward her face. She pulled back, but not far enough to escape the impact.

"You bastard!" she yelled, falling to her knees. She raised a hand to her cheek. Blood dripped from the broken skin.

"Sit on the couch and take off that coat."

Darby did as she was told and dropped it to the floor, then sat heavily.

"Sweet dreams, Princess." He handed her the glass. As she brought it to her lips he raised the gun over her head and swung. Darby pulled back, but not quick enough to avoid impact. She dropped the glass as she fell to the floor.

He pulled the lighter out of his pocket and knelt in front of the fireplace. Within minutes flames ate the paper and nibbled at the wood. Then everything inside the fireplace went up in a blaze and the tinder crackled.

Smoke filled the room. He walked toward the door and lifted the gas can, then poured as he walked behind the couch and crossed between Darby and the fireplace. He made a large circle around his victim. If he were lucky, she would wake up to watch herself burn.

Santos reached into his jacket and pulled out a Marlboro pack and tapped out a cigarette. He stuck it into his mouth and lit it, then stuffed both the pack and the lighter back into his pocket.

He walked to the front door and turned toward Darby taking a long drag.

"I'm going to have to give up these damn things," he said. "They're not good for your health." He flicked the cigarette onto the floor igniting the gas.

Santos unbolted the lock and pushed the door open, then slammed it behind him. He walked down the stairs and grabbed a board. He returned to the porch and stuck it under the doorknob. Then he headed up the hill.

CHAPTER 85

WHEN THE DOOR slammed Darby opened her eyes, rolled to her side and vomited. She lifted to her knees and emptied her stomach as fire crawled about the room. Her head ached and panic swept over her.

She touched her temple. The sticky warmth of blood dirtied her fingers, while the heat scorched her skin and flames darted everywhere. She pulled her shirt up covering her mouth and nose. Breathing into the fabric she assessed the room.

Smoke burned her eyes. Flames encircled the couch and climbed the walls.

She bent down and lifted the couch, pushing it backwards. It tipped over and covered the flames behind it. Grabbing her coat she scrambled over the back of the couch and ran toward the door.

She stopped short as flames blocked her path. She looked left and right and then toward the back of the cabin. Flames danced everywhere. There was no way out. Panic filled her veins

Pulling the coat over her head she ran through the flames to the front door. She turned the knob, but the door would not budge. She slammed her body into it multiple times, then jumped back through the flames, choking, and fell to her knees on the overturned couch. She covered her face with her shirt again and breathed through the fabric.

I am not going to die!

Flames parted and a glass window called to her as the only chance at life. She rushed to the coffee table, lifted it and threw with all her might at the window as a beam crashed down behind her.

The table broke through the window and flew out, and Darby followed.

Falling four feet she hit the ground and rolled. An overwhelming feeling of calm embraced her, as if Keith had caught her and set her down. Then she opened her eyes and began coughing in spasms as pain engulfed her every muscle.

Darby sat up and cried, "Noooo!"

She left her purse with Keith's letter inside, and then...

"Holy shit!" she yelled and scrambled to her feet. She knew where the tape was.

She ran around the cabin to the front door, rushed up the steps and kicked the board out from under the doorknob. Using her shirt to turn the knob, she yanked the door open and jumped back as flames burst out.

She covered her head with her arms and ran into the inferno.

CHAPTER 86

JOHN ARRIVED IN TIME to see the last beam fall into the rubble. A large stone fireplace, surrounded by shells of smoking walls and black soot, stood in memorial. A fire truck hooked up to the lake sprayed the smoldering remains. Rain poured hard and John was never more thankful for Washington's gift.

Please God let her be alive.

If Darby died he would never forgive himself. He parked his car and ran toward the group of police officers.

"Sir, you'll have to stay back," an officer said.

"I'm with the National Transportation Safety Board," John said, flashing his ID, "I'm on an active investigation." He turned toward the cabin. "Was…" He could not get the words out. He sucked a breath of courage and asked, "Were there any bodies?"

"One," said the officer. "They moved her to the ambulance, and…"

John sprinted toward the ambulance and yanked the door open.

"Excuse me?" the paramedic said. He was holding an oxygen mask to Darby's face.

"I'm a friend," John said, and climbed in. He sat on the side of the stretcher and touched her arm. "Darby," he whispered. She opened her eyes and blinked once before she closed them again.

"She was lucky," the paramedic said.

"You're going to be fine, Sweetheart," John said.

He climbed out of the ambulance, and found the officer in charge. "Was anyone else here when you arrived?"

"Nobody."

"What do you know?" John asked.

"I saw a woman run into the building as I pulled in. I honked. Jumped out of my car and yelled at her to stop. By the time I got in there she was lying inside the door, unconscious, gripping this book." He handed the novel, *Flight For Control*, to John.

John took the book. He did a cursory look at the chard covers, front and back, opened and closed it, and then tucked it under his arm. "She almost died for a book?"

"Apparently so. Not sure how she survived either. Beams crashed down everywhere, but they all missed her." He looked at the cabin and then back to John. "They made a barrier protecting her," he said with a sigh. "Never saw anything like it before. I figure it didn't take more than fifteen, maybe twenty minutes to torch."

John had called the police department on his way to the mountains, but they were already in motion because of Kathryn.

Thanks to her quick reaction, they got there in time and Darby was pulled to safety. Seconds longer, this story would have ended differently.

KARLENE PETITT

CHAPTER 87

OCTOBER 1, 2012

Darby lay in a hospital bed being treated for smoke inhalation and minor burns. How the hell she had not been burned to a cinder was nothing short of a miracle. She felt like shit, but finally had the strength to talk. She opened her eyes and took in the room.

"Darby! Oh God. Sweetie, we were so worried about you," Kathryn said.

"How are you feeling?" John asked.

"Good." Darby had made a police statement and Santos was in custody, but John waited until she felt good enough to tell him the entire story.

Darby relayed what happened the best she knew and John taped. It was nothing but hearsay, and Santos was not talking.

When she was done John pressed stop and said, "This is quite a story. But it will be your word against his." He stood and placed his hands on his hips and glared. "What the hell were you doing going back into that cabin for a damn book?"

"Evidence," Darby said glancing at the novel on the windowsill. She had yet to look inside. Half of her was afraid of what she might not find, but she had to believe. She survived for one reason only—to bring the truth to the public.

"What are you talking about Sweetie? Kathryn said, stroking

her hair. "What evidence?"

"My letter," Darby said. "Keith told me where the tape was in my letter."

"He'd said nothing of the sort," John said. "I read it multiple times."

Darby smiled. "Yes he did. He said I was the best chapter of his life. He told me to remember that always. He wrote it twice."

John and Kathryn exchanged a look and Darby sat up and reached for a glass of water.

She took a drink and then said, "Will you hand me my book?"

John handed her the copy of *Flight For Control*.

"I made Keith read this," Darby said, hugging it to her chest. "He'd said chapter four was his favorite chapter and that we needed to..." She grinned. "Well...never mind about that part, but he always said, 'I want my favorite chapter.'"

Darby set the book in her lap and opened it to chapter four. The chapter page was glued to the next, as was the entire middle section. Her eyes moistened. She was right. Darby ripped the page free, and there it was.

Under that page was a carved out section, and his recording pen was nestled deep inside.

Holding the book up she said, "We got 'em!"

CHAPTER 88

D ARBY SAT OFF TO the side of the corporate stairwell, while Kathryn prepared to talk at the press conference. Captain George Wyatt, director of flight operations, Captain Rich Clark, manager of flight operations, and First Officer Dick Foster, director of flying, stood to the side, cleared of all connection to the events. Hanging in the background was the Seattle chief pilot, assistant chief pilot, and her union representative.

After the breaking news of the recording, Patrick Lawrence was cleared of all charges. Santos was sitting in jail without bail, awaiting trial. McDermott was charged with something, but never saw the inside of a cell. He was fired, and the last Darby heard he was interviewing for the CEO position with another airline.

Darby began to unravel their web by speaking out about lack of proficiency on her blog and her concern with their canceling initial ground school. Her post about the Pacific Airlines A330 crash was something McDermott needed silenced.

They all suspected she would be a problem when she first wrote to Mr. Patrick. They never anticipated anyone at Global would go outside the chain of command for anything. Not until Coastal Airlines came on board was that ever an issue.

As it turned out, Wyatt was good friends with Armstrong but

had no idea what he was up to. Wyatt, Clark, and Foster took great pride in maintaining an environment where the rank was kept in place and did exactly what they were told. Most importantly, keeping their mouths shut.

Flight operations tried to put a sledgehammer to Darby's head, and pound her down, for one reason only—she did not play by their rules.

Armstrong enlisted flight operations help without their thinking anything of it, then he told Keith to get something on her. Keith had not initially understood the extent of what Armstrong was up to, yet he took that first flight. But they had fallen in love.

He played their game with motivation to get a position where he could create change for the better. When he learned what they were doing, he blackmailed them to protect Darby.

Why he did not take the tape to the police in the first place, was anyone's guess.

Kathryn had been an equal pain in Santos's ass. She was making too much noise about the shortened footprints and the safety audit. Cleared of all wrongdoing, Kathryn was back on payroll and in line for Santos's position. A reporter stuck a microphone in front of her face.

"How could the people who are tasked to keep our industry safe have allowed this to happen?" the reporter asked.

The crowd rumbled and the wind howled. Darby pulled her coat tight and listened.

"I'm not sure," Kathryn said. "When greed gets involved, anything is possible. What I do know is we must revisit how our airlines are training pilots. We must not cut training because of automation, but just the opposite. Pacific Airlines showed us there are pilots who do not know how to fly. The San Francisco crash told us they're losing skills."

Kathryn told the world her idea on an expanded training program and why it was essential. Emphasizing that pilots needed to be tested on their flying skills. Her greatest concern was the new generation of pilots growing up on a diet of automation. Who could blame them, this was technology in progress.

Darby stood bringing blood back to her knees, and folded her arms, proud of her friend.

"Somebody once said, 'You can teach a monkey how to fly, but you can't teach it how to think,' and they weren't too far off," Kathryn said.

"Yes, but…" a reporter from NBC said, "Statistics show that more people die in car crashes daily than in planes. So how much overkill do you need?"

"None. If you want to accept death in mass as okay," Darby said. Cameras turned her way and she stepped back, but Kathryn waved her forward.

Darby's picture had been on every news channel for the previous 24-hours. Reporters ran to her and stuck microphones in her face. "Do you think pilot training is good enough?"

Wyatt, Clark, and Foster shrunk back from the camera's view.

"We have better equipment and technology than ever before, and flying is still the safest mode of transportation." Darby glanced at her management pilots who visibly relaxed. "But, we don't have enough training."

She winked at Foster and said, "Airlines are cancelling recurrent training and initial ground schools. Pilots are training themselves. We're firing our quality instructors and hiring people off the street to teach in simulators. Some are excellent if they retired off the plane, but excellence and aptitude are not the requirement to work as a pilot instructor. It's the willingness to take the job at low pay."

"What's the answer?" a reporter asked. "How will the public know if their pilots can handle their planes without automation before it's too late?"

Kathryn nodded for her to continue. They had spoken well into the night on this exact issue.

"They don't," Darby said, "but they could."

"How?" the reporter asked.

Darby reemphasized what Kathryn said about the need for more training without automation. She brought up her lack of proficiency and how there are pilots who go for months, even years without seeing the inside of plane who are legal with three takeoffs and landings in the simulator. This needed to stop.

"We also need our checkairman to observe their students on the line flying without any automation, including autothrust and flight directors," Darby said.

"But isn't that what happened in San Francisco?" The reporter asked. "They had an instructor on board and crashed."

"Yes. It is," Darby said. "My point exactly. They did not have the core skills to fly, did not receive the proper training, were nervous about their performance and there was no avenue built into their corporate culture to help them. The pilots on Pacific Airlines 547 were in the same boat."

Wyatt and Clark moved her way.

"I have a challenge," Darby said before she got run out of town. "I challenge every airline to bring each pilot into the simulator, have them lose their autothrust, flight directors, and autopilots at altitude and see if they can land their planes safely."

"You don't think they could?" The report asked.

Darby shrugged. "Could be interesting."

Clark whispered in her ear. "You're treading on dangerous ground."

Wyatt stepped in front of the camera, subtly pushing Darby aside. "We want to thank you all for coming. We will use the lessons learned in this situation to help the industry get better, and we will continue to run the safest airline in the world."

Kathryn stepped forward. "Thank you Captain Wyatt, but this is my press conference. I will the be the person to decide when it's over."

CHAPTER 89
OKLAHOMA CITY, OKLAHOMA

OCTOBER 18, 2012

D ARBY WAITED with Kathryn in the CEO's conference room. They had both been outspoken on the issues, but something needed to be said. The press conference was a good start, but Darby was not sure if her career would survive her outburst. Time would tell. Kathryn, on the other hand, received the promotion she deserved.

The public needed to know what was going on and not until they understood the ramifications of how their pilots were being trained, and cried out, would anything change.

She and Kathryn rolled the dice—land where they may. They both landed in Oklahoma City, with first class tickets and lunch with Mr. Lawrence Patrick.

It was sad to see the old Coastal headquarters close up, but change was a good thing. So they said. Darby slid a hand over the windowsill and gazed out. As the door opened behind her she turned her attention to the man who walked into the room.

Kathryn shook Mr. Patrick's hand and Darby walked over and did the same, giving him her cutest smile she winked.

The old boy's eyes flashed a smile and he said, "Nice to meet you Kathryn, and good to see you again Darby. Please, have a seat. Lunch will be served soon. What can I offer you to drink?"

"Water's fine for me," Kathryn said pulling out a chair.

"I'd like water, too." Darby sat beside her friend. She was planning on giving up coffee for the new year and started early for the weaning process.

"Looks like you two gave the reporters quite a show," he said filling their glasses.

"Ratings are always a good thing," Darby said.

Kathryn elbowed her. "It was what they needed to hear, sir."

"I suppose so." He poured himself a cup of coffee and sat.

Bringing his cup to his lips he watched them both over the rim, which was a little unnerving. When he set his coffee on the table he said, "I want to thank you ladies for clearing my name. I wasn't quite sure how that would pan out."

"You're welcome," Kathryn said, "but it was all Darby."

Mr. Patrick leaned back and folded his arms turning is attention to Darby he said, "Thank you." His eyes smiled, then turned serious. "It appears you both think we have problems. I'd like to hear what you have to say. Maybe we could solve them before we go live on the news next time."

Darby blushed, but jumped on his invitation. She told him her concerns with proficiency, training being cut and the challenges with fatigue and that they should never have taken out the crew bunks. Then she jumped into the culture of flight operations.

"Our flight ops management team is running the department like the military," Darby said. "This is not a war, it's a business. To reprimand anyone for questioning anything in this industry is a contradiction to safety."

Crew resource management came about because of arrogance in the cockpit, when nobody was allowed to say anything—the primary reason why planes crashed. The industry learned its lesson, changed the cockpit to a flight deck and created a system of open communication. Everywhere, except at Global.

"Interesting accusations," Mr. Patrick said when Darby stopped for a drink.

"They're more than accusations. I was told there was nothing I could say that they didn't already know."

"She's right," Kathryn said. "I've watched this for a year. My hands are tied and, quite frankly, the government is running the FAA in a similar manner."

"If we had a different culture, the incidents that have been occurring would have been communicated and we'd have discovered what was happening before you ended up in the slammer. I know of three incidents that should have been hull losses," Darby said with a shiver. "Wyatt and Clark need to listen to the pilots. If they did, they'd realize there's a problem and look into training."

"It's about transparency, sir," Kathryn said.

"We also need fleet training captains who have experience on the equipment they manage," Darby said. "Not someone who was appointed because they're one of the boys."

She leaned forward, her eyes locking onto his. "Our 747 at Coastal that had the rudder hard-over could have been a hull loss without the director's input. The pilots called him because he had experience on the equipment, and together they solved the problem and landed that plane safely."

Mr. Patrick's eyes indicated he clearly remembered the incident.

"If something happened on the A330 out on the line, who would we call for help?"

"Management plots are supposed to be the gatekeepers of safety, Kathryn said. "Somehow the airlines have forgotten the intent as to why we have pilot managers."

Mr. Patrick nodded. "I suspect our management pilots have forgotten that too."

"There's one more thing," Darby said and Mr. Patrick raised an eye-brow. "We need to reinstate ground school."

He opened his mouth to speak, but a knock at the door stopped him and lunch was served. They settled into a comfortable discussion about fatigue and training issues.

Their best attempt to convince Mr. Patrick that more training could justify an increase in airfare, went on deaf ears. As the words came out of her mouth, Darby knew that the public was partially to blame. They always purchased the cheapest fare.

When plates were cleared, Mr. Patrick leaned back in his chair and said, "The reason I asked you both here, is to personally thank you." His eyes moistened. "Without both of you, I'm not sure what would have happened to the airline, or to me." He smiled and said, "I will be forever indebted."

She and Kathryn accepted his thanks, but when he excused himself to take a call Darby said, "I don't think he's going to spend the money needed in training on his own. I'm afraid it's all in your house now."

"You're right," Kathryn said. "Pacific Airlines and San Francisco were our wake up calls, and we haven't heeded the warning. I'm afraid there will be more unless we do something."

"It seems like yesterday when the news touted there hadn't been a major accident in four years," Darby said. "Now we've had two and both attributed to pilots not knowing how to fly. Not to mention the incidents that the public never heard about."

Darby pushed away from the table and walked around the room, looking at the photos hanging on the walls, then turned toward Kathryn.

"The industry is safer than it's ever been. Right?" Darby asked. It was safe, but they were headed into the next generation facing a new set of problems. The concern of what would happen next tugged at her soul.

"It is," Kathryn said. "But the incidents that you witnessed could have been major hull losses, and by the grace of God, they weren't."

"Dumb ass luck," Darby said. "I feel like such a failure. Keith's dead, we had Mr. Patrick's ear, talked to the public, and we really didn't solve anything. We know there were major incidents and why they happened, but what good did it do? We're no better off than we were yesterday."

"You're wrong," Kathryn said. "You created awareness, and not until the public sees a need will anything change. You've opened some eyes, and your blog has been a support system to many pilots who might otherwise have had problems."

With a heavy heart Darby returned to her seat and sighed. "Perhaps, but we can only play Russian Roulette for so long. Eventually a bullet will come out."

EPILOGUE

D ARBY SAT AT HER desk reading blogs about Pacific Airlines flight 574. She was still on reserve on the A330 and not flying. They finally released the official transcript and just as she thought—the pilots did not know how to fly their plane. *Exactly* what she had written.

Despite that everything Darby wrote on her blog was accurate, the letter of reprimand stayed in her file.

Captain Odell, the chief pilot who signed that letter, had just been promoted to director of flying, taking Dick Foster's position. Had Darby taken action against the company for the falsifications in that letter, they would have fired Odell as their scapegoat because his signature was on the document.

Odell was the best person for the director of flying position, so it was probably a good thing she took one for the team.

Dick Foster left the airline, temporarily, to take a position with a Global commuter as the chief operating officer. He retained his seniority number at Global to return whenever he wanted. How ALPO allowed that was beyond her.

Wyatt and Clark continued with status quo. The assistant chief pilot died a natural death. Not literally. He just moved back to the flight line after spending four years in a position that was supposed to be two. The pilot they put in his place was a great guy—so she heard. Before this position, he was the ALPO safety rep. The same union pilot who was indignant when she called about her legality to fly.

Pacific Airlines crashed because pilots did not know how to fly, and another plane crashed in San Francisco because the pilots could not fly without automation.

Kathryn told Darby that thanks to her, the FAA would soon be mandating stall training at altitude, but was that enough?

They were also putting pilots in the simulator to fly visual approaches without the glideslope, but they left the autothrust on. Missing a key point of the San Francisco crash.

Darby sighed. There were pilots in the skies that did not know how to fly. All it took was two to be paired up together and they'd have another crash.

She talked Brock into writing a book about Pacific Airlines flight 574 from a technical aspect and she heard he just posted the synopsis on his blog.

Pushing away from her computer she went to the kitchen and poured herself another cup of coffee. Her New Year's Resolution lasted three months, but she did cut back. Everything in moderation was the modified plan. Life lost flavor without caffeine.

She picked up her cell phone and texted Townsend—*can you send me the link to your blog?*

Within seconds he responded. She returned to her office and typed TrendVector.blogspot.com into her computer.

Pacific Air Lines flight 574

December 14, 2009, an Airbus A330, one of the most modern airliners in the world, with an excellent safety record, had disappeared over the Pacific Ocean. Left behind were a series of maintenance messages that were transmitted during the final minutes of flight. But the sequence of events that followed were anything but normal...

Whether you are a casual aviation observer or a current A330 pilot, this book is for you. It tells the story and shares insights you will not soon forget. The lessons learned may save your life, and those of your loved ones.

Townsend's book will be a hit. The funny thing was, Chief Pilot Odell had placed a letter in her file about her Pacific Airlines post, but he personally gave Brock Townsend permission to publish an entire book on the same subject.

Darby breathed deep. She was living in another world. She had thought those times were gone, but the South still battled for victory.

Where will aviation be in ten years? It was hard to imagine. But one thing Darby Bradshaw knew—she needed to get into a plane and fly to be proficient or something bad was going to happen.

There were two airline crashes at the hands of the pilots.

Things happened in threes, as did plane crashes. It was not 'if' but 'when' crash number three would occur due to inexperience or lack of proficiency.

Darby only hoped it would not be on her watch.

Acknowledgements

A special note of gratitude and appreciation to my technical editors—Roger Olson and Bill Palmer. These A330 check airman not only critiqued the flying scenes to assure accuracy, but they are forever assisting in my ongoing education on the Airbus.

Retired 747 Captain Kathy McCullough took her time to read the 560-page version and provided excellent and honest feedback. Reminding me that some things did not need to be on the page.

A huge Thank You to my readers—John Nance, Chris Broyhill, Mark L Berry, and Eric Auxier. I am honored to have these captains and best selling aviation authors give me so much of their valuable time to read, critique, and support *Flight For Safety*.

Many thanks go to Nathan Everett for his patience, talent, and assistance in bringing my work to life. He is a master of publication. If you want to publish a book, he can help you make your dreams come true. Publisher. elderroadbooks@outlook.com.

Thanks to Big Whitey for his excellent suggestion to aircraft manufacturers, and for bringing great wine to life—Las Madres.

A huge thank you to my daughter, Kayla Wopschall, for the great cover! And to Christine and Darcie for their proofreading talents.

Last, but not least, a special thank you to my husband Dick Petitt. Not only did he read my novel 8 times, but his football games were interrupted with plot points, his meals where discussions over characters, and he read me the novel on our drive to California—all this without complaint, as he is the wind beneath my wings.

Flying a plane takes a team, as does writing a novel. Thank you all so very much!

Discussion Questions

1. Today the FAA recommends pilots to hand fly their planes. Yet with RVSM (Reduced Vertical Separation Minimums) airspace, RNP (Required Navigation Performance) approaches, and arrivals and departures requiring the autopilot, when would international pilots be able hand fly their planes?

2. Which is the safest course of action—utilizing automation to its fullest during approach and landing after the pilots have been awake for 18-hours, or flipping everything off and hand flying the approach? If we know automation is the safest option, should pilots disconnect their planes and hand fly at this time? Better yet, should they be 'practicing' their flying skills while fatigued with passengers on board? When and how should international airline pilots practice their flying skills?

3. The FAA requires three takeoffs and landings every 90-days for pilot proficiency. This came about with long-haul flights and only one takeoff and landing between four pilots. Did the FAA anticipate that pilots might never see the inside of an airplane for 3-months, 6-months, 9-months, a year or longer when they implemented this rule? Are three takeoffs and landings enough to keep pilots proficient in a plane they rarely fly?

4. Fatigue is a never-ending battle. 17 hours awake with crew rest in a passenger seat, flying the back side of the clock across multiple time zones—is it possible to be rested? Did you know 17 hours awake is equivalent to an alcohol level of .05?

5. Corporate culture trickles down to the flight deck. What type of culture do you believe is essential for a safe operation in an airplane? Does a culture of believing you are the 'best' create a work environment conducive to safety? If you think you are better than everyone else, will you have an open mind and encourage others to speak up? Is it possible to have a safety culture that follows a military work environment—do as I say and don't ask questions?

6. What defines a captain? Pilots have moved from flying their planes to managing the flight deck. What traits make a good captain?

7. When airlines merge, how do you think seniority should be dealt with? Some win, some lose, but what system could make everyone feel they were treated fairly? Is there such a system?

8. Where do you see aviation in the next 10 years? What about the next 20? What unique problems will pilots of the future face?

9. What can you do to help improve safety?

Additional Reading

For those of you who have lost a loved one in a plane crash, I recommend you read Captain Mark L. Berry's memoir, *13,760 Feet*. He, too, lost someone, and his journey back to living might help you, or someone you love, move forward.

The accident in the prologue mirrors reality. For those of you who would like to understand the technical details of what happened, I highly recommend Captain Bill Palmer's book, *Understanding AF447*.

Aviation Thrillers by Karlene Petitt. Flight For Series—

Flight For Control
Flight For Safety
Flight For Survival (November 2015)

Flight For Control:

After a ten-year leave, Kathryn Jacobs has been invited back to the N.T.S.B to investigate a series of unexplained airline crashes. But her husband, Captain Bill Jacobs, has his concerns. While her twin daughters are off at camp, and Bill is actively campaigning for the Pilot Union Presidency, Kathryn secretly begins her investigation. What she learns will shock the nation.

Flight For Control is a thriller that reads like a mystery. But there is no mystery on the condition of the airline industry—it's broken. Planes are crashing. Pilots are financially and emotionally bankrupt. Pensions are lost. Fatigue. Cutbacks. Furloughs. Mergers. It's time that someone takes control before it's too late—unless it already is.

Your life is in your pilot's hands—do you know who's flying your plane?

Karlene Petitt is available to host aviation discussion groups, join your book club, or speak at your meetings.

Please email her at Karlene.Petitt@gmail.com to schedule your next event.

KARLENE PETITT IS AN INTERNATIONAL AIRLINE PILOT WHO IS TYPE-RATED AND HAS FLOWN AND/OR INSTRUCTED ON THE B747-400, B747, B767, B757, B737, B727 AND A330. PETITT IS A 35-YEAR VETERAN OF FLYING, AND HAS WORKED FOR COASTAL AIRWAYS, EVERGREEN, BRANIFF, PREMAIR, AMERICA WEST, GUYANA, TOWER AIR, NORTHWEST AIRLINES, AND CURRENTLY FLIES AN AIRBUS FOR AN INTERNATIONAL AIRLINE. BASED IN SEATTLE WASHINGTON, SHE IS THE MOTHER OF THREE, GRANDMOTHER OF SEVEN, HOLDS MBA AND MHS DEGREES AND IS PURSING HER PHD IN AVIATION SAFETY.

CPSIA information can be obtained at www.ICGtesting.com
Printed in the USA
BVOW08s1602040214

343720BV00002B/4/P